# Raising Venture Capital Finance in Europe

# Reach for the sky.

The world is constantly changing. Today's markets are truly international. Competition and opportunities come from new, unexpected places.

Today's successful and ambitious companies must think and act globally. They need credible partners who think and respond in the same way. 3i's extensive networks and connections are providing our portfolio companies access to customers, partners and knowledge worldwide.

3i is a world leader in private equity and venture capital, offering a range of funding solutions.

**www.3i.com**

# Raising Venture Capital Finance in Europe

A practical guide for business owners, entrepreneurs and investors

## Keith Arundale

KOGAN
PAGE

London and Philadelphia

*To my wife, parents and all those entrepreneurial people who have taken substantial personal risks to achieve their dreams*

**Publisher's note**
Every possible effort has been made to ensure that the information contained in this book is accurate at the time of going to press, and the publishers and author cannot accept responsibility for any errors or omissions, however caused. No responsibility for loss or damage occasioned to any person acting, or refraining from action, as a result of the material in this publication can be accepted by the editor, the publisher or the authors.

The material presented in this publication is for information purposes only. It reflects the subjective views of the author and does not necessarily represent current or past practices or beliefs of any organization. In this publication, neither the author nor his past or present employers, nor the editor or the publisher, nor the authors of the individual case studies are engaged in rendering accounting, business, financial, investment, legal, tax or other professional advice or services whatsoever and are not liable for any losses, financial or otherwise associated with adopting any ideas, approaches or frameworks contained in this book. If investment advice or other expert assistance is required, the individualized services of a competent professional should be sought.

First published in Great Britain and the United States in 2007 by Kogan Page Limited

120 Pentonville Road          525 South 4th Street, #241
London N1 9JN                 Philadelphia PA 19147
United Kingdom                USA
www.kogan-page.co.uk

© Keith Arundale, 2007

The right of Keith Arundale to be identified as the author of this work has been asserted by him in accordance with the Copyright, Designs and Patents Act 1988.

ISBN-10   0 7494 4849 0
ISBN-13   978 0 7494 4849 3

**British Library Cataloguing-in-Publication Data**

A CIP record for this book is available from the British Library.

**Library of Congress Cataloging-in-Publication Data**

Arundale, Keith.
  Raising venture capital finance in Europe : a practical guide for business owners, entrepreneurs and investors / Keith Arundale.
    p. cm.
  Includes bibliographical references.
  ISBN-13: 978–0–7494–4849–3
  ISBN-10: 0–7494–4849–0
1. Venture capital–Europe. 2. New business enterprises–Europe–Finance. 3. Corporations–Europe–Finance. I. Title.
  HG5428.A78 2007
  658.15'224094–dc22
                    2007000766

Typeset by Saxon Graphics Ltd, Derby
Printed and bound in Great Britain by Cambrian Printers Ltd, Aberystwyth, Wales

# Contents

# About 3i

### Our Vision
*"To be the preferred Venture Capital partner for the world's best entrepreneurs, corporations and investors."* Jo Taylor, Managing Partner, 3i Venture Capital

We share the ambition of entrepreneurs around the world. We are driven by their vision – to shape the future and make a difference to people's lives.

We will help you grow your winning idea into a successful, fast-growing enterprise. We know how to identify and nurture great innovation because we have been doing it for more than 40 years.

As the world's leading partner for ambitious entrepreneurs, we open doors to new customers, dynamic alliances and fresh talent. We are the only Venture Capital firm that operates globally, bringing you the benefit of fresh insights and techniques from our networks in Asia, the US, Israel and Europe.

Ultimately, your entrepreneurial innovation combined with 3i's professional acumen will build a great company capable of transforming the way we live.

---

*"3i has been supporting EVE for the last three years in France and the USA. Their experience and international reach allow us to accelerate our development and we consider them a true partner. They have been extremely proactive and have been leaders on various items such as financing strategy and international expansion."* Luc Burgun CEO, EVE

*"We are very proud that we have won 3i as our partner for our international expansion. Besides its first class brand name 3i has superior contacts to all relevant players in the internet sector. This constitutes an important advantage to us in the global rollout of Click & Buy."* Norbert Stangl CEO, Firstgate Holding AG

*"We have considered deeply the pros and cons of including a VC at PriceMinister. With 3i, we have discovered that the 'pros' were real (financial means, contacts and International reach) but also that the 'cons' were not real 'cons'. 3i's high level standards have helped us improve our governance and their understanding of the business generates a rich and constructive debate."* Pierre Kosciusko-Morizet CEO, PriceMinister

---

### Investment Criteria
Over the next five years, we will invest $1.5bn to help ambitious entrepreneurs realise their potential to become leaders in their fields – people with life-changing ideas and the drive to turn them into reality.

The businesses we back range from start-ups that are re-writing the rule book, to established innovators seeking rapid growth. They all share:

- exceptional leadership with entrepreneurial flair and proven technical and business expertise
- disruptive technology and the vision to create a new market, or gain significant share of an existing market.

We typically invest between $1m and $50m, from early to late stage. Our expertise in the following sectors is based on years of experience, resulting in a number of billion-dollar companies:

- Healthcare – from new medical devices for minimally invasive surgery in areas such as cardiovascular, orthopaedics, ophthalmology and obesity to disruptive therapeutic platforms, novel aspects of drug delivery and speciality pharma.

- Cleantech – from renewable energy sources, such as solar and biofuels, to water purification and the production of entirely new materials that can radically change the way we use natural resources.

- Consumerisation of IT – from mobile telecoms and intelligent devices, software, internet and online media to electronics and semiconductors.

Once we have committed to you, we back you all the way. We tailor the best global team for you, make the right introductions and offer strategic guidance to accelerate your success.

---

**Interhyp (Germany)**
The number one mortgage broker in Germany, operating online and through call centres and branches.

**Jo Taylor, 3i's Managing Partner:**
*"Interhyp is a great example of what successful venture investment needs: a disruptive business model, excellent management and a major market opportunity."*

**Christian Siegele, 3i investor, Germany:**
*"It was a privilege to work with Interhyp's outstanding management team. In three years they grew the company's revenue seven-fold, positioning it for an IPO that was 30 times oversubscribed."*

---

## Experience

Over the years, we have helped dynamic scientific and business thinkers turn groundbreaking ideas into profitable companies and reap the rewards of their innovation. In the last five years alone, 3i-backed entrepreneurs have achieved over 60 listings on 10 international exchanges and taken part in more than 150 trade sales, for multi-million dollar sums.

We are able to do this because of the calibre of our people, who combine business know-how with a deep personal commitment to every business that we partner.

### Contacts
Head Office – London
3i 16 Palace Street, London SW1E 5JD, United Kingdom  Tel: +44 (0)20 7928 3131  Fax: +44 (0)20 7928 0058

UK – Cambridge
3i 121 Cambridge Science Park, Milton Road, Cambridge CB4 0FZ, United Kingdom
Tel: +44 1223 420031  Fax: +44 1223 420459

Finland – Helsinki
3i PO Box 247, Mikonkatu 25, FIN-00101, Helsinki, Finland  Tel: +358 (0)9 6815 4100  Fax: +358 (0) 9 6815 4451

France – Paris
3i 3 rue Paul Cézanne 75008, Paris, France  Tel: +33 1 73 15 11 00  Fax: +33 (0)1 73 15 11 24

Germany – Munich
3i Rosental 3-4 80331, München, Germany  Tel: +49 89 54 86 2-0  Fax: +49 89 54 86 2-299

Sweden – Stockholm
3i Birger Jarlsgatan 25, Box 7847, SE-103 99, Stockholm, Sweden
Tel: +46 (0)8 506 101 00  Fax: +46 (0)8 506 211 00

# List of case studies
## (in order of appearance in the text)

**Buy this for breakfast**

**Savor this for the rest of the day**

**THE WALL STREET JOURNAL EUROPE IS NOW AVAILABLE IN PRINT AND ONLINE IN ONE SUBSCRIPTION.**
Not only will you receive the world's finest business newspaper delivered to your desk
first thing in the morning, you will also enjoy a 24-hour integrated online package that you can
tailor to your own needs with personalized alerts, regional headlines, and stock quotes
on more than 25,000 regional and worldwide companies.

That's understanding. That's The Wall Street Journal Europe.

# THE WALL STREET JOURNAL.
### EUROPE
P R I N T  &  O N L I N E
Global Business News for Europe

# About the author

Keith Arundale (www.keitharundale.com) is a speaker, author, consultant and visiting university lecturer in venture capital, entrepreneurship and marketing. He is a chartered accountant and chartered marketer and provides business planning and finance-raising advice and support for high-growth ventures, financial and commercial due diligence of potential investee companies, and marketing and business development advice for venture capital and professional services firms. He was with PricewaterhouseCoopers for many years where latterly he led the venture capital and business development programmes for PwC's Global Technology Industry Group in Europe.

Keith is the author of the British Venture Capital Association's *Guide to Private Equity*. He is a Visiting Fellow at Queen Mary, University of London, focusing on venture capital and guest lecturer at Cass Business School in the City of London. Keith is Master of the Worshipful Company of Marketors (City livery company) in the City of London in 2007. He and his wife, Kathy, live in Windsor, Berkshire.

# Foreword by Sir Paul Judge

Historically only large businesses, or very rich individuals, could invest substantially in small companies or buy other large ones. This monopoly has been broken in the past 20 years as the venture capital industry has come of age. Pension funds, life insurance offices, angel financiers and other investors have realized that they can aggregate their resources to act like a large corporation. They have learnt how to employ their money to invest in the development of private firms or in those public companies that would benefit from becoming private.

In order to be credible and successful in becoming involved with private transactions they needed intermediaries, the venture capital companies, who could mobilize their money and employ sector specialists to research and implement the opportunities. This process crossed the Atlantic, first to the UK where privately owned companies have become a growing proportion of economic activity. In recent years it has been increasingly spreading to continental Europe.

The substantial economic returns that have been made by the private equity industry since the mid-1980s, and especially in the past five years, have attracted many new financial and individual funders into the sector. Despite the huge capital losses during the dot.com crash, there remains a proper perception that there are many occasions when economic value can better be added with a private rather than a public company.

There are probably two main circumstances where this is so: 1) when significant restructuring is required involving a short-term reduction in profit, which public markets tend to find difficult to evaluate; 2) when a new concept is at an early stage and the risk of failure is greater than any of the usual investment banking promoters of public share offerings are prepared to contemplate. Both of these types of situation benefit greatly from the availability of professional private equity and venture capital.

This book is an invaluable guide to this vital trend. The author has been involved with the advance of the European venture capital market almost since its inception and his published works have already contributed importantly to the understanding of the dynamics of UK venture capital. In this volume he provides a full description of the venture capital industry throughout continental Europe where it is likely to have as much effect on business attitudes and activities as has already occurred in the United States and the UK.

I would therefore commend this book to everyone interested in the development of European business. Not only does it provide detailed lessons for those hoping to raise money to capitalize on their new idea or to pursue their corporate restructuring, but it also explains to the current captains of industry the power of venture capital to change individual businesses or even entire industries.

*Sir Paul Judge*
*Chairman, Enterprise Education Trust*
*Patron, Campaign for Enterprise*
*President, Association of MBAs*
*Past Master, Worshipful Company of Marketors*

# Foreword by Patrick Sheehan

The world of 'venture capital' in Europe has been changing rapidly. Its terminology, frequently confusing to the outsider, has begun to move towards American norms. The generic terms in Europe are now 'venture capital', for start-up and young hyper-growth companies, and 'private equity', which finances 'management buyouts' and provides 'growth capital' for ambitious established companies.

It is not just the signposts that have been changing though – the whole landscape has. The buyout industry has grown beyond the wildest dreams of its early practitioners to the point where multi-billion-euro 'deals' are commonplace. It has an impact on the lives of the citizens of Europe. Those engaged in the industry strongly argue that they are helping Europe evolve to become more competitive on the global stage, as indeed it must. However, private equity is still, well, pretty private. The dialogue on the role of private equity – its good and ill – has begun to be debated in newspapers and by politicians. Often, however, more heat than light seems to be generated. Keith's book makes a useful contribution to demystifying what private equity actually is and covers the practical aspects of how and why it works.

The main focus of Keith's book is the European venture capital industry. If the private equity industry is often misunderstood, venture capital as its smaller relation suffers more frequently. In part it has suffered in Europe from unflattering comparison with US venture capital, particularly its flamboyant West Coast form. The dramatic successes that, to a European, feel commonplace in Silicon Valley have felt rare in Europe. Entrepreneurs sometimes feel that European VCs are too tentative compared to such counterparts. Investors into venture funds themselves have worried about comparatively poor historic returns from venture capital in Europe. Yet, having worked in both, I would say that these are simplistic and often inaccurate views – of both European and US venture capital. More to the point though, the global venture capital environment has been changing at least as fast as the more visible private equity environment.

The industries whose disruptive innovation drove the venture capital industry – particularly from their epicentre in the United States – are maturing. The storms of disruption are moving on to areas like the media and the environment where Europe, currently, is not at a disadvantage. Indeed Europe now has a lot going for it. Smaller European stock exchanges have become receptive to exciting young companies just when NASDAQ has become, if not actually hostile, then at least unreceptive. Technology transfer from European universities is thriving like never before, Eastern Europe offers the opportunity of 'local offshoring' and in a world of increased mobility, much of Europe offers a stable, well-educated workforce.

So, should we be optimistic about the prospects for venture capital in Europe? Yes, but as a whole it is still a small industry, in some ways too small. It is an industry that makes a real positive contribution to economic growth in Europe and it could do more, but it needs to be nurtured. If you are looking to raise money you will find that the club of active, experienced venture capitalists in Europe is indeed small, particularly as this group frequently works together, syndicating investments. It therefore makes sense to plan your approach carefully. Keith's book gives an excellent and much-needed up-to-date perspective that is worth digesting.

*Patrick Sheehan*
*Founder Partner, ETF (Environmental Technologies Fund)*
*Chairman, Venture Capital Committee, European Private Equity and*
*Venture Capital Association*

# Preface

I have written *Raising Venture Capital Finance in Europe* as a practical guide for the entrepreneur/owner manager who is seeking to raise venture capital financing for a business in the early stages of development in the new and exciting environment in which the European venture capital industry is operating. The book is aimed equally at students in entrepreneurship and finance courses in business schools where a practical approach to the subject will hopefully enhance the more academic and theoretical material from their college professors. It is also intended as background reading for training purposes for people entering, or at an early stage in their careers in, the private equity profession. The book will be useful to professional advisers in Europe who are often approached by persons seeking finance and who could be recommended to the book for further guidance. I hope that the book is also of interest to institutional investors, particularly those looking to enter the European private equity and venture capital industry as investors for the first time and who want to understand more about the European marketplace, as well as to the business angel community.

The book draws on my experience of working in the venture capital and private equity industry as an adviser and commentator over the past 20 years, both in Europe and the United States. I first got involved with the venture capital industry in the early to mid-1980s when I was on secondment to the Pittsburgh, United States office of Price Waterhouse (now PricewaterhouseCoopers). At that time Pittsburgh was attempting to re-brand itself as a high-tech centre following the demise of the traditional steel industry, drawing largely on technology coming out of the local universities. There were a number of venture capital firms operating in the city and the Pittsburgh High-Tech Council was established at that time. Pittsburgh is now an important high-tech and biomedical centre and home of the first robotics institute and of the first simultaneous heart, liver and kidney transplant in the world.

When I returned to PwC's London office from Pittsburgh the British Venture Capital Association (BVCA) had been established for two years. When advising entrepreneurs on preparing business plans and raising finance, I realized that these entrepreneurs often viewed the process of how venture capital firms appraise business proposals and arrive at their required equity stakes as a complete mystery. I was a member of the BVCA's Information Committee at the time and I suggested that the BVCA should have a guide to venture capital – so I was duly asked to write it! The first *Guide to Venture Capital* was published in April 1992 and since then many tens of thousands of copies have been requested from the BVCA or downloaded from the BVCA's website. I have continued to update the guide over the years and it is still published by the BVCA, now as the *Guide to Private Equity*.

One of the first venture capital success stories with which I was involved while at Price Waterhouse in the mid- to late-1980s was that of Century Publishing Company Limited (Century). Century was founded by two publishing industry executives, Anthony Cheetham and Peter Roche, as a specialist trade/consumer publisher, with investor financing of around £750,000 sourced via Venture Link Limited, also a PW client. After three years of trading it merged with the long-established book publisher and distributor, Hutchinson Limited, with no further funds raised. Four years later, Century Hutchinson Group Limited sold out to the Random House Group in the United States for £64.5 million, on a P/E of over 42, making an excellent return for the founders and their investors. The founders stayed on to manage the newly acquired Random Century Group's activities.

But now is also a good time for the European venture capital industry. The year 2005 was a record year for both funds raised and investments. The annual EVCA private equity survey conducted by Thomson Financial and PricewaterhouseCoopers showed that €72 billion funds were raised, the highest ever, of which almost €11 billion was raised for venture, up 24% on 2004, with funds dedicated to high-tech venture doubling in size to €5.1 billion. Overall investments were €47 billion, again the highest ever, with venture experiencing a 23% increase in investment amounting to almost €13 million, which accounted for 75% of the total number of deals. Early indications are that 2006 will see another very good year for both fundraising and investments when the annual data is published in spring 2007. We have seen some recent high-profile success stories such as the sale of venture-capital-backed Skype (the proprietary peer-to-peer internet telephony (VoIP) network) to eBay and the flotation of Q-Cells AG, as well as earlier successes such as Cambridge Silicon Radio which is featured as a case study in this book.

The outlook for the technology sector within the European venture capital industry also looks positive or at least 'cautiously optimistic'. And there is a much-improving entrepreneurial culture in Europe, with many emerging technology centres in key regions of Europe where there are breakthrough companies, top science and technology universities, many with commercial spinout departments, successful managers and engineers with outstanding technology expertise, venture capitalists and other financiers, accountants, lawyers and other advisers and often a whole infrastructure built around science and industrial parks, 'incubator' centres and serviced offices. As we will see in Chapter 6, there is a whole range of entrepreneurial initiatives from the European Commission. It is certainly an exciting time to be setting up a high-growth technology company in Europe.

It is also a good time to celebrate our successes in Europe, something we are often quite shy of doing. Perhaps we can consider showcasing Europe's entrepreneurial and venture capital successes by setting up a 'Museum of Entrepreneurship' (maybe something of a dichotomy!) or even a series of 'museums' with the objectives of:

▌ showcasing European entrepreneurship;

▌ encouraging training for young people in entrepreneurship and familiarizing and interesting others in the subject;

▌ encouraging children to study science at school and university;

▌ holding lectures and seminars on business, finance and marketing topics;

▌ holding seminars from Europe's successful entrepreneurs;

▌ acting as a lobbying forum to encourage new incentives and initiatives for enterprise.

But that is a whole new project – watch this space!

# Acknowledgements

Many people helped in the production of this book. I thank Sir Paul Judge, Chairman of the Enterprise Education Trust and many other organizations, benefactor of the Judge Business School, University of Cambridge and a former Master of the Worshipful Company of Marketors, and Patrick Sheehan, Founder Partner of the Environmental Technologies Fund and Chairman of the Venture Capital Committee of the European Private Equity and Venture Capital Association for their kind comments in the forewords.

I am grateful for the support of the European Private Equity and Venture Capital Association (Javier Echarri and his team) and the British Venture Capital Association (Peter Linthwaite and his team) for contributing material, particularly on European incentives for entrepreneurship from the former and on perspectives on the UK private equity industry and creating success from university spinouts from the latter.

I interviewed several VC firms and entrepreneurs in connection with the case studies featured in the book and appreciate the time that they spent with me. It is the cases that really help the book to come alive. These VC firms and entrepreneurs also kindly contributed their tips for those readers who are seeking to raise venture capital finance and these are included at the end of each case study. I would like to thank the following for contributing cases: Susan Searle and Charlotte Stone of Imperial Innovations, Uli Fricke and Dr Bernd Geiger of Triangle Venture Capital Group, John Cavill of Intermezzo Ventures, Dr Dan Daly of Lein Applied Diagnostics, Frank Kenny and Joey Mason of Delta Partners, Martin Conder of iBase Systems Limited, Jean-Michel Deligny of Go4Venture, Julian Davison and Laurence Garrett from 3i, Dr Phil O'Donovan of Cambridge Silicon Radio, Giuseppe Curatolo of TLcom Capital, Bob Jones of Equiinet, Paul Cartwright of Rutland Partners and Bernard Vogel of Endeavour.

The European Tech Tour Association (Sven Lingaerde, Peter Kazimirski and Johdi Woodford) helped source the Media Lario and Tagsys cases.

Business angel investor Tony Morris shared with me his six questions that investors ask to determine company value. These are included in Chapter 5. Tony also kindly shared with me his approach to investing in high-tech ventures, also included here as a case study.

Nigel Grierson, co-founder of Doughty Hanson Technology Ventures, developed his 'two immutable laws of investing' for the book on the importance of the interpersonal relationship between the management team and the investor.

Jean-Michel Deligny of Go4Venture contributed an extensive case study on Esmertec, in two parts, which explains the challenges of the finance-raising process and the issues that the company faced as it went through, and post, the initial public offering (IPO). I am grateful also to Jean-Michel for his very helpful guidance on non-disclosure agreements and for sharing Go4Venture's Business Plan Scoring Tool with me for inclusion in the book.

My thanks go to all of these individuals for sharing their expertise and giving their invaluable time towards the production of this book.

In addition, Professor John Mullins of London Business School kindly permitted me to feature his seven domains framework included in his *New Business Road Test* (Chapter 8). Joel Kurtzman, former editor of the *Harvard Business Review* and former PwC partner responsible for global thought leadership and innovation, shared his 10 critical factors that will make or break a new company, included in Chapter 5.

Much of the private equity data used in this book is derived from the EVCA and BVCA private equity surveys. I am proud to have been associated with these surveys over the past years and have enjoyed working with the teams, particularly with Mirela Ene at the EVCA, Elissa Brodey at the BVCA and Colin McIlheney and his team at PwC.

I am grateful to Marcia Malcolm, who was a super PA to me during my later years at PwC, for her assistance with the production of the charts, diagrams and graphs.

I also wish to acknowledge the assistance that I have received from the publishers Kogan Page, in particular from Philip Kogan, Chairman, and Ian Hallsworth, Publisher, for encouraging me to write the book in the first place!

Most of all I am indebted to my wife, Kathy, for her enormous encouragement to me during the writing of this book and for putting up with the long hours I spent hidden away in my study. Without her love and devotion I don't think this particular 'venture' would have been achieved! I thank my wife and my parents for their love, support and encouragement in all that I do.

# Why Raise Venture Capital

## by Andrew Myall  www.theIBA.co.uk

Why raise venture capital and what are the issues involved? What is venture capital? People also talk about private equity and everyone loves more tags. Forget private equity. We are talking about relatively small companies seeking to raise typically between £50,000 and £100 million of equity finance when they are not (always!) quoted on a public market like the London Stock Exchange. These are venture capital hunters and it comes in all shapes with varying demands.

Venture capital is sought by companies who need cash, usually to expand or survive, and do not have the cash flow on which to borrow or repay, such as Apple Computers in the early 70s. These companies give up part of their company to venture capital investors. The basic reason for seeking venture capital is to expand businesses more quickly and to achieve personal capital gains from such expansion.

Venture capital seeks such investment opportunities because it thinks it **may** make money from these. It may not. The early investors in Apple probably made about 100 times their money. They certainly made other investments where they lost all their money. Venture capitalists make their money by selling their share of the ownership of a company. They can do that when the shares in their companies become quoted on a stock exchange, hopefully at a higher price than they paid, like Apple or when the company itself is sold to a third party. The venture capitalists in Skype made a great profit when it was sold to eBay. Venture capitalists do of course sometimes sell at a loss or lose all their investment when the particular company goes bust.

So venture capital is risk money. Normally it is not possible to know the outcome of such investments. However venture capital is an established investment group which has developed a lot of expertise in its sector. A good venture capitalist should be able to add advice and insight into industrial sectors and add value to the companies in which they invest. You gain a great advantage if you find such a venture capitalist. Most will claim to add this value, many don't. They will, in any event probably sit on your board and charge you a fee. Good venture capitalists will also help direct your development towards their exit route. This is more jargon for advising you how best to get a stock market quotation for your company or how to sell it. Exit route means a venture capitalist's realisation.

You normally need a business plan showing your company's potential to get a venture capitalist's interest. Some of these investors invest on the quality of the technology only. These are exceptional and you would have to be expert in this area. Most like to see a plan from an existing business wishing to expand. A small minority will invest in start ups. Plans and first impressions are important. It is not unusual for a venture capitalist to look in detail at 20% of the propositions it receives, follow through on 30% of these and consider an investment in 33% of these (i.e. 2) – not a high success rate for a candidate company. To improve your odds you need a quality investment proposal, well presented in a manner with which the venture capitalists are comfortable and a clear strategy for taking them to the exit route with the type of return they seek.

It's harder to find venture capital for smaller investments. For sums of up to £250 to £500,000 private individuals, often known as business angels, are usually the best source. Sometimes these are individuals who have been successful in your industry and can add great management expertise and advice. It then becomes more feasible to consider approaching professional venture capital firms who manage relatively larger sums of third party money. In the UK the best source for venture capitalists is found through the British Venture Capital Association (**www.bvca.co.uk**). About 200 venture capital managers who claim to be in investment mode are registered. Their investment interest varies widely. There are other UK investment sources like Venture Capital Trusts or the UK offices of overseas funds active in the UK. A wider range of managers will be found via the European Venture Capital Association (**www.evca.com**). Business Angels by definition are more individualistic and can be more difficult to find. Internet searching can be productive.

Once identified there is usually a 3 to 6 months process of due diligence, "getting to know" and negotiation of demanding subscription agreements which may be traumatic for first time participants before funds are received. Companies will incur legal and other professional costs in going through this process. Post completion the investment with the venture capitalists has just begun. Typically you will continue to be involved with them for a period of 18 months to 8 years until an exit has been achieved. So when seeking to raise such finance plan for the possibility of failure, accept the requirement to meet some costs in any event, seek the best advice and the most compatible venture capitalist and look forward to a happy exit. Don't go down this route if yours is a lifestyle company only.

CORPORATE FINANCE & STRATEGY

# VENTURE CAPITAL

- **We have over 4500 funding sources within 50 countries covering 25 different industry sectors**

- **We help ensure that your business proposal is investor ready**

- **We short list and contact potential investors and submit your summary**

- **We project manage from offer to legal completion**

- **The IBA is your partner for success**

## CONTACT INFORMATION

The IBA, Quatro House, Lyon Way, Frimley, Surrey, GU16 7ER

Telephone: 01276 804 540
Fax: 01276 804 541

Email: support@theIBA.co.uk
Website: www.theIBA.co.uk

# Introduction

For the entrepreneur with a well-developed business proposition, a team which has previous experience of running a successful business and a properly researched market, where the product or service has the potential to capture a leading stake in the market or a carefully targeted segment of the market, the time has never been better to seek venture capital financing. Knowing how to approach venture capital firms is key and it is also essential to have at least a basic understanding of how they go about appraising an investment proposition.

This book focuses on the entire venture capital process from how to select and approach a venture capital firm, how the venture capitalist goes about appraising the entrepreneur's proposition, how he or she negotiates the terms of the deal, through the due diligence process, dealing with warranties and indemnities, post-investment monitoring by the venture capital firm and, finally, to exit routes including trade sales and stock market flotations.

The book is unashamedly written in layman's terms, with terminology clearly explained. I have included practical advice on preparing a business plan in a form suitable for submitting to a venture capitalist, including the key, but often neglected, areas of the quality and experience of the entrepreneur and his or her management team and the characteristics and growth potential of the market that the product or service is seeking to address. Alternative sources of finance to venture capital are also covered, including government sources, business angel finance and loan and asset-backed finance.

This book expands considerably on the *Guide to Private Equity* which I wrote for the British Venture Capital Association (BVCA), and is supplemented with material that I use in my talks to business school and university students on the private equity process and trends in the industry at Queen Mary, University of London (where I am a visiting fellow) and at Cass Business School (where I am a guest lecturer). The book also includes a series of case histories, drawn from my contacts with venture capital firms and with business angels in Europe, about their criteria for successful venture capital investing, what they look for in a business proposal, and how they seek to add value to their portfolio companies. I have also included cases from the entrepreneur's viewpoint in terms of lessons learnt from approaching and dealing with venture capital firms. The VCs, business angels and entrepreneurs featured in the cases have kindly included their own personal tips for entrepreneurs and management teams seeking venture capital finance. Various summary 'VC tips' are also included in certain chapters; 15 tips in all. There is nothing 'earth shattering' about these, just practical points for you to consider.

The book also includes a detailed assessment of the current status of, and trends and issues in, the private equity and venture capital industries, drawing on my close involvement with UK, European and global private equity and venture capital investment activity and industry surveys of funds raised. While serving as European Venture Capital Leader in PwC's Global Technology Industry Group we were fortunate in securing the opportunity to provide data collection, data analysis and reporting services to first the European Private Equity and Venture Capital Association (EVCA) and then the BVCA on their private equity surveys. I hope that the inclusion of the survey data and my own interpretation of trends and issues in the industry will help the reader to be better informed about the private equity and venture capital marketplace before he or she approaches an investor.

*Raising Venture Capital Finance in Europe* is written to cover all industry sectors, though with a bias towards the technology sectors, and all stages of investment from seed, through start-up and expansion investment. Management buyouts are also addressed, so the central sections on the business plan and the investment process are pertinent to all stages of investment.

## Structure of the book

Chapters 1 to 3 of the book include details on the current status of private equity and venture capital investing in Europe, how the industry is funded and the performance of the different types of fund. Europe's position and influence in the global private equity marketplace are covered, as are the current status of high-tech investing in Europe and the outlook for the industry. The Lisbon Agenda and European Commission initiatives on entrepreneurship are discussed, as are various issues currently affecting the private equity industry in Europe, such as the diversity of returns made by different sectors of the industry, transparency and disclosure by private equity firms and the lack of a pan-European stock exchange. Some common misconceptions of entrepreneurs in raising venture capital are also addressed.

Chapter 4 of the book covers early stage and technology investing, with information on Europe's emerging technology centres, the growing importance of university spinouts and some of the current 'hot' technology sectors for VC investment.

Chapter 5 covers the crucial areas of the management team, the market and the technology – all vital ingredients to a sustainable investment proposition.

Chapter 6 includes information on various sources of finance for a growing business (other than venture capital), including business angels and government grants and assistance in Europe.

How to select and approach a private equity firm, how to prepare a 'winning' business plan, tips on the presentation of the plan to the VC firm, and the whole investment process from how the VC evaluates your proposition to structuring the VC deal, term sheets and the due diligence process are covered in Chapters 7 to 9.

Chapter 10 looks at tax and legal aspects of the private equity deal, including shareholders' agreements and warranties and indemnities.

The ongoing relationship with the investor is covered in Chapter 11, including advice on how to maintain an effective working relationship with the investor and how the VC firm can help the growth and success of an investee company.

Chapter 12 covers the various exit routes open to the management team, with focus on the trade sale and going public.

Finally, in the concluding remarks I draw together the various 'VC tips' that appear in the individual chapters of the book. I hope you enjoy reading the book and I wish you every success in your efforts to raise venture capital finance in Europe.

# 1

# Introduction to private equity

Private equity is medium- to long-term finance provided in the form of share capital to unquoted companies which have the potential to achieve, or are in fact achieving, significant growth and profitability. It is provided by private equity firms, most of which are constituted as limited liability partnerships.

## DEFINITIONS OF PRIVATE EQUITY AND VENTURE CAPITAL

Private equity is the overall umbrella term for the entire industry and includes venture capital, which is financing for the early stage (ie seed and start-up) and expansion or development stages of a business, and equity capital for management buyouts and management buy-ins and also including replacement capital and secondary purchases. This is the context in which private equity is referred to in this book and in all the data to which reference is made.

Some commentators use the term 'private equity' to refer only to the management buyout and management buy-in investment stages. Some others in Europe use the term 'venture capital' to cover all stages, ie synonymous with 'private equity', while in the United States 'venture capital' refers only to investments in early-stage and expanding companies. Even in the United States there are differences in definitions in venture capital, with some people including the later expansion stages in private equity.

In Europe people are starting to use venture capital to mean capital for start-up and young hyper-growth companies and private equity to mean capital for management buyouts and growth capital. All very confusing!

The different definitions of private equity only get to be a real problem when you start to compare data on the private equity and venture capital industry prepared by different data providers and end up comparing apples and oranges. For the purposes of this book, and in line with European Private Equity and Venture Capital Association (EVCA) and British Venture Capital Association (BVCA) definitions, I am using venture capital to include the seed, start-up and expansion stages and private equity as the umbrella term to include venture capital and management buyouts.

# HISTORY OF PRIVATE EQUITY IN EUROPE

Private equity in Europe originated in the late 18th century, when entrepreneurs found wealthy individuals to back their projects on an ad hoc basis. These wealthy individuals were effectively the forerunners to today's so-called 'business angels'. Of course, similar things were happening in the United States, with wealthy industrial families such as the Carnegies, the Mellons and the Rockefellers, who had built up vast fortunes in steel, banking and oil, making investments in entrepreneurial ventures.

Following the Second World War the forerunner to 3i (known as the Industrial and Commercial Finance Corporation or ICFC) was set up in 1945 in the UK, owned by the Bank of England and the clearing banks at the time. ICFC was set up to address the 'equity gap' at the time of between £5,000 and £200,000, popularly known as the 'MacMillan Gap' after the prime minister of the time and the MacMillan Committee. This committee had recognized the existence of such a gap as far back as the early 1930s, whereby unquoted small- and medium-sized firms were unable to afford an approach to the capital markets and were not able to secure bank financing (Coopey, 1994). This equity or funding gap still exists today and is widely regarded as being between £250,000 and £2 million, where it is very difficult to secure venture capital finance for the reasons set out in Chapter 6.

**Table 1.1** Definition of private equity

Private equity = venture capital + management buyouts, management buy-ins and replacement capital/secondary purchases
Venture capital = seed, start-up and expansion stages

From the 1960s onwards, a subsidiary of ICFC, Technical Development Capital (TDC), was set up to invest specifically in high-technology projects. At the same time, the United States was striking a lead as regards the commercial development of high technology, with establishments such as the Massachusetts Institute of Technology (MIT) actively promoting technology 'spinout' companies from its academic research.

Private equity became an industry in Europe in the late 1970s and early 1980s when a number of private equity firms were founded. Professional associations for private equity were then set up with, for example, both the European Private Equity and Venture Capital Association (EVCA) and the British Venture Capital Association (BVCA) being established in 1983.

# DEVELOPMENT OF THE EUROPEAN PRIVATE EQUITY INDUSTRY

The European private equity market has grown enormously over the past decade, from an investment level of around €5 billion in 1995 to a peak of €47 billion in 2005, as shown by the annual private equity surveys conducted by Thomson Financial and PricewaterhouseCoopers for the EVCA.

The previous peak in the industry for funds raised and investments was at the height of the dot.com/internet boom in 2000. At that time there was proportionately more money going into the venture stages of investment than into management buyouts. A number of new venture capital firms were set up to compete with the established venture players. But many did not survive the fallout from this unusual period. Inexperienced investment managers, some of whom had successful backgrounds in buyout investing, ignored the rules of traditional investment proposal decision making, often carried out little or no due diligence and sometimes made investment decisions almost overnight in the extreme competitive market of that era. No wonder they got burnt. There followed a period of extensive write-offs of venture portfolios and a weeding out of the industry. The survivors are the experienced venture players who are going on to raise new funds successfully for technology and venture investing.

Europe has almost caught up with North America in terms of amounts invested. In 2004 Europe represented 39% of global private equity investments by amount; North America represented 41%, as shown by the annual PwC Global Private Equity Report.

Private equity is now a recognized asset class, along with other investments such as bonds, cash, international securities and real estate. Private equity consistently demonstrates superior returns over the medium and long term compared to the principal comparator indices, as shown, for example, in the BVCA's annual 'Performance Measurement Survey' conducted by PricewaterhouseCoopers.

EVCA now has over 925 full member private equity firms and the BVCA has over 180 full member firms. There are some 1,600 private equity firms in all in Europe. One of the issues for the entrepreneur is knowing which of these many firms to approach, and this is discussed in Chapter 7.

The industry's continued development has been helped by an improving entrepreneurial spirit in the UK (one of the positive outcomes of the internet and dot.com 'bubble'), a relatively strong economy, consistent outperforming by the industry of the comparator stock market indices in the medium to long term and an improving environment with regard to government incentives and in some tax areas.

## THE FIREPOWER OF PRIVATE EQUITY

As will be discussed in detail in Chapter 2, the private equity industry is now truly global, though around 80% of investment activity occurs in North America and Europe. The industry raised $248 billion in funds worldwide in 2005, as shown by the annual PwC Global Private Equity Report. The trend appears to be for mega funds, with funds for buyouts in the range of $15–20 billion raised by international private equity firms such as the Blackstone Group, Kohlberg Kravis Roberts (KKR) and Texas Pacific based in the United States, and Permira based in Europe.

A recent study by Deloitte showed that private equity has the firepower to acquire 43% of the FTSE 100 in the UK. In fact private equity firms have already acquired many leading companies in the UK such as Birds Eye (formerly part of Unilever), Debenhams, Travelex, Kwik-Fit, Saga, the AA, Le Meridien hotels (now part of the Starwood group), NCP and many more. With the huge funds now available to private equity, and particularly if the large private equity firms pool their resources in so-called 'club' deals, the industry has the ability to make substantial acquisitions going forward.

# THE CONTRIBUTION OF PRIVATE EQUITY

The creation of value for investors involves more than just funding and, at both the smaller and the larger ends of the investment spectrum, private equity firms can contribute to the growth of the companies that they back in many ways. Whether by using their experience to provide support to the management teams, or by providing guidance on strategic or operational issues, private equity firms will usually be a source of considerable help. As shown in the BVCA's publication *The Economic Impact of Private Equity in the UK*, published in November 2005, four out of five companies sampled felt that their private equity backers had made a major contribution to their businesses over and above the provision of money.

Private equity can promote economic growth and create jobs. Studies by the BVCA show consistently that employment rises by up to 20% when private equity is involved. Around a fifth of UK private sector employees are now employed by companies that have received funding from private equity firms.

# EUROPEAN VENTURE CAPITAL AND TECHNOLOGY INVESTING

Apart from the height of the dot.com/internet era in the year 2000, much of the recent growth in the private equity industry has been focused on management buyouts, with the bulk of the monies currently being raised for the industry designated for this area. In 2005 over 80% of all funds raised in Europe were expected to be allocated to buyouts, compared with just 15% to investments at the venture capital stages. This contrasts with 65% for buyouts in 2004 and 32% for venture capital. However, in terms of the numbers of investments actually made, as opposed to absolute amounts, 8,152 investments were made at the venture capital stages (75% of all investments by number) and 2,366 were made at the buyout stage (22%). This simply reflects the vast difference in deal size between venture and buyout investments.

As we will see in Chapter 3, investments at the venture stages of investment (seed, start-up, other early-stage and expansion) can realize exceptional returns for the experienced venture capital investor. All the criteria are currently in place for an upturn in the venture capital and technology industry, including increased spending on information technology as infrastructure requires renewing, improved earnings of the international technology-based corporations, a more active mergers and acquisitions market, an increase in the number of flotations on the European stock markets (especially on the London-based Alternative Investment Market or AIM) and a less risk-averse, more entrepreneurial approach among Europeans looking to start up and grow their own businesses.

Many of today's leading technology companies have received venture capital backing at some point in their life cycles. In the United States these include Amgen, Apple Computers, Cisco, Compaq, Fairchild Semiconductors, Genentech, Google, Intel, Lotus Development, Netscape, Oracle and Yahoo! In Europe we have perhaps fewer 'big name' success stories. Skype is a recent example. Skype, backed by Index Ventures and others, was sold to eBay for $2.6 billion in 2005. The German solar cell company, Q-Cells AG, was backed by Apax Partners and others, went public in early 2006 and was reportedly the largest single capital gain made by a European venture capital firm since the dot.com boom.

Examples of other venture capital and, in the wider context, private-equity-backed companies in Europe in a variety of industries include: Actelion, Antler, Autonomy, Benjys, Ben Sherman, Cambridge Silicon Radio, Earls Court & Olympia, Filofax, First Leisure, Focus Wickes, Halfords, Kwik Fit, Legoland, Linguaphone, Ministry of Sound, New Look, Nexagent, Oxford Glycosciences, Pinewood – Shepperton Studios, Plastic Logic, the AA, Waterstone's and Yell.

# THE ADVANTAGES OF PRIVATE EQUITY

Private equity is invested in exchange for a stake in your company and, as shareholders, the private equity firm's returns are dependent on the growth and profitability of your business. Private equity is a medium- to long-term investment providing a solid capital base for the future, to meet the growth and development plans of your business. Unlike a bank loan, there is no repayment expected during the term of investment and no interest costs. There are also no charges on your business assets or security required on your personal assets, such as your home, and no personal guarantees required from you or your fellow directors, any or all of which may be required by a bank lender. A bank may in extreme circumstances even bankrupt you, if you have given personal guarantees. Debt which is secured in this way and which has a higher priority for repayment than that of general unsecured creditors is referred to as 'senior debt' (Table 1.2).

The private equity process and subsequent period of investment provides a true business partnership with a venture capitalist who shares in the risks and rewards of the business along with the entrepreneur. A bank lender has a legal right to interest on a loan and repayment of the capital, irrespective of the success or failure of the business.

The private equity firm is rewarded by the company's success, generally achieving its principal return through realizing a capital gain through an 'exit' which may include:

∎ selling their shares back to the management;

∎ selling the shares to another investor (such as another private equity firm);

∎ a trade sale (the sale of company shares to another);

∎ the company achieving a stock market listing.

The provider of debt (generally a bank) is rewarded by interest and capital repayment of the loan.

The private equity firm should also provide you with advice and expertise during the investment period by providing guidance on strategic or operational issues, introducing you to their network of contacts, which may include potential customers and suppliers, or helping to fill gaps in your management team.

The private equity firm will seek to increase a company's value to its owners, without taking day-to-day management control. Although the entrepreneur will have a smaller share of the total equity in the company, within a few years that share should be worth considerably more than the entire company was worth before the venture capital investment.

## HOW THE PRIVATE EQUITY INDUSTRY IN EUROPE IS FUNDED

Before proceeding to look at how the entrepreneur should go about the process of raising venture capital investment to finance his or her own business, an understanding of how and where a private equity firm raises the finance to invest in growing businesses or management buyouts in the first place would be helpful.

Private equity finance derives essentially from the institutions, ie the banks, pension funds and insurance companies. In 2005, according to the EVCA/Thomson Financial/PwC data, a total of €71.8 billion was raised, 54% of which came from the pension funds, banks and insurance companies taken together, some €36.2 billion. Funds of funds (which are funds set up to distribute finance from the institutions among a selection

**Table 1.2** Private equity compared to senior debt

| Private equity | Senior debt |
| --- | --- |
| Medium to long term. | Short to long term. |
| Committed until 'exit'. | Not likely to be committed if the safety of the loan is threatened. Overdrafts are payable on demand; loan facilities can be payable on demand if the covenants are not met. |
| Provides a solid, flexible, capital base to meet your future growth and development plans. | A useful source of finance if the debt to equity ratio is conservatively balanced and the company has good cash flow. |
| Good for cash flow, as capital repayment, dividend and interest costs (if relevant) are tailored to the company's needs and to what it can afford. | Requires regular good cash flow to service interest and capital repayments. |
| The returns to the private equity investor depend on the business's growth and success. The more successful the company is, the better the returns all investors will receive. | Depends on the company continuing to service its interest costs and to maintain the value of the assets on which the debt is secured. |
| If the business fails, private equity investors will rank alongside other shareholders, after the banks and other lenders, and stand to lose their investment. | If the business fails, the lender generally has first call on the company's assets. |
| If the business runs into difficulties, the private equity firm will work hard to ensure that the company is turned around. | If the business appears likely to fail, the lender could put your business into receivership in order to safeguard its loan, and could make you personally bankrupt if personal guarantees have been given. |
| A true business partner, sharing in your risks and rewards, with practical advice and expertise (as required) to assist your business success. | Assistance available varies considerably. |

Source: BVCA, *A Guide to Private Equity*

of private equity fund managers, who in turn invest the capital directly) and government agencies provided a further 13% and 10%, respectively, with the remainder coming from private individuals, corporate investors and academic institutions. Just less than half (47%) of the funds raised for Europe in 2005 came from domestic sources, ie from the country in which the private equity firm is managed, with funds raised from other European countries representing 18% of funds raised and funds raised from non-European countries contributing 34%. After the UK the United States is the largest contributor to European funds and the UK and United States combined contributed 53% of total European funds in 2005.

So the European private equity industry is itself financed in large part by the large pension funds, university endowments and other institutions in the UK and United States. Why should they risk their money in private equity, which is generally acknowledged to have above average risk among the various asset classes? It is basically a question of diversification. A pension fund manager, for example, will wish to place a proportion of funds with different asset classes, with so much in equities, so much in government stocks, so much in real estate, hedge funds, cash and private equity. As noted above, and discussed more fully in Chapter 3, private equity consistently generates superior returns over the medium and long term compared to the principal comparator indices, such as the FTSE 100 and FTSE All-Share indices. So the pension fund manager can achieve a better return on his or her money by investing a proportion in private equity. The amount a pension fund will invest in private equity varies from country to country and is typically between 2½ and 5% in Europe. Other institutions, particularly in the United States, will invest a considerably higher percentage of their assets into private equity. For example, the Washington State Investment Board is considering whether to raise the ceiling on its self-imposed limit of 17% into private equity investment.

## LIMITED LIABILITY PARTNERSHIPS AND THE FUNDRAISING PROCESS

The limited liability partnership is the most common form of structure for a private equity fund in Europe and the United States. It originated in the United States with well-known Silicon Valley venture capital firms such as Kleiner Perkins, Sequoia and Accel and has been adopted in Europe by many private equity firms such as Amadeus, Apax Partners and Advent Venture Partners in the UK, Sofinnova Partners in France, Capricorn Ventures in Belgium and Wellington Partners in Germany.

The pension funds and other institutions invest their money into a private equity fund as limited partners. They are called limited partners because their exposure is limited to the amount that they are investing in the fund. This usually follows a fundraising process by the managers of the private equity firm, who are known as the general partners.

First of all, the general partners determine the investment strategy for the fund, which has to be followed once the limited partners have invested in the fund. The investment strategy determines, for example:

▮ the fund's focus on early- or late-stage venture capital, growth capital or buyout investments or all of these;

▮ the fund's sector focus: software, biotech or other technology, consumer related, industrial products;

▮ whether the fund is to be country specific in terms of the location of the investments that it makes, or pan-European or even global;

▮ the minimum and maximum investment size.

Then the general partners prepare their business plan or fund private placement memorandum. The amount of funds they seek to raise will typically be around €200 million for a technology fund and anything up to €15 billion for a mega buyout fund.

The general partners have total control over what investments are made by the fund. The limited partners have no say over this, though they may sit on an advisory board. Depending on investor interest, the fundraising will either be successful and raise the required amount, maybe even oversubscribed, or the fundraising will be abandoned. Success with fundraising is rather like an entrepreneur trying to raise funds from a venture capitalist: it depends on the quality of the management team, succession issues, the track record or performance of earlier funds and the attractiveness of the sector for which the funds are being raised. If the fundraising is successful then the investors will commit the required amount to the fund, which is then drawn down as needed so that investments can be made.

Fundraising can be a slow process, often taking up to a year or even longer in the current climate, post the relatively 'easy' times of the dot.com/internet period. Even established venture firms with successful track records have been finding it tough to raise new funds for technology and venture capital investing; some have given up but fortunately others around Europe have been successful in raising funds of the order of €200 million. At the other end of the extreme, the mega international buyout houses have been turning investors away as their funds of up to $15 billion become oversubscribed.

The funding process whereby funds flow into the private equity fund from the limited partners and from the fund into the investee companies is illustrated in Figure 1.1.

A limited liability private equity fund usually has a 10-year life. During the first two to four years of the life of the fund the investment executives of the private equity management team are sourcing and making suitable investments. This is when cash flows out of the fund and into the investee companies. During the next three to five years the investment executives or their nominees are serving on the boards of the investee companies, monitoring the investments and hopefully adding value through strategic and hands-on advice so that the investee companies achieve profitable growth. Then in the final years of the life of the fund the private equity managers will be looking for appropriate exit routes for their investment, usually through a trade sale or stock market flotation. When an investment is sold, cash is received back

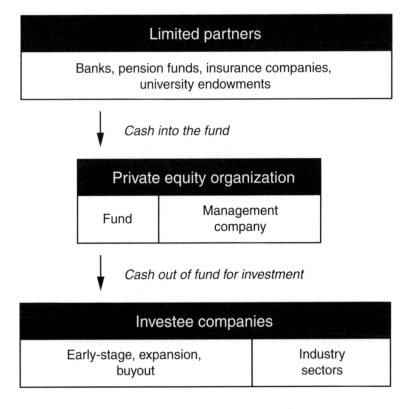

**Figure 1.1** Simplified funding process (injection of funds)

into the fund at a multiple of the amount invested and cash is then returned to the limited partners, generating the internal rate of return (IRR) (Figure 1.2).

About halfway through the life of a fund or even earlier the managers will be looking to raise a new fund, either in the same or different industry and geographic sectors, on the back of the success of the current and earlier funds. As not all investments may have been realized (sold) at the time of this subsequent fundraising, the performance or IRR may be partly based on unrealized returns based on a valuation of the underlying investments using recognized valuation guidelines (in Europe these would be the International Private Equity and Venture Capital Valuation Guidelines, produced by the BVCA, EVCA and AFIC (the French national association) which were introduced in March 2005).

An advantage of the limited liability partnership model, and perhaps the prime motivation for it being set up, is that it is tax transparent for the limited partners who are treated by the tax authorities as if they are

| Limited partners |
|---|
| Banks, pension funds, insurance companies, university endowments |

↑ *Cash returned to Limited partners*
*(generating Internal Rate of Return (IRR))*

| Private equity organization | |
|---|---|
| Fund | Management company |

↑ *Cash received on realization of investment*
*ie IPO or trade sale*
*(at multiple of amount invested)*

| Investee companies | |
|---|---|
| Early-stage, expansion, buyout | Industry sectors |

**Figure 1.2**  Simplified funding process (return of funds)

investing directly in the underlying companies themselves, ie effectively bypassing the fund itself. Otherwise there would be a taxation charge when the underlying investments are sold in excess of cost and the proceeds are received into the fund and again when the fund remits the proceeds to the investors.

# OTHER TYPES OF FUND

Limited liability partnership funds tend to be independent of a parent, institutional body. Captive funds are owned usually by a financial institution, such as a bank or pension fund, and receive their funds for investment as required from the parent. Semi-captive funds raise some of their finance from external investors with the remainder coming from the parent. In Europe in 2005 independents represented 72% of total investments by amount, captives represented 15% and semi-captives 11%.

Some venture capital firms are organized as corporations rather than as partnerships. They have the advantage of a theoretically unlimited life, unlike the typical 10-year life span of a limited liability partnership.

A small number of venture capital firms are quoted. The most well known of these is 3i, which is a quoted investment trust and has been listed on the London Stock Exchange since 1994. Its ability to finance investments from its own capital depends in part on the vagaries of the stock market, although 3i also raises third-party co-investment funds that it manages and which are co-invested alongside its own capital when financing buyouts. The US private equity firm, KKR, listed its $5 billion Private Equity Investors publicly traded buyout fund on Euronext Amsterdam in 2006 and a number of other, mainly US, players, but also including Doughty Hanson in the UK, are considering following suit depending on the stability of the world stock markets.

Venture capital trusts (VCTs) are also publicly quoted. Private investors can invest directly into VCTs on much the same basis as a unit trust. There are various tax advantages associated with VCTs (see Chapter 6). VCTs invest into growth companies in much the same way as a typical venture capital fund.

There are also public sector funds such as the European Investment Fund (EIF), which is part of the European Investment Bank (EIB) and invests into various venture capital funds rather than directly into the underlying investee companies. The Regional Venture Capital Funds in the UK (see Chapter 6) are another example of public sector funds.

# WHAT YOU NEED TO RAISE VENTURE CAPITAL

For the entrepreneur looking to raise venture capital to start up or expand a company, as discussed at length in Chapter 5, you will need to demonstrate to the venture capital firm that you have:

▪ prepared a realistic business plan with a robust business model in place;

▪ a product, using innovative and commercially viable technology, or service with a competitive edge or unique selling point (USP);

▪ protected intellectual property (IP) if applicable;

▪ the ability to take a leading position in a growing market;

▪ evidence of your customer base (and ideally some revenues already generated);

▪ an experienced, complementary management team, including members who have relevant industry sector experience and who have grown successful businesses before, and who are ambitious enough to grow the company rapidly.

# SOME COMMON MISCONCEPTIONS OF ENTREPRENEURS IN RAISING VENTURE CAPITAL

Entrepreneurs and others typically have various preconceived ideas, issues and concerns about the venture capital industry and the perceived willingness or otherwise of VCs to invest in growth businesses. These include, but are not limited to the following:

▪ *'VCs got their fingers burnt in the dot.com bubble. VCs are now totally risk averse. They will not invest in fledgling start-up or early stage companies like mine.'* This is simply not true. Sure there were mistakes made in the 1999/2000 period during the exuberance of the dot.com/internet period followed by hefty write-offs in 2001/2. It's 'back to basics' now and if you have the right elements in place, namely experienced management and a well-thought-out business proposition with a sensible business model, you should be able to raise venture capital finance.

■  *'The VCs will control and completely take over my company. After I
have sweated time and money in developing and building up my
venture, why should I give up part of my equity to an outside shareholder?'* Depending on their assessment of the risk of investing in
your business they may require control in certain circumstances. But
this is rarely the case. In any event, is it better to have a large share of
non-venture-backed business which probably won't meet its
potential or a smaller share of a properly funded venture which has
more chances of successful growth?

■  *'VCs are only interested in achieving a financial return on their
investment, not in adding value to my business.'* Well yes, they do
need to make an adequate financial return for their own investors and
themselves but they will usually seek to add value to your business in
several ways (see Chapter 11) as this will help the company to
achieve successful growth and benefit their investment in your
business as well as yours.

■  *'There is no seed money available these days for young businesses.'*
Wrong! In 2005 in Europe well over 400 pure seed investments were
made by European VCs in over 350 companies amounting to €97
million and that's not to mention the very much greater amount (24
times larger) that was invested in start-up companies. And then there
are many networks of so-called 'business angels' (wealthy individuals) who can invest in seed, start-up and very early-stage enterprises and the various European Commission and national
government support for small, growing businesses (see Chapter 6).

■  *'If I say that I will capture x%, a relatively small share but of a huge,
growing market, that is bound to impress the VCs.'* Sorry, no. You
need to actually demonstrate that a large and/or growing market
exists for your product or service, how you plan to enter and/or
address that market and how much of it you plan to capture in terms
of projected revenues.

■  *'I'm a technical expert with no track record in running companies
before and little management experience. I will never be able to raise
any venture capital finance.'* You ideally need to bring other people
who have the financial, sales and operational expertise onto your
team. If your idea is really disruptive the VC firm may offer to find
these people for you. If you have one or two gaps in your team the VC
will almost certainly help, provided they are keen on your proposition, of course.

■  *'I want to take my company public in three years. That is how I will
achieve my exit and the exit for my investors.'* Many entrepreneurs

say this. However, a trade sale is far more likely these days as an exit (see Chapter 12). Even if you do float, this is not really an immediate exit for you or your investors as you may not be able to actually sell your shares for some time due to the so-called 'lock-up period' that the investment banks will insist upon in order to allow an orderly market to develop in the shares.

■ *'My business plan calls for a finance requirement of €100,000 now. I may need some more capital in a few years time.'* VCs are not interested in putting relatively small amounts of money into a venture. This is more the province of friends and family, business angels and government support. If you really do see the need for substantially more capital as your business grows then build it into your plan and projections so the VC can see the total funding requirement.

■ *'There's a wall of money out there for investing. Why can't the VC take a gamble on my proposal? If it doesn't work out they have plenty more money available to try something else.'* As we will see in Chapter 2, there is about a year and a half's supply of private equity finance in Europe based on current investment levels and considerably less in terms of funds available for venture capital investments in technology enterprises. In any event this is not how VCs invest. Each investment decision they make is based on a very careful evaluation of an investment proposal, followed by extensive due diligence. They are not in the business of throwing darts at a dartboard, so to speak, and hoping that one dart will hit the bull's-eye!

■ *'I'm not going to reveal anything about my proposal to a potential investor unless he or she signs a non-disclosure agreement.'* Then he or she may well decline to show any interest in your proposition. NDAs are a tricky area, which is why I take some considerable space in discussing them in Chapter 9. They are of course appropriate in certain circumstances.

■ *'As I've put so much time and effort into developing my business I don't need to make a further financial commitment when the VC invests.'* You can't expect a VC to invest if you are not prepared to make a financial commitment too at the time of investment, despite the years you may already have put into building the business.

■ *'I'll save time by sending my business plan to a whole series of VC firms at the same time.'* Don't adopt the 'scattergun approach'. Be selective in which VCs you approach, make it personal and wait for constructive feedback before you approach too many more.

▌ *'The VCs can make an immediate decision on whether to invest in my company. If they decide to go ahead we can get the deal done almost overnight.'* Well, maybe this might have been the case in the dot.com era but no longer. It's 'back to basics' and a very careful evaluation of your business proposition will be made. This is not to say that the VCs can't and won't move very quickly if necessary. Otherwise expect the process to take up six months or more!

## Assume nothing!

One of the most common mistakes in raising venture capital finance is to make false assumptions along the process, ie that people will take the time to read your business plan, that you will receive constructive feedback on your plan, that you will actually control your company post-investment, that your first customer will come in on time, that the sales and profit projections in your plan will actually materialize, that your key management and other employees won't get cold feet or attracted away to other, potentially more lucrative employment. A whole host of uncertain areas. Ask as many questions as you can during the funding process, of your potential investors, of your fellow team members, of your suppliers. And most of all 'assume nothing'.

I first came across this motto 'assume nothing' when I was carrying out an investigation assignment for a banking client of Price Waterhouse in the United States on a Miami-based yacht marina and supplier. The Miami business was owned by a lawyer who was also the bank's legal adviser in Florida. He had a substantial loan from the bank to finance the marina and an associated restaurant and was paying neither interest nor principal back to the bank on the loan. He had the words 'assume nothing' emblazoned on a plaque behind his desk. It turned out that he was also one of the largest cemetery operators in South Florida. It also turned out to be one of my most interesting assignments at the then Price Waterhouse and his motto has always stuck with me and been of great value on many occasions.

# VC Tip #1

### Assume nothing!

Things may not be what they seem. Don't be afraid to ask questions and get feedback as you go through the venture capital raising process.

# 2

# Growth and trends in the European private equity marketplace

## EUROPEAN PRIVATE EQUITY ACTIVITY

By all accounts 2005 (the most recent year for which full year data is available) was a very successful year for the European private equity industry (Figure 2.1). Funds raised soared to a record €71.8 billion in 2005, more than two and a half times the amount of €27.5 billion raised in 2004.

Total amounts invested by European private equity firms reached an all-time high of €47.0 billion in 2005, representing a 27% increase compared to the amount invested of €36.9 billion in 2004, and the number of investments increased slightly to 10,915 from 10,236 in 2004. Europe may even have caught up with North America in terms of amounts invested when global data for 2005 is available. As mentioned earlier, in 2004 Europe represented 39% of global private equity investments by amount; North America represented 41%.

Divestments at cost (ie exits such as trade sales and IPOs) also reached a record level at €29.8 billion in 2005, up 52% from 2004's total of €19.6 billion.

Indications are that 2006 will follow 2005 as another successful year, particularly with regard to fundraising, with some major fundraisings already having taken place.

### Key countries for private equity activity in Europe

Private equity activity around Europe varies enormously. The UK is by far the biggest player (Figure 2.2), with UK-headquartered private equity firms

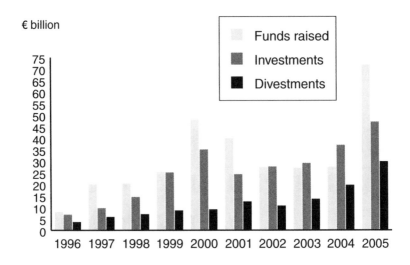

Source: 2005 European Private Equity Survey
Conducted by Thomson Financial and PricewaterhouseCoopers on behalf of EVCA

**Figure 2.1**  European private equity – summary activity

raising some €45.6 billion in 2005, or 64% of the European total. France was in second position with €11.5 billion raised (16% of total funds raised) and Germany third with €2.9 billion raised (4% of total funds raised).

The private equity industry in the UK has grown rapidly from the mid-1980s and is second in importance globally only to the United States. It continues to be the driving force of the UK enterprise economy. Around one-fifth of UK private sector employees are now employed by companies that have been invested in by private equity firms. The industry's success has led the Financial Services Authority (FSA) in the UK to consider scrutinizing the larger private equity groups as the regulator grapples with the perceived possible risks to the stability of the financial system posed by the private equity industry's growth. The FSA has said recently that it will be looking at disclosure by private equity firms and their impact on the transparency of the financial markets. Prior to this, in 2005, the FSA scrutinized private equity firms' compliance and anti-money laundering controls.

# SOURCES OF EUROPEAN FUNDS RAISED

The institutions provide the bulk of the European funds. The pension funds overtook the banks in 2005 as the largest single source of funds at

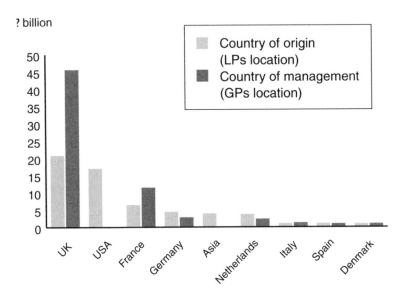

Source: 2005 European Private Equity Survey
Conducted by Thomson Financial and PricewaterhouseCoopers on behalf of EVCA

**Figure 2.2** European funds raised in 2005. Country of origin and country of management of European funds raised

€16.9 billion, or 25% of total funds raised. The banks contributed €11.9 billion, or 18% of total funds raised; funds of funds contributed 13% at €8.9 billion; insurance companies were the fourth largest source at 11% of total funds raised at €7.5 billion. Other funds came from government agencies (10%), private individuals (6%), corporate investors (5%), academic institutions (2.5%) and capital markets (1%).

## ALLOCATION OF FUNDS RAISED

For the entrepreneur it is where these funds intend to allocate their resources which is perhaps more important than the absolute amounts raised. Not surprisingly, the proportion of funds raised for buyouts continued to increase; in fact by over three times in 2005 from €17.8 billion in 2004 (65% share) to €57.7 billion or 80% of total funds raised in 2005 (Figure 2.3). Encouragingly, the proportion of funds raised for high-tech early-stage and expansion investments doubled, now representing 7% of total funds raised at €5.1 billion, up from €2.5 billion or 9% of funds raised in 2004. However, the proportion raised for non-high-tech early-stage and expansion investments decreased by 8% to €5.8 billion, representing 8% of total funds raised.

Funds raised that are expected to be invested in early-stage high-tech companies increased over 2½ times to 5% of funds raised at €3.5 billion from €1.3 billion in 2004, while funds raised expected to be invested in high-tech companies at the expansion/development stage increased almost 1½ times to €1.5 billion.

Funds raised expected to be invested in non-high-tech companies at the early stage increased almost 1½ times to €0.9 billion, while funds raised for non-high-tech companies at the expansion/development stage decreased by 13% to €4.9 billion.

For the larger countries, in terms of funds raised, there are some quite large differences between countries in the split between funds allocated to buyouts and funds allocated to high-tech, although, with the exception of Switzerland, substantially more funds tend to be allocated to buyouts. For example, the UK allocated 93% to buyouts and just 1% to high-tech venture capital. France allocated 66% to buyouts and 9% to high-tech venture capital; Germany allocated 43% to buyouts and 26% to high-tech. Italy allocated 37% to buyouts and just 2% to high-tech venture capital (over 50% going to non-high-tech venture capital). Switzerland

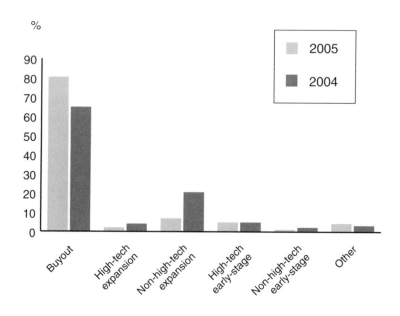

Source: 2005 European Private Equity Survey
Conducted by Thomson Financial and PricewaterhouseCoopers on behalf of EVCA

**Figure 2.3**  Expected allocation of European funds raised

allocated just 13% to buyouts and 87% to high-tech venture capital (all at early stage). This could mean that, as a high-tech entrepreneur, you might be better off approaching a Swiss firm for investment rather than a UK firm, all other conditions being equal (which of course they will not be). In Switzerland the total amount allocated to high-tech venture capital was €1.3 billion, more than double the €0.6 billion allocated to high-tech venture capital in the UK.

## EUROPEAN INVESTMENT ACTIVITY

As noted above, total amounts invested by European private equity firms reached €47.0 billion in 2005 (Figure 2.4). Management buyouts represented 66% of the total amount invested in Europe in 2005 at €32.1 billion, an increase of 25% from their 69% share in 2004 (€25.7 billion). Buyouts represented 22% of the total number of investments, compared to their 18% share in 2004. Venture capital investments represented 27% of total investments in 2005 at €12.7 billion, up 23% from €10.3 billion in 2004. Replacement capital represented the balance at €2.2 billion.

UK private equity firms invested 51% of the total European investment amount at €23.8 billion in terms of the country of management of the private equity firm making the investment, followed

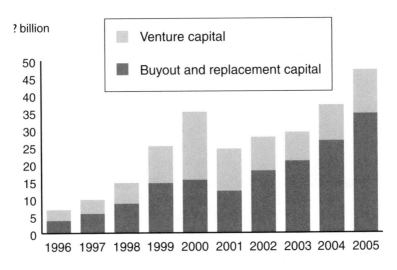

Source: 2005 European Private Equity Survey
Conducted by Thomson Financial and PricewaterhouseCoopers on behalf of EVCA

**Figure 2.4** European private equity investments

by France with 16% of the total investment amount at €7.3 billion and Sweden with 6.5% at €3.0 billion, followed by Germany and Spain, both of which had investments representing 6% of the total at €2.7 billion. In terms of the country of destination of investments (ie the country in which an investment as made by a private equity firm is located) the UK was still in the lead, although to a lesser extent as shown in Figure 2.5.

Seed investments fell again in 2005, in terms of both their share of investment amount and the absolute amount. Seed investments represented just 0.2% by amount at €97 million in 2005 compared to 0.4% by amount at €148 million in 2004. Seed again represented 4% by number of investments in 2005 at 416 investments, up slightly from 405 in 2004.

Start-up investments increased slightly in 2005 from €2.2 billion in 2004 (6% share) to €2.3 billion (5% share). Start-ups represented 29% by number (30% in 2004) with 3,175 investments.

The largest category of investments by number in 2005 was the expansion stage at 42%, as in 2004 (45%), which represented 22% of the total investment amount at €10.2 billion, up 29% from €7.9 billion in 2004.

Among the larger countries the predominance of buyouts was most marked in France, where buyouts represented 77% of the total amount invested, followed by the UK at 73%. Mega buyouts (ie those greater

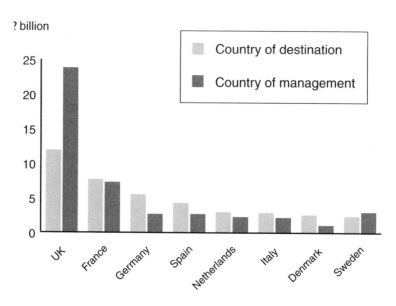

Source: 2005 European Private Equity Survey
Conducted by Thomson Financial and PricewaterhouseCoopers on behalf of EVCA

**Figure 2.5**  European private equity investments in 2005. Country of destination and country of management

than €300 million in equity value) took place in the UK (where they represented 31% of buyouts by amount), Spain (20% of buyouts) and France (8% of buyouts).

Most countries had relatively little investment by amount at the seed stage, with the exception of Finland where seed investments represented 10% of investments by amount, and Portugal with 5% seed investments by amount. Countries with the highest proportion of start-up investments were Belgium, where start-ups represented 30% of total investment amount, Switzerland at 21%, and Austria and Portugal, each with 20%.

Countries with a high proportion of investment at the expansion stage include Hungary, where expansion represented 87% of the total investment by amount, Denmark at 69%, Switzerland at 66%, Norway at 61% and Portugal at 56%.

The majority of investments are made within the private equity operators' home countries – 86% by number and 62% by amount of investment in 2005. Investments made in other European countries (eg outside the host country) represented 10% by number and 35% by value, while investments made outside Europe represented 4% by number. Overall, in 2005, 96% of the total amount invested went to investments that were managed in Europe.

## SIGNIFICANCE OF EUROPEAN PRIVATE EQUITY IN THE GLOBAL MARKETPLACE

Eight European countries appear in the listing of top 20 countries worldwide based on levels of private equity investment. As shown in Table 2.1, the United States leads the global ranking with $43.8 billion invested in 2004 (latest year for which global data is available). The UK follows in second position with $22.4 billion invested. Taken together, European countries represented around 39% of global private equity investments; only two years previously they represented just 25%.

The Asia Pacific countries taken together represent 16% of global private equity investments; Africa and the Middle East represent 3% and South America represents 1% (Figure 2.6).

## LEADING COUNTRIES FOR PRIVATE EQUITY GROWTH

If we look at the growth of countries' private equity investments over the six-year period from 1998 to 2004 we see that much of the signif-

**Table 2.1** Top 20 countries (based on total private equity investment)

| Country ranking | | Investment value US $ billion | Funds raised US $ billion |
|---|---|---|---|
| 1 | United States | 43.76 | 84.74 |
| 2 | UK | 22.36 | 11.78 |
| 3 | Japan | 7.06 | 5.54 |
| 4 | France | 6.12 | 2.82 |
| 5 | Germany | 4.41 | 2.32 |
| 6 | Spain | 2.30 | 1.85 |
| 7 | Australia | 2.17 | 1.86 |
| 8 | China | 2.06 | 0.44 |
| 9 | Netherlands | 1.94 | 3.76 |
| 10 | Sweden | 1.90 | 4.28 |
| 11 | Italy | 1.73 | 1.95 |
| 12 | Korea | 1.56 | 0.37 |
| 13 | India | 1.34 | 0.66 |
| 14 | Singapore | 1.29 | 0.92 |
| 15 | South Africa | 1.26 | 0.40 |
| 16 | Israel | 1.22 | 0.72 |
| 17 | Canada | 1.19 | 1.13 |
| 18 | Malaysia | 0.76 | 0.12 |
| 19 | Denmark | 0.46 | 0.63 |
| 20 | Pakistan | 0.40 | – |

*Source*: PwC Global Private Equity Report (2004 data)

icant increase in activity levels has been in the Asia Pacific countries (Figure 2.7). Pakistan leads growth over the six-year period with 141% growth, followed by Denmark with 62% growth, India with 56% growth and Malaysia with 56% growth. Of course, some of these countries were starting at relatively low investment levels. By contrast, the United States does not appear in the list of top 20 countries by growth as its growth rate was just 2%, but then it was starting with the highest investment levels at the beginning of the six-year period.

The private equity community is showing considerable interest in India and China (which had a 9% growth rate in private equity investments over the six-year period to the end of 2004). Firms such as 3i and Carlyle have opened offices in both countries and are making substantial investments in sectors such as healthcare, engineering, media, energy and financial services. KKR recently completed its largest deal in India – the $1 billion buyout of Flextronics' Indian software unit.

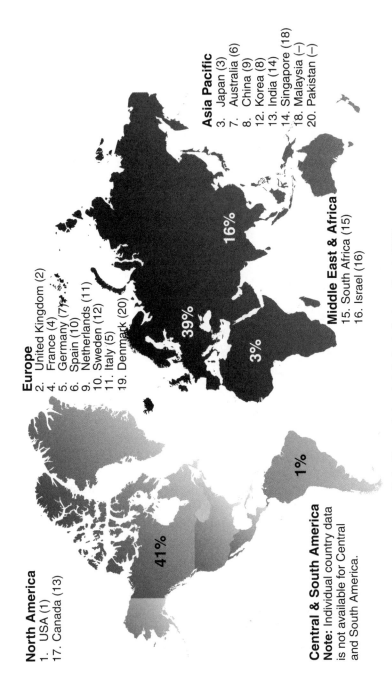

**North America**
1. USA (1)
17. Canada (13)

**Europe**
2. United Kingdom (2)
4. France (4)
5. Germany (7)
6. Spain (10)
9. Netherlands (11)
10. Sweden (12)
11. Italy (5)
19. Denmark (20)

**Asia Pacific**
3. Japan (3)
7. Australia (6)
8. China (9)
12. Korea (8)
13. India (14)
14. Singapore (18)
18. Malaysia (–)
20. Pakistan (–)

**Middle East & Africa**
15. South Africa (15)
16. Israel (16)

**Central & South America**
**Note:** Individual country data is not available for Central and South America.

41%

39%

16%

3%

1%

**Note:** Figures in brackets indicate their position in 2003
Source: PwC Global Private Equity Report 2005 (2004 data)

**Figure 2.6** Global private equity investments (2004 data). Top 20 countries (based on total private equity investment)

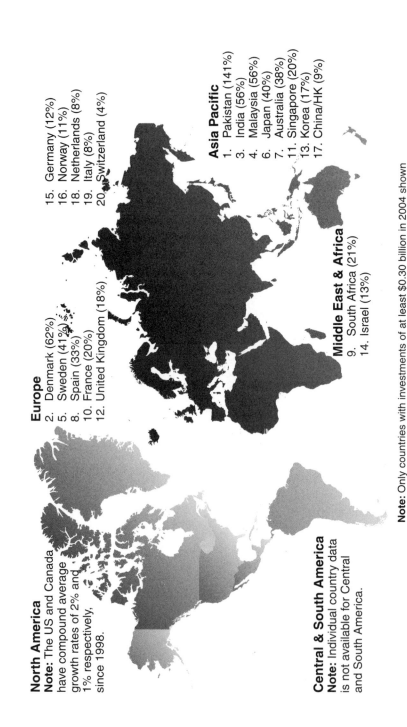

**North America**
**Note:** The US and Canada have compound average growth rates of 2% and 1% respectively, since 1998.

**Central & South America**
**Note:** Individual country data is not available for Central and South America.

**Europe**
2. Denmark (62%)
5. Sweden (41%)
8. Spain (33%)
10. France (20%)
12. United Kingdom (18%)

15. Germany (12%)
16. Norway (11%)
18. Netherlands (8%)
19. Italy (8%)
20. Switzerland (4%)

**Middle East & Africa**
9. South Africa (21%)
14. Israel (13%)

**Asia Pacific**
1. Pakistan (141%)
3. India (56%)
4. Malaysia (56%)
6. Japan (40%)
7. Australia (38%)
11. Singapore (20%)
13. Korea (17%)
17. China/HK (9%)

**Note:** Only countries with investments of at least $0.30 billion in 2004 shown
Source: PwC Global Private Equity Report 2005 (2004 data)

**Figure 2.7** Global private equity investments (2004 data). Top 20 countries (based on growth (CAGR 98–04))

## India

India's heritage as a former British colony has given it a common law legal system (which affords greater protection to investors than the civil law system, drawn from Roman law, which is prevalent in continental Europe), multiple stock exchanges, and English widely spoken at least among the educated classes. There has been much inflow of foreign investment into India. There are a number of very good universities and technical institutes and a wealth of highly skilled professionals. Much of the growth in India has been in the IT sector, business outsourcing and call centres.

## Pakistan

A private equity fund focused on Pakistan was also due to be launched later in 2006. Pakistan has similar characteristics to India but is perceived as a third-rate country and has largely been ignored by investors. Hamilton Bradshaw aims to raise up to $100 million to invest in asset-backed businesses in Pakistan.

## China

China is the fastest-growing major economy in the world but private equity and venture capital have played little role in its development, largely because the country lacks the basic legal infrastructure to support a venture capital market, the Chinese stock markets are inefficient and highly political, and there is no Chinese stock exchange to provide exits for VC-backed companies à la NASDAQ in the United States. There are also little protection for intellectual property and a general lack of stability in business regulations. However, since China was admitted to the World Trade Organization in January 2003 the Chinese government has improved the status of its foreign investors and relaxed the rules governing their activities.

## Singapore

In Singapore the government has instituted various tax breaks, guarantees and seed-stage investment matching, through its Startup Enterprise Development Scheme, as part of its investor-friendly approach.

Some European VCs see Asia as sales channels for their European portfolio companies' technology products or even to provide the opportunity to European start-up companies to commercialize their technology. Others see Asia as an exit route via trade sales to Indian companies. Some private equity and venture capital firms have set up funds dedicated to Asia. Sequoia Capital has set up a $200 million China fund, IDG Ventures and Accel Partners have jointly launched a $250 million IT China fund and Intel set up a $200 million Capital China Technology Fund. Carlyle raised a $1.8 billion buyout fund for Asia in 2006 which will invest in companies across Asia, excluding Japan. It is largely the West Coast US VC firms who are looking to Asia, due to their nearer proximity than their East Coast colleagues and the cultural linkage from, for example, a relatively high proportion of Asian students in West Coast universities such as Stanford and Berkeley. There have been several IPOs of successful venture-backed Chinese companies on NASDAQ.

## Middle East

There is also increasing activity in the Middle East. Carlyle announced plans in 2006 to launch a $500 million fund to invest in the Middle East. Local private equity firms are also raising funds, such as Abraaj Capital, the Dubai-based private equity firm, which closed its second buyout fund at $500 million in late 2005 and is raising a $2 billion fund in 2006. The Dubai Islamic Bank and Dubai World announced the launch in 2006 of a $5 billion family of private equity funds that will invest globally. The Gulf Venture Capital Association has recorded over 40 private equity funds operating in the region and funds raised could be substantial in 2006, possibly as much as $17 billion according to some sources.

## Russia

While there have been few private equity deals to date in Russia, activity is increasing despite the unpredictability of doing business there and the risks inherent in the country, such as weak financial controls, political instability and poor legal protection for investors. The Russian government announced in 2006 that it is planning to invest some $555 million into a series of privately managed venture capital funds which will invest in early-stage Russian companies. The government will have a stake of up to 49% in each fund, with the remainder provided by private investors.

With all this increasing activity in developing regions of the world, the question can be posed as to whether a truly global market is emerging for venture capital and private equity. This is probably still some way off due to legal and fiscal regimes that are country specific and not easily transferable. Even in Europe there is still no pan-European fund structure despite the efforts of EVCA and others. But there has been progress, with cross-border stock markets for growth companies, such as AIM in Europe, following the demise of earlier efforts like EASDAQ and NASDAQ Europe. Private equity firms themselves are becoming increasingly global, opening offices and making investments outside their core countries.

# HIGH-TECHNOLOGY INVESTMENTS GLOBALLY

Looking at high-tech investments in the global context, the top 20 countries for investment have some similarities to the top 20 countries for all private equity investments – see Figure 2.8 which shows the amount of private equity investments (all stages of investment) by country. However, Israel, whose venture capital industry is dominated by high-tech investments, moves up to 6th place, and the Asia Pacific countries of Korea, India and Malaysia move up to 7th, 11th and 13th place, respectively. Switzerland, Belgium and Finland join the top 20 in 18th, 19th and 20th place, respectively. China on the other hand (with perhaps more of a focus on manufacturing and buyouts) drops to 14th place.

Israel's emphasis on high-tech investments can be traced to policy decisions to commercialize defence-related technology developed with public funding. An influx of trained engineers and scientists from the former Soviet Union also helped, as did the steps taken by Israeli entrepreneurs to go public on the US markets.

The United States remains the leading country for high-tech venture capital investing. The PwC National Venture Capital Association MoneyTree™ report (data provided by Thomson Financial) measures venture capital investments into all industry sectors in the United States. However, over 80% of these investments by amount are in the high-tech sectors. Total venture capital investment is running at around $5–6 billion per quarter, with the key sectors for investment being software (22% of all venture capital investments by amount), biotechnology (14%), medical devices and equipment (12%), and telecommunications (11%).

# HIGH-TECH INVESTMENTS IN EUROPE AND OUTLOOK FOR THE INDUSTRY

High-tech investments in Europe were €8.0 billion in 2005, representing 17% of the total amount invested by European private equity firms in that year, down from a 20% share in 2004. A total of 4,882 investments

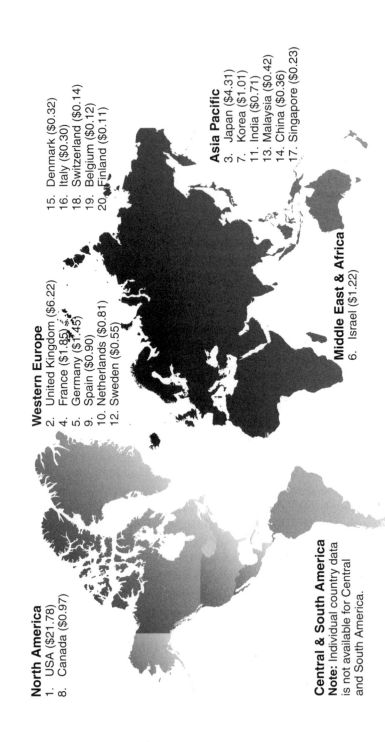

**North America**
1. USA ($21.78)
8. Canada ($0.97)

**Western Europe**
2. United Kingdom ($6.22)
4. France ($1.85)
5. Germany ($1.45)
9. Spain ($0.90)
10. Netherlands ($0.81)
12. Sweden ($0.55)

15. Denmark ($0.32)
16. Italy ($0.30)
18. Switzerland ($0.14)
19. Belgium ($0.12)
20. Finland ($0.11)

**Asia Pacific**
3. Japan ($4.31)
7. Korea ($1.01)
11. India ($0.71)
13. Malaysia ($0.42)
14. China ($0.36)
17. Singapore ($0.23)

**Middle East & Africa**
6. Israel ($1.22)

**Central & South America**
**Note:** Individual country data is not available for Central and South America.

Source: PwC Global Private Equity Report 2005 (2004 data)

**Figure 2.8** Global private equity investments (2004 data). Top 20 countries (based on high-tech investment)

were made, representing 45% of the total investments by number, up from 4,799 investments in 2004 which represented 47% of total investments by number.

Within the high-tech sectors, investments in the computer-related area (computer software, computer hardware, computer services and semiconductors) were €2.4 billion (5% of all investments by amount, up slightly from €2.35 billion in 2004), biotechnology investments amounted to €0.9 billion (2% share, up from €0.7 billion) and medical/health related-investments increased to €3.5 billion (7% share, up from €2.8 billion).

On a country basis, there are marked differences in the amounts invested in high-tech in relation to the total investment amount, with the larger countries, in total investment terms, having a relatively smaller share of high-tech investments. Ireland led in 2005 with an 85% high-tech share, followed by Greece with 62%, Austria with 52%, Switzerland with 49% and Finland with 48%. The Netherlands had a 10% high-tech share, the UK 15%, France 16%, Spain 26% and Germany 32%.

Funds raised allocated to high-tech venture capital were €5.1 billion in 2005, representing 7% of all funds raised, an increase of more than double on 2004 funds raised for high-tech venture capital. So while the proportion of funds raised for high-tech is far less than funds raised for buyouts, for example, at least the confidence of investors in high-tech funds is increasing again after the dot.com/internet fallout.

The performance of high-tech (and early-stage) funds is still well down on the comparator indices, such as the FTSE 100 and FTSE All-Share index (see Chapter 3), in the medium to long term. Those high-tech venture funds in the top quartile of performance returns and with track records of success are still attractive to institutional investors. Over the past year there have been successful fundraisings by European venture capital firms specializing in high-tech and with the appropriate track records, with firms such as Advent Venture Partners in the UK, Sofinnova Partners in France, Wellington Partners in Germany and Index Ventures in Switzerland raising funds of the order of €150–300 million.

The other encouraging development is that write-offs are back towards normal levels. This is where venture capital firms have made investments in portfolio companies that have subsequently proved worthless; perhaps projected revenues or other aspects of business plans have not materialized as envisaged, the management team has been weak, competitors have stolen the market, financial controls have been weak or major cash flow problems have occurred. Or the venture capital firm simply failed to carry out appropriate due diligence and other vetting proceedings in the rush to invest in the highly competitive environment of the dot.com/internet period. Write-offs reached 30% of all divestments (exits) by amount at cost in 2001. They now stand at around 5%.

Venture capital firms in Europe remain somewhat risk averse. They usually will not assume any risk as regards the technology used in the business proposition in which they are considering investing. The technology must be proven, innovative (or better still 'disruptive'), commercially viable (with evidence of this ideally in terms of customer revenues already being generated or at least customer contracts in place) and with all relevant intellectual property suitably protected, preferably owned by the company with appropriate licences in place. The venture capital firms take on the market risk, ie will the product actually sell in the marketplace to the extent set out in the projections in the business plan? The entrepreneur/management team will be expected to demonstrate that their product has the ability to take a leading position in a fast-growing marketplace.

The 'back to basics' investment approach which venture capital firms now adopt requires the team to have prepared a detailed business plan (see Chapter 8) around a realistic and robust business model. The team itself should be experienced in the industry, and possess complementary management and operational skills. Ideally at least one senior member of the team, usually the CEO, should have set up and run a successful business before.

There has been some consolidation in the European private equity industry and this is likely to continue, with a focus on the international, cross-border, private equity houses (which invest predominantly in buyouts and public to private deals) and on the niche, stage and/or industry-specific venture capital firms such as the leading technology venture capital players.

The lack of a pan-European stock exchange for growth companies, along the lines of NASDAQ in the United States, also hampers progress in the European venture capital industry, though this is being helped with the internationalization of the AIM and the new junior markets for the Deutsche Borse and Alternext.

Despite the issues raised above, the outlook for the European technology venture capital industry looks positive or at least 'cautiously optimistic'. It helps that VCs are usually themselves positive/optimistic people. There has been a more active mergers and acquisitions market over the past year and some successful IPOs of venture-backed companies in Europe. Several of the large, multinational technology companies have shown improved earnings, though this is very variable, with some leading companies cutting revenue forecasts for consecutive quarters. And there is more spending on IT, although not necessarily in terms of hiring IT staff due to the increased trend for outsourcing of IT services in an attempt to cut costs. Part of the reason for the increased spending on IT is the need to replace outdated resources that have been kept in service due to previous attempts to cut IT costs. It is also partly due to the emergence of new technologies, such as RFID (radio frequency identification) tags, which is extending market growth. And there is unlikely to be any cut in demand for security surrounding IT systems.

There is an improving entrepreneurial culture in Europe – one of the benefits of the dot.com/internet era was the great impetus this period gave to people of all ages and experience seeking to set up their own businesses, leaving the perceived security of employment in established companies and willing to take risks as entrepreneurs. We have not quite reached the culture of the United States where to succeed in a venture-backed business you are almost expected to have failed once, twice even three times, and where the price of failure is not automatic abandonment by the business community.

The time is now right for successful venture investing and raising finance for well-developed business propositions.

## EUROPE CLOSES THE GAP ON THE UNITED STATES IN TECHNOLOGY INVESTING

One of the areas I used to review each year at PwC was a comparison of technology venture capital investments in Europe compared to the United States. Called 'Money for Growth', the report compared the figures for technology venture capital investment in the United States and Europe and highlighted the differing sizes and stages of development of each market.

Despite some difficulties in comparing the two sets of figures directly, it is clear that US technology venture capital investments in 2004, at €14.0 billion (as shown in the PwC/NVCA MoneyTree™ report (data provided by Thomson Financial)), were just under four times the size of the comparable European investments of €3.7 billion. This marks a narrowing of the gap from 2003, when the US total was about 4.5 times that of Europe, and reflects a continuing trend. In 2000, US technology venture capital investments were almost nine times greater than in Europe, in 2001 about six times greater, and in 2002 about five times greater – so there is evidence that Europe is steadily reducing the United States' lead, although this does not take into account currency fluctuations.

The US MoneyTree™ and European Money for Growth surveys are not directly comparable due to the inclusion of all private equity and unsecured and secured debt (but only if the debt derives from private equity funds) in the European survey, whereas the US survey includes venture capital only and no debt (except on conversion to equity). In addition, the industry categories of the MoneyTree™ survey do not directly correspond with those used in the European survey.

# LISBON AGENDA

The gaps between Europe and the United States in terms of an entrepreneurial culture, attitudes to risk by both entrepreneurs and VCs, and commercialization of innovation (including university spinouts) are well recognized by governments and policymakers.

In March 2000, the EU Heads of States and governments agreed to make the EU 'the most competitive and dynamic knowledge-driven economy by 2010'. The Lisbon Summit was designed to mark a turning point for EU enterprise and innovation policy, with practical steps to strengthen the EU's research capacity, promote entrepreneurship and facilitate take-up of information society technologies. The main issues for achieving the goals set out in the Lisbon agenda were the necessary investment in research and development (set at 3% of GDP), a reduction of red tape to promote entrepreneurship, and achieving an employment rate of 70% (60% for women).

The European Commission's action plan on entrepreneurship was designed to provide a strategic framework for boosting entrepreneurship and aims to encourage more people to start businesses and to help entrepreneurs succeed, proposing actions in five strategic policy areas:

1. promoting entrepreneurial mindsets and awareness of the entrepreneurial spirit by presenting best practice models and fostering entrepreneurial attitudes and skills among young people;
2. providing better incentives for entrepreneurs which recognize the need for a fairer balance between risk and reward, dealing with the negative effects of business failures (as noted above) and amending social security systems for entrepreneurs;
3. promoting growth and competitiveness, including improving access to support and management training for entrepreneurs from all backgrounds, especially women and ethnic minorities, and encouraging cross-border trading and support networks and strategic partnerships between entrepreneurs;

4.  improving access to finance, including the availability of venture capital, business angel finance and investments by private individuals to create more equity and stronger balance sheets as well as efforts to lower capital taxes;
5.  creating a more SME-friendly regulatory and administrative framework.

When the Lisbon agenda was re-launched in 2005 some progress has been made on innovating Europe's economy but there was growing concern that progress with reforms was not going fast enough and that the ambitious targets set in the agenda would not be reached by 2010. In many European countries the economic outlook had got worse, with unemployment in France and Germany, for example, at around 10%. While some of this was related to the downturn in the world economy following the bursting of the dot.com/internet bubble, recovery has been much slower in Europe than in the United States. There is also the problem of ageing populations and growing competition from Asia.

The year 2005 saw the production of 25 National Reform Programmes (NRPs), in which each member state sets out its key challenges and priorities for action in the context of Lisbon.

The 2006 Spring European Council of the EU called for a number of specific priority actions to be implemented by the end of 2007, including investment in knowledge and innovation, unlocking business potential (especially of small- and medium-sized enterprises (SMEs)), increasing employment opportunities, the reduction of the average time to set up a company to a maximum of one week, the promotion of entrepreneurship education and training in national education systems, and moving towards an efficient and integrated EU energy policy.

Specifically with regard to entrepreneurship there are a large number of European Commission initiatives. I would like to acknowledge the help I have received from EVCA who provided the detail for me to prepare the following summary.

# SUMMARY OF EC INITIATIVES ON ENTREPRENEURSHIP

Many of the following initiatives are based on the EC's 'Action Plan: The European Agenda for Entrepreneurship' prepared in 2004. This action plan contained five strategic policy areas and gives priority to a focused set of key actions.

## 1. Fuelling entrepreneurial mindsets

### Key action: Fostering entrepreneurial mindsets through school education

The EC produced a booklet, 'Helping to create an entrepreneurial culture', in 2004, and an EC conference on 'Entrepreneurship in Europe' held in the autumn of 2006 discussed how to better implement those recommendations. The 2004 charter for small enterprises had education for entrepreneurship, specifically in secondary education, as a priority area. The EC's proposal for an integrated action programme in the field of lifelong learning included the promotion of an entrepreneurial spirit among its objectives.

The EC Communication on Entrepreneurship education was adopted in early 2006. It provides member states with recommendations aimed at enhancing the role of education in creating a more entrepreneurial culture in Europe. Also, the proposed Youth in Action Programme 2007–2013 will include among its main objectives encouraging young people to be creative and to adopt a spirit of initiative and enterprise.

## 2. Encouraging more people to become entrepreneurs

### Key action: Reducing the stigma of failure

The fifth report of the implementation of the European charter for SMEs, prepared in 2005, had better regulation, especially bankruptcy law, as a priority area. Also in 2005, the EC held a workshop on bankruptcy laws and identifying best practices. The EC held a conference on insolvency in 2006.

### Key action: Facilitating business transfers

The EC communication on business transfers issued in 2006 called on member states to ensure that tax systems are transfer-friendly, to provide adequate financial conditions, to raise awareness, consider soft factors and support mentoring and to organize transparent market for technology transfers.

### Key action: Reviewing social security schemes for entrepreneurs

This key action was also included in this strategic policy area.

## 3. Gearing entrepreneurs for growth and competitiveness

### Key action: Providing tailor-made support for women and ethnic minorities

An EC conference on 'Women-led businesses: Overcoming barriers to growth and improving access to finance' was aimed at facilitating female entrepreneurs to access finance. There is an EU web portal available which gathers all the initiatives promoting female entrepreneurship.

### Key action: Supporting businesses in developing inter-enterprise relations

This key action includes EC support to pan-European business cooperation schemes and has also resulted in a report produced in 2006 which identifies four good practices for cooperation between innovation cluster initiatives and Innovation Relay Centres (IRCs). The mission of the IRCs is to support innovation and transnational technological cooperation in Europe with a range of specialized business support services. IRC services are primarily targeted at technology-oriented SMEs but are also available to large companies, research institutes, universities, technology centres and innovation agencies.

## 4. Improving the flow of finance

### Key action: Creating more equity and stronger balance sheets in firms

In 2004 the EC met with national experts and data collection was carried out to evaluate the state of business angel financing in Europe. An EC working group prepared a report on 'best practices in accessing early-stage finance' in 2005. A Risk Capital Summit was also held in 2005, which was a joint UK–EU conference to debate and make recommendations on how risk capital should support the establishment of Europe as a leader in innovation, growth and enterprise.

The new Competitiveness and Innovation framework Programme (CIP) will come in early 2007 and will promote entrepreneurship and innovation, energy efficiency and renewable energy sources, environmental technologies and the better use of information and communication technology. It will increase SMEs' innovative capacity through an easier access to capital through loans, equity, venture capital and guarantees as well as technical assistance and grants.

JEREMIE (Joint European Resources for Micro to Medium Enterprises), a joint initiative of the Commission and the European Investment Fund (EIF) with the European Investment Bank, was launched in 2006 in order to improve access to finance for entrepreneurship and improve capacity in the field of financial engineering in member states and regions.

The EU has produced a guide on how to work with banks. It provides guidelines for SMEs applying for loans from banks.

The EC communication 'Financing SME growth, Adding European Value' published in 2006 includes a set of measures proposed by the EC to improve the flow of finance to innovative SMEs and to promote their growth. The EC has invited member states to join in promoting finance for innovative SMEs. It aims to triple early-stage venture capital investment by 2013.

The Commission has also reviewed its State Aid rules to allow greater flexibility and to provide better targeted aid in favour of SMEs, such as in relation to innovation.

Recently adopted guidelines for regional aid for 2007–2013 introduce a new form of aid in order to provide incentives to support business start-ups and the early-stage development of small enterprises in assisted areas.

## 5. Creating a more SME-friendly regulatory and administrative framework

### *Key action: Listening to SMEs*

The EC has held a conference on 'Consultation of stakeholders in the shaping of small business policy at national/regional level'.

### *Key action: Reducing the complexity of complying with tax laws*

Here the EC has produced a communication on home-state taxation and issued a proposal for VAT 'one-stop shops', both aimed at eliminating the additional burden of cross-border business from small enterprises.

The Action Plan has also led to the 'EC Communication on SME policy' which sets out a single policy framework for Commission action on entrepreneurship and SME businesses for the years to come. The Commission has proposed specific actions in the following areas:

- promoting entrepreneurship and skills;
- improving SMEs' access to markets;
- cutting red tape;
- improving SMEs' growth potential;
- strengthening dialogue and consultation with SME stakeholders.

The final impact of these EC initiatives will now depend on the degree of follow-up given in member states at national and regional level.

# EUROPEAN VENTURE CAPITAL AND PRIVATE EQUITY ASSOCIATION

The European Private Equity and Venture Capital Association (EVCA) is a member-based, not-for-profit trade association with over 925 members. Established in 1983 and based in Brussels, it represents, promotes and protects the interests of the European private equity and venture capital industry. EVCA aims to enhance the understanding of, and create a more favourable environment for, equity investment and entrepreneurship in Europe. Its activities cover the entire range of private equity, from venture capital (seed, start-up and development capital) to buyouts and buy-ins.

## Representing the European private equity and venture capital industry towards a variety of stakeholders

On behalf of its members, EVCA undertakes public policy activities and maintains a dialogue with policy institutions and regulatory bodies at European, international and national levels, often in coordination with national trade associations.

EVCA promotes and increases the understanding of the key roles that private equity and venture capital and entrepreneurship play in creating and protecting jobs and enriching the European economy.

## Raising professional standards

EVCA is at the forefront of developing guidelines for professional standards and best practice, contributing to harmonization across the industry. EVCA has produced a range of widely used guidelines for the professional conduct of private equity and venture capital fund managers, both in respect of the management of their activities and in their relationships with investors and portfolio companies.

## Networking opportunities

EVCA provides opportunities for members from across Europe to meet together, exchange information and ideas, and discuss the latest industry trends and issues. Throughout the year EVCA holds regular networking events with leading practitioners and industry participants from all over Europe, including the EVCA Investors' Forum, the EVCA Symposium and the EVCA Venture Capital Forum, as well as workshops on ICT, life sciences, buyouts and corporate venturing topics.

## Enhancing professional development

Since its foundation in 1987, the EVCA Institute has built a reputation as Europe's premier provider of courses for private equity practitioners. The Institute's comprehensive range of private equity management training courses is designed to enhance the professional skills and expertise of a private equity practitioner at all stages of his or her career. The group-based courses provide an opportunity to network with peers from across Europe and to profit from the experience of instructors drawn from leading senior industry professionals and academics.

The 'Entrepreneurship Education Toolkit on Private Equity and Venture Capital' is available for European universities and Institutions of Higher Education to help them teach a class explaining the basics of private equity and venture capital.

## Conducting and publicizing industry research

EVCA conducts and commissions a wide variety of private equity and venture capital research. Through its partnerships with Thomson Financial and PricewaterhouseCoopers, EVCA collects quarterly and annual statistics, based on rigorous and transparent methodologies, and publishes annual statistics covering the activity in, and performance of, the European private equity industry. EVCA members have the EVCA library and Research Helpdesk at their disposal, with access to industry data and information at no extra cost.

On 1 February 2005, EVCA hosted its third annual Policy Meeting in Brussels. The meeting brought together over 200 leading EU and national policymakers, industry representatives, academics and stake-holders who were invited to exchange views on the ways to move forward in supporting sustainable European innovation, growth and job creation through private equity and venture capital.

In 2005, EVCA presented its Public Policy Priorities for the forth-coming years, including nine priorities and measures for policymakers to help achieve the European Union's Lisbon objectives of growth, competitiveness and innovation, through the private equity and venture capital industry.

EVCA's Public Policy Priorities deal with:

▌ fostering Europe's entrepreneurial environment, culture and education;

▌ boosting innovation, research and development (R&D);

▌ easing the raising and deployment of private equity and venture capital funds to drive a high-growth entrepreneurial economy.

Further information on this can be found on: www.evca.com/html/public_affairs/whitepaper.

For more information on EVCA please visit www.evca.com or telephone +32 2 715 00 20.

Many European and overseas countries have their own private equity and venture capital associations. These usually publish directories of members, data on funds raised, investments and divestments in their countries and often useful guidance material for investors and entrepreneurs. Many act as lobbying organizations with their governments for better incentives for those raising finance and for the tax treatment of private equity organizations.

# BRITISH VENTURE CAPITAL ASSOCIATION

The BVCA (British Venture Capital Association) is one of the largest country associations. It covers all stages of private equity and has over 360 members (full member private equity firms and associate member professional adviser and consultancy firms). The BVCA represents private equity and venture capital in the UK and is devoted to promoting the private equity industry and improving the performance and professional standards of member firms and the individuals within those firms.

The BVCA publishes a Directory of Members which lists the member firms and their investment preferences and contact details. A fully searchable version of the Directory is also available free of charge to those seeking private equity investment on www.bvca.co.uk. It also lists financial organizations, such as mezzanine firms, fund of funds managers and professional advisers, such as accountants and lawyers, who are experienced in the private equity field.

---

### British Venture Capital Association

The following is the BVCA's perspective on the UK private equity industry:

> The BVCA is the industry body for the UK private equity and venture capital industry. Our membership, of over 360 firms, represents the overwhelming number of UK-based private equity and venture capital providers and their advisers.
>
> The BVCA has over 23 years of experience representing the industry, which currently accounts for over 50% of the whole of the European market (in terms of the total amount of private equity invested in Europe), to government, the European Commission and Parliament, the media, regulatory and other statutory bodies at home, across Europe and around the world. We promote the industry to entrepreneurs and investors, as well as providing services and best practice standards to our members.
>
> In the UK, continental Europe and much of the rest of the world, 'private equity' means the equity financing of unquoted companies at

many stages in the life of a company. 'Venture capital' is a subset of private equity, covering the seed to expansion stages of investment.

In 2005, worldwide investment by our members increased by 21% to an unprecedented £11,676 million, with investment in overseas companies growing for the third consecutive year. Investment in continental Europe increased to its highest ever level in 2005, totalling £3,858 million.

The smaller, entrepreneurial end of the market is a key driver of economic growth in the UK and is an important area of focus. Over 490 early stage businesses attracted private equity funding to the tune of £380m in 2005, a 35% increase on 2004 levels. This increase was largely driven by start-ups, with equity commitments to these new ventures increasing by 67%.

In recent years a number of vehicles have evolved focused on investing in smaller entrepreneurial businesses. There are a number of UK Government-backed schemes, targeted at early-stage enterprises, which tend to be match funded with private sector capital. These provide a vital initial cash injection for early-stage growth businesses, often enabling them to reach the critical mass necessary to attract later-stage institutional venture capital. Government-backed equity investment funds are run on a commercial basis by experienced venture capital fund managers, which means that the process of securing investment from these sources follows the same principles as pitching for traditional institutional venture capital funding.

Individual investments from Government-backed funds range from small tranches of £50,000 to £100,000 provided by vehicles such as the 'Regional Growth Funds' to larger tranches of up to £2m provided through the newly formed Enterprise Capital Funds. Other initiatives include Regional Venture Capital Funds, which provide initial equity investments of £250,000 with the potential to commit a further £250,000 in 'exceptional circumstances', and VCTs, which can invest up to £1m in smaller unquoted businesses and AIM-listed stocks with a net asset value of no more than £7m. The UK Government has also enabled small, growth businesses to access loans of up to £250,000 through the Small Firms Loan Guarantee Scheme, whereby lenders are provided with a government guarantee against default in certain circumstances.

The suitability of each of these funding sources very much depends on the size and stage of development of your company, its medium-term capital requirements and its projected growth. Most funding sources are limited in the amount they can commit to any one business. Therefore, for a business that is likely to require more than £1m of capital in the first year to 18 months it might be wise to consider an Enterprise Capital Fund or a venture capital fund manager, both of which are likely to have the capacity to invest larger tranches of equity. To help you narrow down your search, the BVCA Directory of Members can offer details of UK venture capital investors and their preferred investment remits.

When it comes to the process of attracting venture capital funding, there are a number of 'golden rules' that will help you to optimize your chances of getting onto a potential investors' radar. Venture capital investors receive hundreds of proposals a year and the initial screening process tends to be speedy. A strong proposal may be overlooked if it is badly presented, overly technical or lacking focus. One good way to avoid presentational 'bear traps' is to seek some feedback on your proposal before you begin approaching investors.

The business plan itself should focus on market, strategy and financials without getting too bogged down in technical detail. A venture capital group is concerned with market and positioning, competition and supply/demand dynamics; striking the right balance between this industry perspective and the technical briefing is essential. The provision of a set of detailed and up-to-date financials is an absolute must, as is a realistic valuation of your business.

When it comes to presenting, ensure that you are fully prepared. Involve other members of your management team but make sure each is equally briefed. Key issues should be covered in an incisive and logical manner. It is no good getting straight to the numbers until you have explained what your company does and where its market is going. Equally a logical inter-relationship between the overall market and forecasts is important – if the market is static and you are showing growth then you must be able to show a robust case for how increased market share to be achieved.

For venture capitalists the creation of value involves more than just funding. Guidance on strategic and operational issues and providing support to the management team are just some of the ways venture capitalists use their experience to grow businesses. So the final golden rule must be to be clear about what you want and expect from the relationship.

Contact: Sarah Eaton, Head of Membership and Marketing, BVCA. Telephone: +44 20 7025 2950; www.bvca.co.uk

For information on using the directories of members of national venture capital associations to select which private equity or venture capital firms to approach for financing see Chapter 7.

# 3

# Issues facing the European private equity industry

For the entrepreneur or owner manager looking to raise venture capital it is useful to have some knowledge of the issues that the private equity industry as a whole is facing. This should be helpful when you come to choose which venture capital firms to approach and set up your first meeting with the VC. At least you will be aware of some of the recent developments in the industry and the current areas of debate, which will provide evidence that you have thoroughly researched the industry before approaching a VC.

## PREDOMINANCE OF MANAGEMENT BUYOUT FUNDRAISING VERSUS VENTURE FUNDRAISING

I have already referred to the preponderance of funds in Europe for management buyouts as opposed to early-stage venture financing. Consequently there are rather more firms that specialize in later-stage financing than early-stage and they focus on much larger deals. In Europe the average size of a buyout deal (equity component only) is around €14 million. Seed investments are around €250,000, start-ups around €750,000 and expansion capital around €2 million. A venture capital firm will want to carry out full investigatory and due diligence procedures before they invest in a proposition whether they are financing €500,000 or €50 million. This all takes a vast amount of a VC's, and their external advisers', time. Hence some firms will focus only on the larger deals. In their view it is not worth their management team's efforts to work on the smaller deals in view of the time/reward ratio, not to mention the higher returns that have been achieved by the later-stage funds. So, if you are a start-up or early-stage business, you need to search carefully for those venture capital firms willing to take the time to investigate your proposition.

The industry is becoming even more skewed towards buyouts with the advent of the mega buyout funds. Funds of upwards of €10 billion are being raised. For example, the US buyout house, Blackstone, closed its new global private equity fund at $15.6 billion in July 2006, the largest private equity fund at that time. Its previous fund closed in 2002 with commitments totalling $6.45 billion and is now fully invested. And one senior private equity leader has forecast the advent of the $100 billion fund within the next 10 years. If the large private equity firms pool their resources in so-called 'club' deals, the industry has the ability to make substantial acquisitions going forward.

Club deals in the United States became the source of investigation by the Department of Justice in 2006 as the Department launched an inquiry into alleged cartel practices among the large private equity funds and whether this constitutes anti-competitive behaviour. In Europe, in the UK the Financial Services Authority has been studying the private equity industry, concerned by the industry's rapid growth and possible risks to the stability of the financial system. In Germany the finance ministry has outlined plans to subject private equity firms to stricter regulations.

In Europe the European Union's Markets in Financial Instruments Directive (MiFID), which comes into effect by November 2007, is an attempt to standardize financial services in order to create a single European market for investment bankers, stockbrokers, corporate finance firms, banks and any other organizations selling investment products to customers, and currently encompasses private equity firms. MiFID extends the coverage of the current investment services directive regime and introduces new and more extensive requirements to which firms will have to adapt, in particular in relation to their conduct of business and internal organization. MiFID contains provisions to ensure investor protection and market transparency and integrity. These cover the same topics as the current professional guidelines endorsed and applied by European private equity and venture capital investors. However, private equity and venture capital specificities do not fit with several of its other obligations, for example best execution constraints where there is no market comparison possible, and such requirements could potentially have a negative impact on private equity and venture capital funds acting on a discretionary client-by-client basis for non-listed securities. EVCA is seeking clarification from the European Commission on the relationship between private equity and venture capital in respect of MiFID.

Fortunately for the early-stage entrepreneur, there will always be the specialist venture firms with their €200 million funds who are prepared to invest in what the industry perceives to be riskier deals, and still make good returns in doing this. The key is specialization. These smaller firms are usually run by investment executives who have practical, hands-on experience of creating and running successful growth companies themselves and/or have worked at senior executive level in specific industry sectors, such as software, telecommunications or semiconductors. They will understand your sector and the market in which it operates. They know how to structure and advise on venture capital deals. Those that have survived the dot.com/internet period have the proven track record to go on making appropriate investments and successfully raising new funds. In general they were not set up by buyout executives who thought they would join the dot.com fund 'gold rush' and subsequently went on to write-off most of their ill-conceived investments.

## DIVERSITY OF RETURNS MADE BY DIFFERENT SECTORS OF THE INDUSTRY

Since 2000 PwC has been collecting data for the BVCA on the performance of 'independent' UK private equity funds, ie funds raised from external investors for investment at the venture capital and management buyout (MBO) stages, in conjunction with Capital Dynamics. The survey achieves a 100% response rate from BVCA member firms, which makes the survey the most complete country-specific survey on the performance of private equity funds in the world.

The BVCA Performance Measurement Survey consistently shows that private equity funds outperform the total UK pension fund assets index (as shown in the WM All Funds Universe) and the FTSE 100 and FTSE All-Share indices over the medium to long term. In recent years this strong performance by private equity funds has been mostly fuelled by buyout funds and by pan-European funds in particular.

UK private equity funds significantly outperformed total UK pension funds assets, as shown in the WM All Funds Universe, in 2005 and over 3-, 5- and 10-year periods (Figure 3.1). UK private equity also outperformed the FTSE 100 and the FTSE All-Share indices in 2005 and over 3, 5 and 10 years, and outperformed all other principal FTSE indices in 2005 and over 5 and 10 years.

For the more recent funds, those with 1996 vintages onwards (the vintage year is the year of a fund's first closing, ie the year in which a fund has raised an initial sum of money with which to commence its investment programme) and large MBO funds (those which invest in management buyouts and buy-ins with more than £100 million of equity invested) were the best performing funds in the 2005 data over 3, 5 and 10 years, achieving 26.2% pa over 3 years, 18.7% pa over 5 years and 18.5% pa over 10 years and outperforming the FTSE 100 and FTSE All-Share indices over 3, 5 and 10 years (Figure 3.2). All private equity returns quoted are the net returns to investors, after all costs and fees.

However, venture funds (1996 vintages onwards) and technology funds had negative returns on average over 3, 5 and 10 years, largely because they are still heavily influenced by the weight of funds raised in 1999/2000, the height of the dot.com/internet era. Performance of these funds does continue to improve gradually. Pre-1996 vintage early-stage funds, while negative over 3 and 5 years, showed a positive return of 17.6% pa over 10 years in the 2005 data.

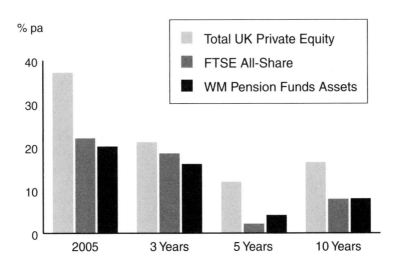

Source: BVCA Private Equity and Venture Capital Performance Measurement Survey 2005

**Figure 3.1** UK private equity performance versus principal comparators

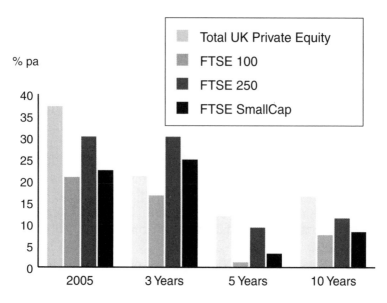

% pa

Legend:
- Total UK Private Equity
- FTSE 100
- FTSE 250
- FTSE SmallCap

Source: BVCA Private Equity and Venture Capital Performance Management
Survey, 2005

**Figure 3.2** UK private equity versus FTSE indices

Funds investing outside the technology sector performed much better
than technology funds over 3 (23.2% pa), 5 (14.4% pa) and 10 (17.8%
pa) year periods.

Large MBO funds for both pre-1996 and 1996 onwards were the best
performing category of funds since inception (inception of a fund is the
date of a fund's first drawdown) to 31 December 2005, at 18.2% pa and
18.0% pa, respectively, followed by mid-MBO funds (which invest in
management buyouts and buy-ins with £10 million to £100 million of
equity invested) pre-1996 and 1996 onwards at 15.8% pa and 9.3% pa,
respectively (Figure 3.3). Early-stage funds performed least well of the
pre-1996 vintage funds since inception to 31 December 2005, at 8.8%
pa, and venture funds performed least well of the 1996 vintage funds
onwards at –1.9% pa (Figure 3.4).

UK-focused funds achieved a 14.0% pa return since inception
compared with non-UK funds at 14.9% pa. Technology funds achieved
just a 0.1% pa return since inception compared with that of non-tech-
nology funds of 15.7% pa (Figure 3.5).

While the average returns of early-stage, venture and technology
funds are nowhere as good as the MBO funds, if we look within the
ranges of the early-stage, venture and technology funds we find some
exceptional performances. For example, returns for pre-1996 vintage
early-stage funds ranged from a high of 148.4% pa to –12.6% pa over 10

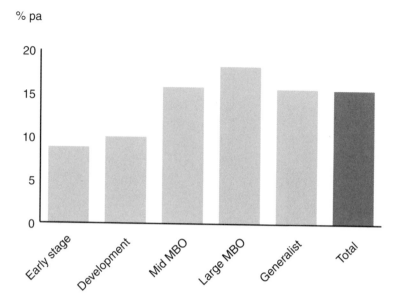

Source: BVCA Private Equity and Venture Capital Performance Measurement
Survey 2005

**Figure 3.3**  UK private equity: since inception performance of pre-1996 funds
by stage to December 2005

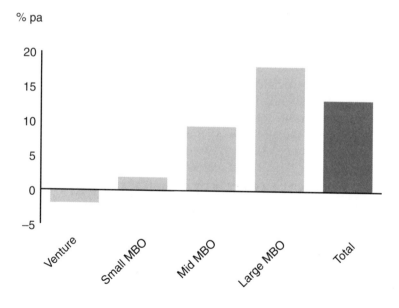

Source: BVCA Private Equity and Venture Capital Performance Measurement
Survey 2005

**Figure 3.4**  UK private equity: since inception performance of 1996–2001
funds to December 2005

% pa

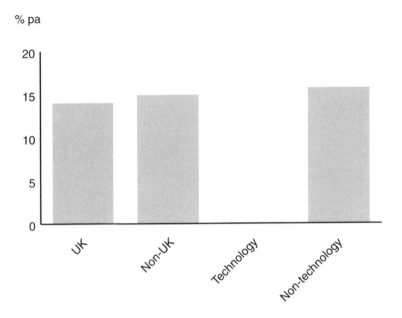

Source: BVCA Private Equity and Venture Capital Performance Measurement
Survey 2005

**Figure 3.5** UK private equity: since inception performance by subcategory to
December 2005

years. Technology funds (all vintages) ranged from 75.3% pa to –15.8%
pa over 10 years. It is, however, true to say that the top quartile
performance for technology funds is not as good for other industry
sectors for funds since inception to 31 December 2005 and for early-
stage funds pre-1996 vintages and venture funds 1996 vintages onwards
as compared to mid- and large MBOs for the same period.

# MANAGEMENT FEES PAID TO PRIVATE EQUITY FIRMS

Private equity funds have historically received an annual management
fee of around, but not more than, 2.5% based on the amount of funds
committed, as opposed to actually invested, by the investors to the funds
(the limited partners). The management fee is meant to cover the costs of
the private equity management team in running the fund, executive and
staff costs, sourcing deals, appraising investments, reporting to the
limited partners and office administration costs.

The management fee is not meant to provide an element of profit or return to the private equity managers. This is provided by 'carried interest', which is usually around 20% of the total profits made by the fund after all the investments have been realized and the limited partners have received their distributions due from the fund.

The management fee has historically been at around the 2.5% level no matter what the size the fund on which it is calculated, whether it is a typical venture fund at €50–300 million or a buyout fund of considerably more. More recently, management fees on these large buyout funds have been nearer 1.5%. The issue is whether private equity managers should expect to receive as much as 2.5%, or even 1.5%, on mega funds of over €10 billion; after all, this would amount to the rather substantial amount of €150 million in fees per year! Also, there are those who argue that most of the work of the managers is when investments are being sourced, made and then monitored and grown. As the fund becomes fully invested there is less work for the managers to do, other than to seek exits for the investments in due course. So maybe the managers should receive a reduced, tapered fee in the middle to later years of a fund's life, ie after the investments have been made but before the exits are achieved. Or maybe a whole new basis for refunding managers' fund administration costs and incentivizing the investment executives and other private equity firm management needs to be developed.

Carried interest is usually paid right at the end of a fund's life after all investments have been realized. Some of the larger European funds are negotiating with their limited partners for carried interest to be paid on a deal-by-deal basis. This would require a claw-back provision in case carried interest paid on successful investments is followed by unsuccessful investments later on in the fund's life. The overall performance over the life of the fund is what matters in the long term, not one or two spectacular investments, though occasionally, and typically with early-stage venture funds, a successful, multi-times-return exit can lead to the overall fund achieving the required return and entitling the private equity executives to their 20% carry.

Because of the high demand from investors to take part in new buyout funds, some managers have been able to negotiate a higher level of carry of 25% and in some cases 30%. These tend to be the exceptions for some really outstanding funds whose management teams not only have excellent track records but are also sufficiently differentiated to allow for above average returns.

# TRANSPARENCY AND DISCLOSURE BY PRIVATE EQUITY FIRMS: RELATIONSHIPS WITH LIMITED PARTNERS AND THE PRESS

The private equity industry is often accused of being too secretive, lacking transparency in its deals and performance. These accusations usually come from the media. There is considerable transparency between a private equity fund and its limited partners, such as the pension funds, banks and insurance companies. Not only do the limited partners receive quarterly and annual reports on the progress of each of a fund's investments, they are hopefully in fairly close communication with and from the general partners (GPs). The extent of this informal communication may vary depending on the depth of relationship between the general partners and the limited partners. Some GPs may prefer to keep this to a minimum; others may have more of an ongoing dialogue. While the written reports are confidential to the limited partners, the limited partners do represent the public ultimately, for example through employee pension funds investing in private equity.

The industry as a whole publishes annual reports on the performance of private equity funds, such as the BVCA Performance Measurement Survey referred to above, which shows the performance of funds over 1, 3, 5 and 10 years and since inception, split by venture, small, mid- and large buyouts, with ranges of returns also given for each category. These reports are provided to the members of the VC associations but are also made available to the press and can be purchased by the public. Of course, for reasons of confidentiality and to ensure complete reporting by all firms no matter how well or how poorly their funds have performed during the year being reported on, the performance of individual funds is not made public, not even to the VC associations. The industry is after all 'private'.

This whole issue of lack of transparency by the private equity industry came to a head in 2001 when a journalist at the San Jose Mercury News requested information on the performance of the California Public Employees' Retirement System (CalPERS), which is the largest pension fund in the United States. CalPERS initially refused to provide the information, citing non-disclosure clauses in its investment partnership agreements, although CalPERS had published selective private equity performance data on its website. The San Jose Mercury News then filed a request under California's Public Records Act, which is that state's version of the national Freedom of Information Act. CalPERS' argument that private equity performance data are trade secrets did not wash with the courts, partly because CalPERS had already published the selective information on its website, and CalPERS agreed to a settlement whereby it agreed to disclose how much it had earned or lost in each of the private equity funds that it had invested in, but would not disclose the identities or valuations of individual portfolio companies.

Other groups such as student bodies, in the case of the large endowment funds such as Yale and Harvard, and labour unions, in the case of pension funds, have been pressing for more disclosure on the performance of their endowments or pension funds performance in private equity funds.

General partners are concerned that providing details on the performance of their funds, ie. the internal rates of return (IRRs), could lead on to sensitive, confidential data on individual portfolio companies, such as individual company performance or details of a strategic, competitive nature, being given, which could be commercially harmful to those companies. Or if certain portfolio companies are not performing particularly well, information on this could discourage potential business partners of those companies.

Also, the performance data is meant to be studied by sophisticated investors who understand the long-term nature of the private equity industry. Current year (or one-year) returns are extremely volatile and inappropriate as a realistic measure of private equity performance. It is not possible to invest in a private equity fund for just one year. Private equity is a long-term investment spanning the life of a fund. At best, the one-year return indicates only if the year was 'good' or 'bad'. Also, IRRs have little meaning until a fund is at least halfway through its typical 10-year life, when realizations (exits) through IPOs or trade sales start to occur. So forced disclosure on a one-year or even quarterly basis too early in the life of a fund would not be meaningful to investors. Interim results are likely to look bad because they reflect the management fees charged to the fund and the possible failure of some start-ups, which is likely to occur earlier in the life of a fund than the longer-term successes.

The pressure for greater transparency has paradoxically led some general partners to limit the information that they provide to certain of their limited partners, eg the public pension funds in the United States, who are subject to Freedom of Information Act requirements. Or even, in the case of Sequoia Capital and the University of California, to ask the limited partners to withdraw from investing in a new fund.

# LACK OF PRIVATE EQUITY LEAGUE TABLES

Unlike in the United States where there are league tables for just about every aspect of life, let alone private equity, Europe suffers from a lack of publicized information on the relative standing of private equity firms. True, there are directories of members and overall aggregate information on investment activity and performance published by the European and national private equity and venture capital associations, but there is a lack of disaggregate information – largely on the grounds of confidentiality. I have been pressing for disclosure of at least league tables on say the top 10 most active venture capital firms in the technology sector across Europe, but to no avail. In the United States, each quarter the PwC NVCA MoneyTree™ survey publishes information on the most active venture investors, showing name of firm, location and number of deals done. On the performance side most firms will tell you that they are in the top quartile but information as to who exactly is in the top quartile is not available, at least from the national venture capital associations.

   Deal-specific information can be obtained by subscribing to one of the private equity data houses, such as Thomson Financial's VentureXpert (www. venturexpert.com) which includes statistics for all aspects of the venture process, including information on venture funds, private equity firms, executives, venture-backed companies and limited partners as well as the analytical source for fund performance, commitments, disbursements and statistics.

   What does all this relative lack of no-cost publicly available disaggregate information on the private equity industry mean for the entrepreneur/owner manager looking to raise venture capital? It means you need to be very careful when selecting which VCs to approach. Get recommendations from a knowledgeable intermediary, such as an accountant or lawyer who is active in the private equity industry and knows the top firms at each stage and in each sector well, knows which firms are really top quartile and who is most active in deals in the sectors in which you are working and looking to raise finance. For more on this, see Chapter 7.

# GUIDELINES FOR VALUING UNQUOTED INVESTMENTS

One of the issues in calculating the performance of a private equity or venture capital fund is that, unless all the underlying investments have been realized through an exit such as an IPO, trade sale, secondary sale or write-off (heaven forbid), it will be necessary to ascribe a value to any unrealized, ongoing investments. Historically, risk-averse accountants prescribed that such investments should be held at cost unless there had been an impairment in value, in which case the investments should be written down or even written off. Conservatism was the key. With accountants now more forward-looking, there is a drive for fair value accounting and the avoidance of artificially low asset valuations.

Consequently, the private equity industry in Europe, taking a lead on the United States, has published International Private Equity and Venture Capital Valuation Guidelines which were developed by the BVCA, EVCA and AFIC (the French national association). These guidelines were launched in March 2005 to reflect the need for greater comparability across the private equity industry and for consistency with IFRS and US GAAP accounting principles which adopt the overall principle of 'fair value'. These valuation guidelines are used by the private equity and venture capital industry for valuing private equity investments and provide a framework for fund managers and investors to monitor the value of existing investments. Fair value is the amount for which an asset could be exchanged, between knowledgeable willing parties in an arm's-length transaction.

The European valuation guidelines have been endorsed by 30 national venture capital associations throughout Europe, including Russia. In the United States the Private Equity Industry Guidelines Group (PEIGG) had previously published valuation guidelines and the European guidelines are largely consistent with these. Both the US and the European valuation guidelines have been endorsed by the Institutional Limited Partners Association (ILPA). The US National Venture Capital Association (NVCA), which represents VC firms rather than buyout firms, has chosen not to endorse the PEIGG guidelines, probably due to the NVCA's underlying caution of prudence in implementing specific elements of the guidelines such as valuation write-ups of early-stage companies in the absence of market-based financing events.

So with the current exception of the NVCA in the United States there should now be much greater consistency in how investments are valued in private equity firms' portfolios, which will permit better comparability of performance across funds. Of course, in the old days, when investments were held at cost less any required write-downs, there was probably reasonable consistency, but with the adoption of fair value accounting there is much greater scope for subjectivity.

# CREATION OF A SINGLE PRIVATE EQUITY MARKET FOR EUROPE

Currently, despite lobbying from EVCA and other bodies, the legislation that governs the way private equity investing is conducted in Europe is determined on a national level. In 2006 a group of 14 private equity and venture capital experts from 10 European countries submitted a report urging European Union institutions and national policymakers to create a uniform framework conducive to private equity investment across Europe. The aim is to allow European private equity investors the freedom to run their operations and raise funds across country borders, while respecting each country's fiscal and regulatory requirements, and to avoid double taxation and legal uncertainty surrounding private equity fund interests.

In 2006 Apax Partners and the Economist Intelligence Unit conducted a survey which benchmarked the attractiveness of the business environment in 33 countries to international and local private equity firms. Not surprisingly, the United States came out first in the overall rankings and first for its financing environment, market opportunities and entrepreneurial environment. The UK came second overall but was first for its legal and policy environment. Italy came 24th overall and 24th for its legal and policy environment, with its complex bureaucratic and legal procedures and inadequate infrastructure which continue to deter investors, as well as a high tax burden on firms and a rigid labour market. China came out 33rd (out of 33) overall and 33rd for its legal and policy environment.

The legal, tax and operating environment in which private equity operates in Europe is very much based at the local, country level. The maturity or otherwise of private equity development in the country is largely directly proportional to the 'friendliness' of regulators and the availability of incentives for private equity investing, as the more experienced with private equity and venture capital the more the benefits of this asset class to the wider economy are known and appreciated. However, there is much more to do in terms of recognizing the cross-border, international aspects of the European private equity industry, including being reasonable about the taxation of private equity business originating from other member states and the recognition of fund structures across member states. The current fund structuring environment does not support cross-border investing and changes need to be made so that, for example, capital gains on cross-border investments are taxed only in the home country of the investor.

# LACK OF PAN-EUROPEAN STOCK EXCHANGE

Attempts to create and maintain a pan-European stock market in the past with EASDAQ and then NASDAQ Europe failed. The current plethora of individual country exchanges is not conducive to Europe's venture capital industry being competitive with the United States. The European Union has more than 20 stock markets and most lack the critical mass to be effective. Each exchange has its own set of regulations, listing requirements, disclosure requirements, IPO market practices, under-writing fees and trading systems. EVCA argues that while the individual country exchanges may be adequate for large-cap European companies, they are not able to provide the capital and liquidity requirements of small-cap growth companies, such as the companies that the European venture capital industry supports. An efficient pan-European high-growth stock market would improve the ability of young companies to raise capital.

Most entrepreneurs, although not all, will be looking to exit their successful businesses at some stage, usually via a flotation on a stock market or a sale to another company (trade sale). Others will want to continue to grow and expand their businesses and eventually pass the business on to their heirs.

Venture capital firms similarly, and essentially exclusively, need to exit their investments, though some will retain a shareholding when a company is floated. Access to the capital markets and subsequent trading liquidity is therefore important to both entrepreneurs and venture capital firms so that publicly traded equity, resulting from the flotation of the venture-backed company, can be ultimately sold for cash.

EVCA is therefore lobbying hard for the creation of a pan-European stock market for young, high-growth companies in Europe. This could be achieved, not by imposition by European policymakers, but by close collaboration between the existing country exchanges or the broadening of one exchange to be pan-European.

The recent 'internationalization' of AIM, whereby the London Stock Exchange is developing AIM to accommodate the demand among small- and medium-sized companies across Europe for equity growth capital, may help with this. The LSE's goal is to develop AIM into a single pan-European trading platform for young, high-growth companies and it is seeking the support and commitment of the investment community in the other major European financial centres, developing a network of links with investors, advisers and intermediaries as well as the issuers themselves in markets across Europe. Local nominated advisers (Nomads) across Europe will act as a pipeline for companies coming to

AIM, and local member firms will provide liquidity, ongoing research and local distribution to investors.

Also, new junior markets have been created for the Deutsche Borse in Germany and Alternext was set up in 2005 by Euronext to meet the needs of small- and mid-sized companies seeking simplified access to the stock market. Alternext's streamlined listing requirements and trading rules are suited to the size and business needs of small- and mid-cap firms. The New York Stock Exchange and Euronext agreed in June 2006 to complete a €15 billion merger creating the largest, and the world's first transatlantic, stock exchange. NASDAQ holds a 25% stake in the London Stock Exchange. LSE rebuffed a bid approach from NASDAQ in 2006.

Listing on AIM versus the main market in the UK is covered in Chapter 12.

# DEBT LEVELS

A typical buyout deal might comprise debt of at least twice, and maybe up to five times, the equity component. So a €150 million buyout deal could be €50 million of equity and €100 million of debt. As funds get ever larger and deal sizes increase there are some who are concerned that debt levels will rise to unacceptable and dangerous levels. High leverage is fine when interest rates are low but becomes an issue when interest rates increase. Is the business able to generate the cash flow from sales to service the high debt levels? In many cases this would not be the case and the business would have to be refinanced, which may be difficult in a slowing economy or interest-rate-hike situation.

The debt financing is not just provided by banks. Much of it is collateralized debt and is sold on to hedge funds or other investors. So this means the debt risk is more widely spread than if the banks were just the main lenders. On the other hand, the new 'lenders' such as the hedge funds are looking for high returns and if these are not achieved this new source of debt funding could rapidly dry up. So there is concern in some quarters that the private equity market may be overheating.

# ENCROACHMENT OF HEDGE FUNDS

There has been a recent trend of executives leaving the private equity industry to join hedge fund operations, and some private equity firms have accused the hedge funds of 'poaching' their executives. Hedge funds have been attracted to private equity by its high returns, growing liquidity from the advent of secondary purchases and the lower returns of the hedge fund industry. Hedge funds have been taking large equity positions and adopting shareholder-activist stances. Is all of this a serious threat to private equity from the hedge fund industry?

Sources put the number of hedge funds worldwide in excess of 8,000, with the hedge funds controlling well over €800 billion in assets. Traditionally, hedge funds have focused their investment strategies on securities and other assets that are liquid and are susceptible to pricing at marked-to-market values. As the assets can be valued and reduced to cash, the hedge funds permit investors to join or withdraw at regular intervals, and managers take fees based on marked-to-market values. However, variations on these traditional concepts have been introduced, and it is these variations that make it possible for hedge funds to participate in what have traditionally been viewed as private equity investments. Hedge funds have historically been more interested in shorter- and medium-term deals than the long-term value that private equity brings to its deals in terms of close working with the investee company management team post-investment.

For their part the larger private equity firms are clubbing together with other private equity firms and forming alliances with banks and hedge funds in order to pursue multi-billion-dollar takeover opportunities. As the mega funds continue to grow and multi-billion-dollar funds are raised, private equity will be able to bid for such opportunities in their own right; in the meantime, clubbing together and alliances are seen as the solution.

Additionally, some larger private equity firms, such as KKR, have set up so-called 'funnel' funds which are listed and allow smaller investors and hedge funds to invest in a private equity fund. KKR's funnel fund is listed on the Euronext Amsterdam stock market.

So private equity is more likely to be working in partnership with the hedge fund industry than in competition with it.

## INDUSTRY CRITICS

As well as the accusation of secrecy and a lack of transparency, the private equity world is often criticized for heavy-handed dealings (the term 'vulture capitalists' springs to mind), destroying employment, only being interested in 'mega' deals and having a 'wall of money' available for investment; even worse, some large private equity firms together with other financiers were accused of being 'locusts' by a former chairman of Germany's Social Democratic Party. The press picks up on all of this, of course, and the public is left with the impression of a greedy, secretive, powerful world of private equity.

Private equity firms have not done much in the past to counter some of these accusations, rather coyly refusing to talk to the press about anything, using the excuse of their investors not wanting publicity, but the industry is now starting to speak out. For example, in late 2005 EVCA published the first Europe-wide study of the impact of private equity and venture capital, an independent survey, conducted by the Centre for Entrepreneurial and Financial Studies at the Technische Universitat Munchen, which revealed that both venture-capital-backed and buyout companies had increased their staffing levels four times higher than the average among EU member states. Venture-capital-backed companies created a net new 620,000 jobs in the period covered by the survey of 2000 to 2004, while companies that had been subject to buyouts created a net new 420,000 jobs. The highest growth in employment was seen by venture-backed firms (more than 30% growth in employment between 1997 and 2004) and in particular by venture-backed biotechnology and healthcare firms (more than 45% growth).

Private equity needs to build up its public relations efforts to get the positive messages out about its contribution to the European economy and that the creation of value for investors involves more than just providing the funding. Whether by using their experience to provide support to the management team, or by providing guidance on strategic or operational issues, the private equity firm will usually be a source of help in a number of ways. As shown in the BVCA's publication *The Economic Impact of Private Equity in the UK*, published in November 2005, four out of five companies sampled felt that their private equity backers had made a major contribution to their businesses over and above the provision of money. The private equity industry in Europe plays a crucial role in promoting successful enterprises as well as providing attractive returns to its investors. In the UK around a fifth of UK private sector employees are now employed by companies that have received funding from private equity firms.

As regards the 'wall of money', the funds raised in Europe in 2005 will last for only 18 months based on 2005 investment levels. And the industry is not only interested in 'mega' deals. Although 68% of investments by amount went into buyouts in 2005, 78% of investments by number went into companies that employ fewer than 100 people.

# European early-stage and technology venture capital investing

## FIRMS SPECIALIZING IN EARLY-STAGE AND TECHNOLOGY INVESTING

There are relatively few venture capital firms in Europe that focus on investing in early-stage and/or the technology sectors. Finding them is a case of searching the directories of the European or national private equity and venture capital associations, as explained more fully in Chapter 7 which covers how to select and approach the most appropriate private equity and venture capital firms for your business proposal. Or better still, discussing appropriate firms to approach with a knowledgeable professional adviser such as your accountant or lawyer. To start you off, Table 4.1 lists a sample of well-known venture capital firms that specialize in these sectors, by country. I must stress that this is by no means fully inclusive. I list them here because I know several of the executives at these firms and know of their interest in the technology/early-stage sectors. Many of them also invest at the expansion and MBO stages but there are many more firms who invest at the expansion and MBO stages but not at the early stages. Do visit the websites of these firms for more information.

**Table 4.1** European venture capital firms that specialize in the technology sectors

**Benelux**

AlpInvest Partners
www.alpinvest.com

Capricorn Venture Partners
www.capricorn.be

European Investment Fund
www.eif.org

GIMV NV
www.gimv.com

**Central and Eastern Europe**

3TS Capital Partners
www.3tsvp.com

**France**

Partech International
www.partechvc.com

Sofinnova Ventures
www.sofinnova.com

**Germany**

BayTech Venture Capital
www.baytechventure.com

Extorel
en.extorel.de

PolyTechnos Venture Partners
www.polytechnos.com

Siemens Venture Capital
www.siemensventurecapital.com

Triangle Venture Capital Group
www.triangle-venture.com

TVM Capital
www.tvm-capital.com

Wellington Partners
www.wellington.de

**Ireland**

ACT Venture Capital Ltd
www.actventure.com

Delta Partners
www.delta.ie

Trinity Venture Capital
www.trinity-vc.ie

**Netherlands**

AlpInvest Partners
www.alpinvest.com

Gilde Investment Management
www.gilde.nl

**Nordic**

CapMan
www.capman.com

Investor Growth Capital
www.investorab.com

Nexit Ventures
www.nexitventures.com

SEB Foretagsinvest Venture Capital
www.foretagsinvest.seb.se

Sitra
www.sitra.fi

**Spain**

Mercapital
www.mercapital.com

**Switzerland**

Conor Venture Partners
www.conorvp.com

Index Ventures
www.indexventures.com

Techno Venture Management
www.tvmvc.com

Vision Capital
www.visioncap.com

**UK**

3i
www.3i.com

Abingworth
www.abingworth.com

Accel Partners
www.accel.com

Add Partners
www.addpartners.com

Advent Venture Partners
www.adventventures.com

Alta Berkeley
www.altaberkeley.com

Amadeus Capital Partners
www.amadeuscapital.com

Apax Partners
www.apax.com

Ariadne Capital
www.ariadnecapital.com

Atlantic Bridge Ventures
www.abven.com

Atlas Venture
www.atlasventure.com

Avlar BioVentures
www.avlar.com

Benchmark Capital
www.benchmark.com

Capital Partners Private Equity
www.capital-partners.co.uk

Crescendo Ventures
www.crescendoventures.com

DN Capital
www.dncapital.com

Doughty Hanson Technology Ventures
www.doughtyhanson.com

Eden Ventures
www.edenventures.co.uk

Elderstreet Investments
www.elderstreet.com

Environmental Technologies Fund
www.etf.eu.com

Esprit Capital Partners
www.espritcp.com

e-Synergy
www.e-synergy.com

European Venture Partners
www.evp.co.uk

European Technology Ventures
www.etvcapital.com

Finance Wales Investments
www.financewales.co.uk

go4venture
www.go4venture.com

IDG Ventures Europe
www.idgve.com

Imperial College Innovations Limited
www.imperialinnovations.co.uk

Intel Capital
www.intel.com

Kennet Venture Partners
www.kennetventures.com

Merlin Biosciences
www.merlin-biosciences.com

MTI Partners
www.mtifirms.com

Noble Venture Finance
www.noblegp.com

Northern Venture Managers Limited
www.nvm.co.uk

Oxbridge Capital
www.oxbridgecapital.com

Oxford Technology VCTs
www.oxfordtechnology.com

Pond Venture Partners
www.pondventures.com

Prime Technology Ventures
www.ptv.com

Quester Capital Management
www.quester.co.uk

Scottish Equity Partners
www.sep.co.uk

Softbank Europe Ventures
www.softbank.com

TLcom Capital Partners
www.tlcom.co.uk

Top Technology Ventures
www.toptechnology.co.uk

TTP Venture Managers
www.ttpventures.com

YFM Venture Finance Ltd
www.yfmventurefinance.co.uk

Zouk Ventures
www.zouk.com

Some of the firms included in Table 4.1 specialize in specific technology sectors, such as software or biotech. Some will specialize at various stages of investment, such as seed, start-up, other early-stage or expansion/development capital. The important issue is to target your business proposal to those firms which are known to invest in your particular sector and to target the investment executive(s) who specialize in your sector at those firms.

## DIFFERENCES IN APPROACH BETWEEN EUROPEAN AND US VENTURE CAPITAL FIRMS

We looked at the current trends in technology investing in Chapter 2, including the fact that VCs in Europe no longer assume any risk as regards the capabilities of the technology underlying the business proposal and only take on the market risk; the emergence of niche, stage/industry-specific technology VCs; and the issues some firms have been facing in raising new funds for investment in view of the average relatively poor performance of early-stage/technology funds in terms of returns generated as compared to the funds focusing on small, medium and large buyouts. I also mentioned the overall approach to risk in Europe as compared to the United States, with Europe's greater caution manifesting itself especially via the aversion to technology risk, and a readiness to accept only market risk where possible – and even then ideally with revenue generation, or at least, customer contracts, in place. In contrast, US private equity houses appear much more prepared to take a punt on technology.

Venture capital firms in Europe tend to 'drip-feed' money into investments, investing relatively small amounts at inception and further amounts only if the investee company meets various criteria or milestones as set out in the business plan and documented in the investment agreement with the VC. In the United States there is more likelihood of a VC coming up with the total required funding as envisaged in the business plan at inception. This difference in approach to initial investing between European and US VCs may be because venture capital firms in the United States have been active in the industry for rather longer than those in Europe, maybe because there are generally more funds in total in the United States for early-stage and technology investing than in Europe and possibly because VCs in the United States tend to be closer geographically to their investee companies (the so-called 'zip code' investors). This difference in approach can lead to funding problems as the business grows; maybe milestones are not met in the required timeframe so the VC delays or cancels future finance provision, maybe milestones are met but the VC refuses to continue funding for some other reason such as management issues. The more risk-averse approach protects the VC's interests but subjects the investee company to much more uncertainty as to whether funding will be forthcoming.

Various studies of the industry demonstrate this difference in approach to investing by European and US VCs. The study I referred to in Chapter 2, 'Money for Growth', showed that, while Europe may gradually be closing the gap on the United States in terms of venture capital technology investments, the most striking contrast between Europe and the United States remains in the size of average investments/deals, where the average US deal remains seven times the size of an investment in Europe. The report concludes that, as set out above, this reflects a fundamental difference in the approach to investment, with Europeans tending to drip-feed investment as and when various hurdles are crossed, rather than entrusting the management with a large tranche at an early stage. There were about twice as many investments by number in Europe as deals in the United States in 2004, with Europe's 4,203 investments during 2004 coming in at not far from double the US total of 2,308 deals during the year. This is partly a reflection of the different definitions of an investment/deal in Europe versus the United States. In Europe each separate investment by each venture capital firm is classed as a separate investment or deal, whereas syndicated investments in the United States are classed as just one deal.

The average deal size for technology-related investments in the United States was € (equivalent) 6.1 million in 2004, down 2% from the €6.2 million average deal size recorded in 2003. The average investment/deal size for European technology venture capital investments was €0.9 million in 2003, up 23% from the average size of €0.7 million in 2003.

# EUROPEAN EMERGING TECHNOLOGY CENTRES

One of the areas where Europe is certainly leading on the United States is the proportionately greater number of emerging technology centres. The United States has its Silicon Valley in the San Jose, California area as well as tech centres in San Diego, California; Seattle, Washington; Austin, Texas; Minneapolis, Minnesota; Boston, Massachusetts; and Raleigh, North Carolina.

Europe now has many emerging technology centres, many with 'Silicon' nicknames analogous to Silicon Valley in the United States, of which Silicon Fen in the Cambridge area is perhaps the most famous.

## Characteristics of the technology regions

What do these areas have in common? Breakthrough companies (eg Nokia in Finland), top science and technology universities (eg Imperial College in London, University of Cambridge) usually with experienced technology transfer offices, managers and engineers with relevant technology expertise, venture capitalists and other financiers, accountants, lawyers and other advisers and often a whole infrastructure built around science and industrial parks, 'incubator' centres, serviced offices etc. The informal and formal networks that are created between these people and entities provide the collaborative support structures that entrepreneurs and innovation need to flourish.

Some of Europe's leading technology areas are listed in Table 4.2.

## Example of a European technology region

The Thames Valley region in the UK (sometimes rather unkindly referred to as 'Silicon Ditch') is where I am based so I use it here as an example of the ingredients that these technology centres have in common around Europe. The Thames Valley is the European headquarters for many of the world's largest IT companies as well as several companies involved in the biotech sector. Global technology companies with major operations in the Thames Valley include Cisco, Dell, LG Electronics, Microsoft, Oracle, Siemens and Vodafone. The Universities of Oxford and Reading are located here with their science, technology and engineering departments, business schools and entrepreneurship centres.

The Thames Valley is home to Europe's largest trading estate in single ownership – Slough Trading Estate was the world's first trading estate set up in 1920 and now has over 20,000 people working for around 400 companies on the estate. The Thames Valley has its network of VCs and legal and accounting firms and other advisers. It has excellent links to London and the rest of the UK through the motorway networks and to the rest of the world through Heathrow airport. And there are several networking organizations in the area for both established companies and early-stage companies and entrepreneurs, including the Thames Valley Economic Partnership and its Innovate Thames Valley initiative whose aim is to stimulate and promote innovation and enterprise by working closely with businesses at the cutting edge of new technology (both

**Table 4.2** European technology regions

| | |
|---|---|
| • **UK**<br>Thames Valley ('Silicon Ditch')<br>London<br>Cambridge ('Silicon Fen')<br>Glasgow ('Silicon Glen')<br>Newport, Wales ('Cwm Silicon')<br>Birmingham/Manchester<br>Newcastle/Leeds<br>Belfast | • **Israel**<br>('Silicon Wadi')<br><br>• **Czech Republic**<br>Prague ('Czech Tech')<br><br>• **Sweden**<br>Kista (science/industrial area largely<br>spun out of Ericsson) |
| • **Germany**<br>Stuttgart/Munich<br>Frankfurt<br>Dusseldorf<br>Dresden ('Silicon Valley of the East')<br>Heidelberg/Karlsruhe | • **Finland**<br>Helsinki ('Oulu Technopolis') –<br>spun out of Nokia<br><br>• **The Netherlands**<br>Amsterdam and Eindhoven (where<br>Philips is headquartered) |
| • **Ireland**<br>Dublin ('Silicon Isle')<br><br>• **Switzerland**<br>Geneva/Neuchatel | • **Spain**<br>Madrid<br><br>• **Poland**<br>Krakow |
| • **France**<br>Grenoble<br>Paris<br>South of France (Sophia Antipolis) | • **Romania**<br>Bucharest<br><br>• **Russia**<br>Moscow, St Petersburg, Perm |
| • **Belgium**<br>('Flanders Language Valley') | |

entrepreneurs and established corporates) and with scientists, technologists and investors and the Thames Valley Investment Network which links investors, such as business angels, to companies with high-growth potential.

# UNIVERSITY SPINOUTS

One of the usual features of emerging technology areas is the existence of leading-edge science and technology universities. The interest of academics and research staff, university management and investors (early-stage VCs and business angels) in the commercialization of new technologies being developed at these centres has never been stronger.

For example, Imperial Innovations, the technology commercialization and investment company, based at Imperial College, London, sources its opportunities primarily from academic staff at Imperial College and Imperial Innovations is responsible for managing intellectual property for Imperial College. Imperial Innovations has a portfolio of around 60 spinout companies. Technologies commercialized include therapeutics, medical devices, diagnostics, software, renewable energy and low carbon, mechanical devices and recycling, which reflects the diverse research activity at Imperial College and also complementary IP sourced from third parties.

How Imperial Innovations works with its spinout companies is addressed in the first of two case studies later in this chapter on Ceres Holdings plc, where Imperial Innovations drafted the original scope of the business plan and then brought in three MBA students to work with an experienced Innovations technology transfer project manager to further develop the plan. In the second case study on InforSense Limited we see how the founding academic is continuing to lead the company as CEO and has been joined by a strong management team including a chief business officer and president.

## Definition of a university spinout

The definition used here is taken from a book on university spinouts to which I contributed, entitled *Taking Research To Market: How to build and invest in successful university spinouts*, edited by Kenny Tang, Ajay Vohora and Lord Roger Freeman (Euromoney Books 2004). It is: 'A startup company whose formation was dependent on the intellectual property (IP) rights of the university and in which the university holds an equity stake'.

## Characteristics of university spinouts

The characteristics of university spinouts are as follows:

▌ the value of the spinout is linked primarily to long-term growth potential, derived from scientific knowledge and IP;

▌ the spinout company may lack tangible assets in its early stages;

▌ the underlying products have little (or no) track record; and

▌ the products are largely untested in the marketplace.

Well-known university spinouts include: Genentech, Google, Lycos, Digital Equipment Corporation (DEC) and Chiron.

## Stakeholders in university spinouts

The stakeholders in a university spinout include:

▮ Academics (technology researchers/ developers) – usually have less developed commercial skills, knowledge of markets, financial returns than for corporate spinouts. Academics may also have a conflict of interest in terms of withholding research findings to pursue personal gain rather than publishing to the scientific community.

▮ Institutions (universities) – usually with ownership interest in the IP and in spinout process through a technology transfer office (TTO). The university may take an equity stake in the spinout or license the IP to the spinout.

▮ Investors (VCs and business angels) – have specific requirements for the returns on their investments.

The university technology transfer office (TTO) may have considerable delegated authority but usually reports to the senior management group of the university. The TTO is unlikely to have line management authority over the academics who are generating the IP.

## Issues relating to university spinouts

An investor dealing with a university spinout company will have several issues to deal with including:

▮ Equity ownership – who gets what between the founders, university, management team and the investors?

▮ IP ownership – will spinout company own it and if not, eg if owned by the university, what are the terms of any licences?

▮ Use of university facilities – does spinout need these to continue, for example office space and equipment, administrative services?

▮ Management team – does the team have the complement of the right skills for the stage of development of the spinout and are people in the right roles? A key issue will be whether the founder CEO of the spinout (usually an academic) will be prepared to hand over to an external CEO as the company grows. If not, he or she probably should not be made CEO in the first place.

▮ Time – can university work within commercial timescales or will investors walk away from deals?

A key step in the early life of a spinout is achieving proof of concept, ie a feasibility study that converts the theoretical to the practical and usually occurs after the filing of a patent application but before full-scale demonstration of the technology and well before any product development. An assessment of the market potential/market size for any products should also be made at this stage.

Funding for proof of concept studies may be available from the university itself, possibly via the University Challenge Funds (see Chapter 6). Proof of concept is pre-seed stage. At the seed stage business angel or seed specialist VC money might be available.

How to encourage more businesses to spin out from universities is a key challenge. This is addressed in the UK context in the following article from the British Venture Capital Association.

## BVCA: Creating success from university spinouts

How to create profitable businesses from university-developed technology is one of the great challenges of our time. Everyone agrees how important it is to the future success of the UK economy but there is much wrangling and frustration about how to achieve it. Scientists blame venture capitalists for being too greedy or refusing to invest in palpably brilliant projects. Government ruminates on whether there is an equity gap and, if there is, where is it and how do we solve it? VCs say scientists are unrealistic in their expectations, just don't understand the needs of business and are pretty sure there is not so much of an equity gap as much as there is an opportunity to invest gap. All these are gross generalizations but they crudely encapsulate the areas of dispute.

The development and exploitation of innovative technology is not a new challenge that has materialized in our time but has been an important part in the development of mankind throughout time. As technological development has become increasingly complex and sophisticated, so it has required more investment to make it possible. Bluntly, the development of modern science is an expensive undertaking and it requires rigorous and thoughtful investment processes.

We know that in the UK we have some of the best science and technology development in the world. We also have in this country the largest and most vibrant venture capital community in Europe. The UK accounts for over 50% of the European VC market and is second in size in the world only to the United States. The challenge then is how to improve the understanding and relationship between these two communities for the benefit of all.

How to tackle this issue has been one of the recent priorities of the BVCA. The BVCA commissioned a report, 'Creating Success from University Spin-outs', to look at ways in which things could be improved. The only remit for the report was that it should not be critical of any organization and that it should propose practical and realistic initiatives that could be taken. The eight principal conclusions of the report included recommendations for action for the VC industry and the BVCA, the universities and the government. They included:

- the government and the universities measuring what is happening not simply by the quantity of activity but by more rigorously looking at the quality of what is going on;
- a clearer demonstration by the universities of the value and importance of entrepreneurship;
- that access to and the management of intellectual property rights should be simplified;
- that the aims, objectives and incentives across a university, its individual departments, researchers and the technology transfer offices should be more closely aligned;
- that VCs and business angels should do more to help universities understand more clearly what it takes to secure their backing;
- that better relationships should be built between universities and the business community so there is a better understanding of customer needs and market opportunities;
- that funding should be secured from government for proof of market and technology qualification for spin-out candidates;
- that experienced entrepreneurs and managers should be recruited into spin-outs at an early stage to help share experience and knowledge.

None of these recommendations are complicated and they should not be controversial. Most are simply common sense. Together we have to find a way of moving the debate on from where it is, which is why are we not doing better, to where it needs to be, which is how together can we find the answers.

For the full report 'Creating Success from University Spin-outs' please go to www.bvca.co.uk

Jo Taylor
Chairman, BVCA Technology Committee
Director 3i

# Case study 1
## Ceres Power Holdings plc – Imperial College university spinout

Ceres Power Ltd was founded in 2001 to develop and commercialize research carried out by Professors Brian Steele, John Kilner and Alan Atkinson of the Department of Materials and Dr Nigel Brandon of the Department of Chemistry at Imperial College London. The company is a developer of fuel cell technology that generates electricity from natural gas.

Ceres Power is developing fuel cells that combine practical operating temperatures (around 550 °C) with affordable materials and deliver electrical power in the range from 1 to 25 kW. The cells are made from stainless steel components and thin ceramic coatings. They are constructed in such a way as to make them modular using standard sealing technology. Consequently, they can be manufactured affordably and are extremely robust.

Imperial Innovations drafted the original scope of the business plan and then brought in three MBA students to work with an experienced Innovations technology transfer project manager to further develop the plan. The final submission won first prize at the European Business plan competition. Innovations subsequently brought in Ludgate Financial Advisors, as fundraisers experienced in the energy sector.

The sum of £4.25m was raised as initial first-round funding in 2002 and a further £5m in 2003 from additional investors including Cazenove, FNI, Newton Investments, Fleming Family and Partners, the Carbon Trust and Imperial College. This was the first major later-stage investment made by Imperial College. Prior to second-round fundraising an experienced CEO, Peter Bance, was appointed.

Having won the Carbon Trust Innovation award in 2003, Ceres Power's fuel cell impressed the judges as a design with considerable commercial potential aimed at small-sized units for use in the home and applications where the fuel cell can replace internal combustion engines and lead acid batteries.

The company is now widely recognized to be developing a major technology that has potential to transform power generation and is recognized as a leader in low carbon technologies.

Ceres Power floated on the Alternative Investment Market of the London Stock Exchange at the end of 2004 and placed 13.3 million new shares at £1.20 per share, valuing the company at £66m.

In 2005 the company extended its commercial relationships with important partners having secured a third contract with BOC, the global industries gases producer, and a £2.7 million programme with British Gas in March 2006. Ceres has also developed its platform technology for a range of market applications, and grown its manufacturing capabilities.

Ceres Power has played a significant role in putting fuel cells and micro-power generation on to the UK's energy agenda. In the year of the UK's Energy Review, Ceres Power represented the industry in the development of national energy policy through membership of the Chancellor's Energy Research Partnership and Chairmanship of the newly formed UK Fuel Cell Industry Association. Ceres Power has also received direct support from national and regional bodies including the DTI, the Carbon Trust and the South East England Development Agency (SEEDA).

Imperial Innovations currently holds 9.3% of Ceres Power Holdings plc.

www.imperialinnovations.co.uk

# Case study 2

## InforSense Limited – Imperial College university spinout

InforSense was founded in November 1999. The business sells a suite of data-mining software tools which have been developed by Professor Yike Guo and his team in the Department of Computing. After extensive market analysis, it realized that the best way to commercialize this technology would be to create a spinout company that could sell and develop the data-mining software to many different organizations and businesses in the sectors of life science, healthcare, financial services, and sales and marketing.

The technology enables organizations (scientific and business) to integrate data sources, information and analysis tools, and also to capture and orchestrate companies' decision-making processes. This delivers improved productivity for businesses and organizations that use it. InforSense's technology can offer scientists the ability to access a variety of software packages and data sources to construct their own integration processes without having to manually transform data or program interfaces. Its proprietary-platform-powered 'Discovery Net' was the winner of the High Performance Computing Challenge at the International Supercomputing Conference and Exhibition in 2002.

Professor Yike Guo has continued to lead the company as CEO but has been joined by a strong management team, including Joseph F. Donahue as Chief Business Officer and President in 2005. In April 2003, Frank Jones, Chairman of Schlumberger Plc, joined the company and was appointed by Imperial Innovations as non-executive chairman. Frank Jones has significant experience managing and directing companies in the IT industry.

InforSense maintains a European headquarters in London and a North American headquarters in Cambridge, Massachusetts. In addition, Professor Guo continues his research activities at Imperial College and there has been a continuous transfer of knowledge from his team here to the company and vice versa. In the financial year 2004/2005 the company had a more than threefold revenue growth over the previous fiscal year. Revenues increased in each of the key global markets – Europe, North America and Asia. In 2005, the company also won its first customers in the financial services sector.

In June 2006, InforSense established a distribution network in Japan with CTC Laboratory Systems (parent company Itochu Techno-Science Corporation). It also has a joint venture with the Shanghai Centre for Bioinformatics Technology and IBM China to create a laboratory for bioinformatics research and applications in Shanghai. The company also has distribution deals with companies in the United States and a co-selling agreement with IBM in Europe.

Holding its first global users' conference in the United States, in April 2006, InforSense had over 85 participants from industry and academia sharing insights into working with InforSense products. In addition to extensive discussions and live demos, InforSense and a number of its partners, including Apple, ChemNavigator, Daylight,

DeltaSoft, Elsevier MDL, Oracle and Spotfire, showcased their collaborations and integrated product offerings.

InforSense has had considerable success signing a number of high-profile global customers for the software in the drug discovery field. Customers include the world's top pharmaceutical companies, AstraZeneca, Bayer, GSK, Procter & Gamble and Syngenta, as well as research institutes such as National Cancer Institute USA, Oxford University and Windber Institute. They also work with large financial institutions managing billions of dollars of client investments, and represent some of the Fortune 500 companies. InforSense was selected to participate in a major EU-funded Cross-Industry Grid Computing project in 2005 and in the same year won 'Best of Show' in 'BioIT World' for Knowledge Management and Collaboration.

A number of InforSense's customers have stated that by committing to InforSense software, they have empowered more scientists across their organizations to use information-driven analytics effectively to inform and accelerate their research. InforSense's technology has enabled scientists to translate their research into real decisions that impact patient care.
www.imperialinnovations.co.uk

# 'HOT' TECHNOLOGY SECTORS FOR VC INVESTMENT

The EVCA and Money for Growth reports referred to in Chapter 2 show in which fairly broad technology categories European VCs are actually making their investments. The VCs are always on the look-out for the 'next big thing', following the dot.com/internet era. Of course, by the time the 'next big thing' has been identified it is usually too late for a VC to make a cutting-edge investment, stealing the lead from its competitors. And the danger then is that the VC is simply jumping on the investment bandwagon. Also, as referred to above, VCs are no longer keen to take on technology risk but focus instead on proven technology, IP protection and global market potential. The more disruptive the technology the more interested the VC is likely to be in the investment proposition surrounding the technology. A disruptive technology is a new technological innovation, product, or service that eventually overturns the existing dominant technology or product in the market, eg as digital photography has almost replaced film photography.

The following are just some areas in which VCs are actively investing or are looking at with close interest (if not necessarily substantiating this with hard investment at the present time, as in the case of nanotechnology).

## Software

The computer software sector in Europe consistently represents around a quarter of total technology investments in Europe both by amount and number. The rebound in corporate IT spending over the past two years has fuelled a general recovery in the software industry. The search continues for opportunities in niche software technologies, with the main focus areas including security, analytics, vertical market applications and wireless as well as document security, search marketing and knowledge management systems.

There is stiff competition for deals in the UK and continental Europe has become a logical hunting-ground for VCs seeking value.

## Computers and networking

The IT landscape is largely dominated by large-scale, monolithic, centralized systems. These are increasingly at odds with the globalized, multifaceted, distributed and fast-moving environment in which multinational businesses now operate.

The new generation of componentized technology architecture is all about aligning technology to business requirements, not the other way around. The development and adoption of web service components marks a move away from traditional enterprise architectures and towards service-oriented architectures, which will enable the creation and delivery of technology service bundles mapped directly onto business processes.

The current outsourcing trend, plus the resurgence of the application service provider (ASP) models and the advent of software as a service, is hastening the move towards commoditization of IT infrastructure. New software-as-a-service and pay-as-you-go models will emerge, ultimately leading to utility computing models, with standardized processing power provided on tap complete with service applications and infrastructure on a pay-per-usage basis. Opportunities for VCs are in the areas of the componentized IT environment of the future which will not only be component developers but also enablers in areas such as data virtualization, networking, intelligent storage and search engines. There is also a drive towards utility computing whereby computer resources are provided on an on-demand and pay-as-you-go basis. Users are billed only for the actual use of resources. As the provider of the utility computing facility can spread users' different requirements for computing resources, the utilization of those resources can be optimized.

## Wireless technology

Europe is still leading the United States on wireless technologies, particularly 3G. The industry has had to deal with how the multiple wireless technologies in various stages of maturity all fit together, such as WiFi and WiMax, DSL, Bluetooth and 3G. The aim overall is for seamless mobile connectivity. There is still a need for better collaboration such as with GSM roaming. Other issues to be sorted out include interconnectivity, security and authentication. There are plenty of opportunities for VC investors in all of these areas.

Voice over Internet Protocol (VoIP) is another area of interest. This is where telephone conversations are carried out over the internet or a private network using internet protocol (which is a packet switching technology whereby the voice data is sent in packets rather than over an end-to-end circuit) instead of via a dedicated voice circuit. Skype is Europe's most famous success story in this area.

There is also the integration of VoIP and cellular technology to produce a dual-band phone that operates as a wireless phone outside an office building and connects through the WLAN while inside. Other areas include multimedia networking software; software that helps consumers find and buy songs, movies and other types of content on the internet, ring tones linked to video clips of the caller, and the easier transfer of music from PCs to mobile phones.

Then there is the whole area of broadband connections going into people's homes and innovations in the consumer electronics market, including electronic equipment, computers, e-mail software, multimedia software, display panels and semiconductor technology.

Of course, it is necessary to ensure that consumers want these new services and not to put the technology cart before the consumer horse, as with WAP, for example, which has never really taken off. On the other hand, few people predicted the success of SMS messaging or mobile phone ring tones.

## Web 2.0

Web 2.0 has arisen out of the ashes of the dot.com/internet period in 2000/1, with new applications and websites for a second generation of services on the web that enables users to collaborate and share information online. Web 2.0 includes application services in which users access software through the web from any device anywhere in the world: a global wireless internet.

## Medical instruments and devices

An underlying move towards more risk-averse investing has meant that over the past two years or so there has been a decline in biotechnology investment and a rise in medical instruments/devices investment. Medical devices have shorter health regulatory approval cycles, such as the FDA in the United States, making development much more cost effective and time to exit much more rapid. Key areas for investment in the medical devices field are medical imaging, remote diagnostics and robotic surgery.

## Radio frequency (RFID) tags

These are passive electronic circuits that can be powered and read remotely. RFID tags have been operational in security systems and some motorway tollbooths for some time. RFID has many applications, including the potential for tracking, controlling and replenishing stock more cheaply and effectively. Since the start of 2005 Wal-Mart has required its top suppliers to place high frequency tags on cartons and pallets shipped to its stores and warehouses, though there have been issues such as who will pay for the RFID tagging of supplies and technical problems such as UHF (ultra high frequency) interference with other RFID readers, even from a distance of a few kilometres, and the lack of a single RFID standard, as well as different regulations about radio frequency use. This has resulted in delayed RFID implementation in some of Wal-Mart's stores. Tesco has also been trialling RFID tags.

## Nanotechnology

Nanotechnology is the design, characterization, production and application of structures, devices and systems by controlling shape and size at the nanometre scale. A nanometre is a billionth of a metre or roughly the length of ten hydrogen atoms. A human hair is approximately 70,000 to 80,000 nanometres thick. There is no single field of nanotechnology. The term broadly refers to the fields of biology, physics, chemistry and other scientific fields, or a combination thereof, dealing with the manufacturing of nanostructures.

Current nano products tend to add value by adding a nanomaterial to an existing product. Nanotechnology has been put to practical use for a wide range of applications, including stain-resistant clothes (which build spill resistance into the fibres of the fabric of the cloth), enhanced tyre reinforcement and improved suntan lotion. The technology is also being pushed forward into new areas such as carbon nanotubes and nanobots.

Carbon nanotubes are sheets of graphite rolled up to make a tube, of down to 0.4 nanometres in diameter. Apart from remarkable tensile strength, nanotubes exhibit varying electrical properties (depending on the way the graphite structure spirals around the tube and other factors). Nanotubes can be insulating, semiconducting or metallic conducting. In due course they could replace standard silicon-based computer memory systems, becoming a disruptive technology.

PIN inversion nanotechnology creates a minute drug carrier for the systemic absorption of drugs that present major absorption challenges using existing techniques. Drug delivery and diagnostics provide opportunities for VCs now.

Other applications are more evolutionary than disruptive, such as those referred to above that add value by adding a nanomaterial to an existing product.

Much of the investment in nanotechnology to date has been by governments – over \$18 billion of public funding has been made in nanotechnology. In 2005, according to Tim Harper of Cientifica (www.cientifica.com), around \$375 million was invested in nanotechnology by North American VCs, much of this to fund further development at existing companies. Many of the early nanotech investments were made in the first waves of enthusiasm for a new industry without much technical due diligence being performed, not unlike the dot.com era. Cientifica has reported that US VCs outspent their European counterparts by a factor of six in 2005, despite operating in a similar-sized market and with similar amounts of nanotech funding by their respective governments. The Europeans tend to be more concerned at the risks associated with nanotechnologies such as unknown markets, consumer resistance (eg health concerns over carbon nanotubes) and lack of investor understanding of the industry. The way forward is likely to see nanotechnology unlocking further value within existing markets rather than creating whole new markets in its own right.

## Grid computing

Grid computing is an emerging computing model that uses the resources of many separate computers connected by a network (eg the internet) to solve large-scale computational problems. The networked computers can be widely distributed geographically and their resources can be used depending on their availability, capability, performance and cost. Grid computing can therefore be used in the downtime when these disparate facilities are not otherwise being used for their 'normal' purposes.

## Quantum computing

Progress is being made towards quantum computing – a radical new technology that could deliver billions of times the world's combined computing power in a single device. Quantum computing is developing as a result of a concern that Moore's Law is reaching its physical limits and alternatives to silicon-based, transistorized processors are being explored. (In 1965 Intel co-founder Gordon Moore predicted that the number of transistors on a chip would double every 18 months without increasing cost of power use.) Quantum computers make use of molecules stored in a liquid to represent bits of data termed 'qubits', or quantum bits, which are the building blocks of a quantum computer. Quantum computing will provide huge capacity increases in processing and storage with the added benefit of a huge reduction in size. It is, however, still a long way, maybe 10 years or so, from being a commercial proposition.

## Semiconductor technology

Advances in semiconductor technology, for example digital video processors as used in display panels such as LCDs and plasma screens, provide the ability to add more functions onto a piece of silicon without increasing the size of the chips.

## Plastic solar cells

These are new photovoltaics that provide an efficient and flexible way to generate electricity from virtually any surface exposed to the sun.

## Printable mechatronics

This is an adaptation of inkjet technology that can be used to 'print' mechanical parts and electronic devices (eg Plastic Logic – a 2000 start-up from Cambridge to develop inexpensive computer chips using inkjet printing techniques).

## Clean technology

With environmental issues and concerns right at the forefront of lobbying groups and political agendas, clean technology is a hot new area for VC investment. Clean technology is basically industrial processes with intrinsically lower levels of pollution. Much of the historic investment by companies was the 'end-of-pipe' variety which involves adding a new piece of equipment which reduces the toxicity of releases. This of course adds to overall costs. But clean technologies today are much broader and forward-looking than this and include wind and solar energy, power storage and energy management, water purification, industrial process controls and hybrid electric vehicles. Clean technologies use energy, water and raw materials and other inputs more efficiently and productively and create less waste and/or toxicity, deliver equal or superior performance to environmentally unfriendly technologies and improve customer profitability, through cost reduction and/or increased revenues. Clean technologies are currently of interest to VCs because of the large, fast-growing markets which they serve and the economic and environmental/political push to adopt these clean technologies.

# Case study 3

## Triangle Venture Capital Group – points to consider and some tips for the entrepreneurial start-up company

Triangle Venture Capital Group is a German-based venture capital partnership which focuses on investment in seed and start-up companies primarily active in the information and communication technology (ICT) and medical device industries.

In this short article Uli W Fricke and Dr Bernd Geiger of Triangle Venture Capital Group illustrate how founders can establish their position in a high-tech start-up and how venture capitalists assess the prospects for the economic success of the start-up, illustrated by a brief case study at the end of the article. They offer practical tips for budding entrepreneurs in the technology sector – all from the from the practitioner's perspective.

### Product and technology

*A question of substance – the product*

Consider the 'top-down' view: what kind of issues does the market have as regards the industry and the end-users? Generalized topics to consider include mobility, adaptability, efficiency and size. Does your technology have enough substance to play a substantial part in these areas? Analyse the existing problems and solutions in the marketplace that your product is attempting to address and hold your technology up for comparison with others.

## Freedom to operate, intellectual property and copyright

When regards to technology, nothing is more dramatically underestimated than the intellectual property aspects because you cannot actually touch 'ideas' as opposed to physical entities and the former therefore require a much higher abstraction of the term 'property'. Some people, however, reject this ideologically. This ideological influence has resulted in Europe becoming a legal 'black hole' for the software sector, in particular, which has led to severely distorted competition and general disadvantages for the region.

As an illustration, Open Source became established because, in the life cycle of technologies, specialties often turn into commodities after a while. Founded in the 1970s, today the basic functionalities of the relational database, for example, are a commodity and 'open source' (eg MySQL). However, for transaction performance and high security only special proprietary systems are available to date. This illustration also demonstrates the practical use of the open source concept: adapt commodities, save on development costs and then market one's own proprietary technology on top of it.

It is debatable how many patents a start-up must generate per year, when a large corporation produces, say, one patent per department per month. But what happens if a research institute invests 20 person-years in the development of a technology when someone else has patented the key process? That's like having a luxury car in the garage but no licence to drive it; in other words, no freedom to operate. Freedom to operate does not just apply to 'far-off' America or companies that are not comparable, such as RIM/Blackberry. Even in a publicly funded research project with partners from industry and science it can happen that after the project ends one industrial partner will have patented it without being noticed because the scientific partner had neglected the issue. And if this happens then the founder's spinout dreams will have come to an end.

## USP (unique selling proposition) and IPR (intellectual property rights)

Proprietary technologies for the key functions of the product, which are safeguarded through patents, function as hurdles for imitators and copycats and are the key to success. Of course, there are exceptions but these are very rare. This is even true for software. You should be pragmatic in your use of the open source principle and ignore the ideologies.

Another important question: How big is your technology's share of the value creation chain – 10%, 50%, 100%? The immediate value of the technology is always the sum of this share plus the technology's indispensability. If you have only 1% of the value creation chain with your technology, then in reality the technology is not indispensable – and with that, a USP quickly becomes pointless!

## Target market and business model

### Problem-solving capacity and target market

Strategies for defining a target market fill books – and yet there is no universal answer. It is important that 1) you know the problem-solving capacity of the technology and 2) you are familiar with the features of your potential market.

Regarding 1): Do you have vertical competency in a single market or is it horizontal, across various markets? Is the technology used as part of a primary product, or as infrastructure for the manufacture of the product? Is the technology applied close to the end-user, or in an industrial environment?

Regarding 2): Have you already been active in this market? What are its growth rates? How is the 'food chain' structured and what is its half-life/volatility? Do you know the market's key opinion leader? Is it known who is already in the market and what the market participants are prepared to spend their money on? Do you know what the established companies said in their last meeting with analysts?

Owing to their high degree of consolidation, mature markets are much more difficult for an entrepreneur to penetrate and capture than adolescent markets. But there are mature markets that include young innovative submarkets and these can gain appeal (for example, retail is becoming innovative thanks to e-commerce). Redefining a mature market can become very expensive, and is best left to someone else. For this reason, the question is pertinent as to where technologies find themselves in the 'hype cycle' regarding the degree of maturity, public attention, and time remaining to productive application. Must the market be 'educated' (with a technology push)? Or can you benefit from a market pull?

### Business model

The right business model is mainly determined by three parameters: trading profitability, lag time of trading profitability and scalability. The decision for or against a business model (including consulting, projects, licences, maintenance, leasing, item, volume sales, etc) should be made with an eye to optimizing the three parameters and not because a particular business model is currently in vogue.

### Investment requirements – do you even have any?

If you sell a service, then you're really selling yourself and don't need to invest in product and significant market development. Initial investment and the scalability of what you sell must demonstrate a high correlation within a foreseeable timeframe. Therefore, it is less likely that an investor will finance a service company.

An investor always looks for the lever – the initial investment must compare with a significant increase in value. Generally, that can only be achieved with scalable products, ie developed once and sold many times!

## Team

Personality profile:

- Are you the type to raise yourself by your own bootstraps?
- Do you put a lot of stock in capitalism?
- Do you view your glass as half full, or half empty?
- Can you excite your listeners today about something that you won't have finished for 9 months?

If you want to become an entrepreneur, you should have answered the above questions in the affirmative. Your family, friends and surroundings will probably try to dissuade you from doing so because of the risks, but you should weigh possible difficulties against the advantages:

- As an entrepreneur, your income is wide open (up as well as down) – that is the opposite of an employee whose basic needs are always met.
- You will only bump up against your own limitations. No one can tell you 'that's not the way we do things'.
- As an entrepreneur, the speed at which you learn things is many times higher than it is in a big company.

Seek out contact with people who have already become entrepreneurs and learn from them.

### Teamwork – Or would you rather always do everything by yourself?

Don't even try to go it alone – find people in your environment and if possible, from elsewhere in your industry, who complement you. You need a core team of two to three people who stick together like a family. College graduates are a good infrastructure to have in your development department, and if you are starting a spinout get your professor involved – that will further ensure a solid connection to research resources.

## Conclusion

Our advice for technology founders seeking finance is to talk to various VC investors to discuss commercialization paths early on. Then select your investor according to the following criteria:

- Work with professionals only. Investing is not a hobby.
- The professionals should be specialists in your area. It is clear that investors who have been active mainly in marketing model-driven consumer segment investments will have less experience with technology research spin-offs and vice versa.
- Avoid investors that can only help you start up. The investor must be in a position to bring you to your first breakeven position, and even participate in additional financing rounds.
- Determine whether the investor's fund size is a good fit for you. For the marketing-intensive consumer market, the investor's fund should be well over €100 million to be able to participate in additional rounds. With technology-driven research spinouts, a fund of more than €100 million may not be ideal as there are high-tech start-ups that can be built into successful companies with a high degree of capital efficiency. These companies usually are better advised to have investors with smaller fund sizes, since with large fund sizes the amount invested could be triggered by the total fund size. If this results in larger funding rounds for the company than necessary, this might get the company off the track from being capital efficient.

## X-aitment GmbH case study

The following case study illustrates some of the above points:

- Technology: Software, autonomous agent systems.
- Technology origins: German Research Center for Artificial Intelligence (DFKI), Saarbrücken.
- Motivation for business/business idea: Agent systems have been a subject of research at DFKI for a long time. Managers, founders and former doctoral candidates at the DFKI recognized

that the problems caused by the lack of flexibility of today's computer games could be solved very well with agent systems.

- Value-added contribution: X-aitment's agent system has a dual benefit: 1) the bulk of all programming expenses in computer game development today lie in scripting all movements and scenes – an enormous effort; 2) the number of different scenes correlates directly with the excitement of the game or how long it takes after market launch for the game to appear on eBay at a much lower price. Through the introduction of autonomous software agents by means of an artificial intelligence engine, the number of scenes is in theory unlimited while at the same time decreasing the programming expense.
- Growth strategy: A new game generation is being developed with the first customer, one of the biggest game designers in Europe. The impact of the artificial intelligence engine already indicates a quantum leap in realism in the alpha phase. Additional customers in Europe and the United States are currently being acquired.
- Intellectual property position: As early as the first investment assessment, six months before the agreement was concluded, three strategic patent families were applied for, for hedging purposes, in advance of attending the leading gaming industry trade fair. This was very easy to do because mainly internal white papers were used. The fine-tuning for the patent office was finished later. The strategy is to apply for three to four patent families per year in the most important gaming markets in the world.
- Financing decision: VC financing of €3 million to last until break-even was given priority over the high-tech founders' fund which could have provided start-up financing of €500,000, because the latter would have required another search for financing in the short term. (The high-tech founders' fund is a seed fund initiated by the German government and is tax funded in order to provide seed funding for high-tech start-ups. In 2005 it was one of the few active investors in seed and series A funding rounds for German high-tech companies.)

www.triangle-venture.com

# 5

# What venture capitalists look for from a potential investee company

Early-stage venture capital financing remains very difficult to obtain. The very best early-stage ideas can get venture capital backing, and are doing so. But it remains a tough task. And it confirms the importance to any early-stage venture of a professional, well-presented and well-informed approach to potential investors with ideally revenues already being generated and well-rounded management expertise.

## SOURCES OF INVESTMENT PROPOSITIONS

Before approaching a venture capital firm you need some idea of what the firm will be looking for in your investment proposal. VC firms receive hundreds of investment propositions each year. These originate from several sources, including the following:

■ 'cold' or unsolicited approaches direct from entrepreneurs and others seeking finance, perhaps having seen entries in private equity firm member directories such as those available from EVCA or the BVCA or other country private equity associations;

■ responses to venture capital firm websites, corporate brochures or advertising;

■ introductions from intermediaries, such as accountants and lawyers;

▌ referrals from management of their own portfolio companies and from other entrepreneurs who have dealt with the VC firm;

▌ introductions from other VC firms, maybe as part of a proposed syndicated investment;

▌ approaches at investment forums, during which entrepreneurs seeking finance make short presentations to VCs and other forum attendees, such as the annual UK Technology Innovation & Growth Forum organized by the European Technology Forum.

The VCs are not just waiting for interesting investment opportunities to come their way. They are actively sourcing ideas themselves, as we will see in the case of TLcom Capital and Media Lario (case study 12).

## WHAT THE VCS ARE LOOKING FOR

Of the several hundreds of investment propositions received each year a typical VC firm will probably actually invest in fewer than 10 projects. Of course, the quality of propositions will vary enormously and those that are well thought out and positioned appropriately, with an effective means of introduction to the VC, will have the best chance of making it through to actual investment. It is therefore essential that you meet the VCs' criteria in terms of what they are looking for in an investment proposal. Not just from the perspective of what needs to go into your business plan (which is covered in Chapter 8) but more from the point of view of the VCs themselves, ie what they are seeking to get out of an investment in your business.

In a typical early-stage venture capital portfolio it's the 80/20 rule (or worse) that pertains. Half the companies will probably not return their cost of investment while companies representing maybe no more than 5% of the cost of all investments will return 80% of the final value of the fund.

Assuming your proposal falls within the VCs' investment criteria in terms of stage of investment, industry sector, size of investment and geographical focus (I cover investment criteria in Chapter 7), what else are they looking for?

First of all, they are looking for the opportunity to make a substantial return on their investment, commensurate with the risk they are taking in investing in your business. The risk they attach to an investment in your business depends on several factors, including the stage of investment (start-ups and other early-stage businesses have inherently higher risk than later-stage businesses such as management buyouts), the industry sector (certain technologies such as drug discovery having considerably higher risk than traditional manufacturing industries, for example), the market opportunity and the extent to which this has been demonstrated to exist in your business plan, and the quality of the management team. Generally speaking, the higher the risk in your business proposal (as perceived by the VC firm) the higher the return the venture capital firm will expect to make. For an early-stage technology deal they might be looking to achieve a return of over 50% per annum, seeking to make several times their investment (maybe even as high as 10 times) over the period in which they invest (typically around five years). For a buyout investment the desired return may be nearer 30% and upwards. The VC firm also needs to satisfy itself that it will be able to exit from its investment in the requisite time frame, usually via a trade sale or IPO.

Within the overall aim of seeking to make a large return on their investment the VC will be focusing on the quality of the management team, the soundness and commercial viability of the technology, the depth of research you have conducted into the marketplace (can the product or service take a significant share of an expanding market?), whether any intellectual property (IP) is properly protected and the overall strength of your business proposition. It basically boils down to three elements: people, technology and market. The weightings which VCs place on these three areas vary from VC to VC.

## TEN CRITICAL FACTORS FOR A START-UP COMPANY

In their book *Startups that Work*, Joel Kurtzman and Glenn Rifkin list 10 critical factors that will make or break a new company. These are derived from research carried out by Joel Kurtzman and a team from PricewaterhouseCoopers which included studying 350 companies and interviewing hundreds of VCs, CEOs, boards of directors and angel investors. The companies studied, from the United States, Europe and Israel, received seed and first-round financing in the years 1999, 2000 and 2001 – ie during the dot.com/internet boom. They studied companies in the biotech, telecommunications, semiconductor, software and services industries. A model called 'Paths to Value' was constructed which captures the state of a company at a point in time through measurements of distinct components of performance, capability and business focus. The model attempts to identify specific strategies for sustained value creation among early-stage companies operating in various industries, regions and under different market conditions. The Paths to Value model provides a diagnostic tool that can be used to identify key developmental milestones that companies should strive to achieve at various rounds of financing.

So what about the 10 critical factors for a start-up company? Kurtzman and Rifkin list these as:

1. Start with a large group of three or four founder members of the management team, if possible founders who have worked together before.
2. Make certain a marketing or sales person is a member of the founding team. Companies make big mistakes when they focus all their resources on their products and services but not their markets.
3. It's all about teams. Whether you are starting with a group that's worked together in the past or hiring a team from scratch, successful entrepreneurs get that way because they can create teams.
4. When building the business, don't worry about your exit. Concentrate on creating value. The best VCs look for bigger, longer-term payoffs, not just quick results.
5. Manage your cash. Start-ups in the bubble years burned through money, but companies today have to be run much more tightly.
6. Start with a market. Occasionally a product or service will be so innovative or revolutionary it will create a market on its own. But for the most part, start-ups become successful not by creating markets but by going into markets that already exist and by developing products or services that are better, easier or cheaper.
7. Find a great first customer. This creates confidence in the market.
8. Build a board that is a great 'sounding board', not just a good watchdog. The best boards are those that really focus on helping management solve its thorniest problems and then get out of the way.
9. Make your product or service high quality and unique, then brand it in a way people won't forget.
10. Enjoy the ride. The entrepreneurs and the people who funded them interviewed by Joel Kurtzman and the team loved what they did and, for the most part, enjoyed being with other people.

It's all about People, Markets and Technology and these are the three key areas that VCs will be looking at as they review your proposition.

# PEOPLE (AND MANAGEMENT TEAM)

Many VCs cite the strength and experience of the management team as the most important factor. After all, you can have the most wonderful technology and a proven, ready market for your products but if the team is either not complete, or otherwise inadequate in some way, or inexperienced in running a business, disaster is likely to strike either through poor financial and systems controls, or through inability to meet demand or provide superior customer service, or to expand the business into new products and markets. The management team needs to have team members who have relevant industry sector experience, ideally in the same sector as the business proposition for which VC financing is currently being sought. It needs a clear leader and a team with complementary areas of expertise, such as marketing, sales, operations, finance, etc. The leader, who is typically, but not necessarily, the entrepreneur behind the project, needs to have vision, enthusiasm, a strong work ethic, staying power and the ability to motivate and manage his or her team effectively. The team needs to have the skills required to convert the business plan into reality. The team has to have the ability to actually run the business in practice, not just the theoretical knowledge. If the team has experience of running a venture-capital-backed business before, so much the better.

The more complete, experienced and well-rounded the team, the better. Surround yourself with the best possible people. As Paul Cartwright of Rutland Partners points out in case study 15 on H&T Group, don't feel threatened by people who might be more qualified than you.

Depending on the stage of the business and its size, it is not always necessary to have every single executive member in place when you present your plan to the VC. Clearly a small, but growing, start-up needs less of a full team than an established business seeking development capital, though in the case of a start-up the entrepreneur or CEO would be expected to have a fairly broad range of business skills. Gaps in the team should be identified and, if the VC is keen on your proposition, he or she may be in the position to help source missing team members from his or her network of contacts. You shouldn't expect to have more than one or two positions unfilled, however, and key roles such as strategy, sales, operations and finance should have been addressed. Again, depending on the stage and size of the business it may not be necessary to have a full-time professionally qualified accountant on board as finance director. An experienced and reliable bookkeeper, with support from a financial non-executive director, may suffice in the early years of a business, as long as appropriate management information systems are in place to provide the CEO and other members of the team with the financial and operating information that they need to run the business.

If it turns out later that the team is not performing as expected the VC will make changes. As we will see in case study 16 on Tagsys, the VC investor, Endeavour, changed the board of directors and several members of the management team post-investment.

With a small start-up it's usual for the founder(s) to be technically orientated. One of the founders should also be the company's sales, marketing and PR person. It is not always necessary to hire expensive marketing people until you have proved that your business can generate cash from sales. But sooner or later you will need specialist product marketing people on board.

Individual team roles should be clearly defined with objectives and responsibilities set out for each team member. It is important that the team members do operate collectively as a team, however, so pay attention to the personal chemistry between executives as you recruit or otherwise select them and, as we will see in case study 4 on Logical Networks, founded by serial entrepreneur John Cavill, you need to ensure that the team is well balanced in terms of its skills and personalities, collectively operating as an 'entrepreneurial team' in John's words.

## Case study 4

### Logical Networks – the importance of the integrated entrepreneurial team

John Cavill founded Logical Networks plc, a UK networking services business, in late 1988. Logical Networks was funded by 3i and grew rapidly at over 55% compound annual growth rate over nine years until it was acquired by Datatec in 1997 when sales reached £50 million and staff numbered around 200.

John remained with Datatec as a main Board director until 2000 when he left to set up Intermezzo Ventures Ltd, a new venture research and consultancy company. John is also a visiting fellow at Henley Management College where he is currently carrying out doctoral research into the characteristics of entrepreneurial teams (see www.intermezzo-ventures.com).

Here is the story of John's experience in raising venture capital backing at Logical Networks and his initial tips on the importance of effective entrepreneurial teams in high-growth venture-backed businesses.

## Complete team identified up front

When John Cavill first approached potential investors in 1988 he had already identified his management team. The Sales Director and Finance Director had worked with him previously at Data Translation Inc, a US manufacturer of scientific and industrial micro-computer products. John was managing director of the UK subsidiary which he had set up for the parent company. The marketing director was also known to John as they had worked together at Fairchild Test Systems. The project director, who joined from Kleinwort Benson, was someone introduced to John by an industry contact. All were highly experienced in their fields and John felt that they would work effectively together as a team.

John had grown the UK subsidiary of Data Translation to the point where sales of the computer networking products that he had intro-duced were outstripping the sales of the parent company's own products. As a result, Data Translation decided to sell its networking business in the UK, so John offered to do an MBO. As talks neared conclusion the parent company's board changed its mind and decided to hold on to the business as it was generating cash that was required in the United States. Data Translation subsequently offered John two choices: either a position developing another part of the group's business or severance from the group with a golden handshake, which included a two-year non-compete clause. John didn't like either option, told them so and was fired! He then spent the next six months writing the business plan for his new venture with Logical Networks and pursuing a claim for wrongful dismissal against Data Translation, which he won.

## Innovative business model

While he had his team identified when he approached the VCs, the commercial viability of Logical Network's proposed systems inte-gration offering was not proven. The UK subsidiary of Data Translation was a specialist reseller of industrial and scientific products for microcomputers but there was no systems integration business anywhere in the UK at that time. Local area networking technology was still quite new, with products only available from three or four manufacturers in the United States. There was no company, only a business plan, when John obtained initial venture capital finance. The USP of Logical Network's business model was to provide a technical centre of excellence, through a separate division, branded Calibre Network Services. This served both the direct sales network integration side of the business and new resellers to the market via a separate division, branded Unity Distribution, with network technology training and support services. Competing companies in this sector were not providing both systems integration to end-users and value-added distribution via resellers. Logical Networks' model was effectively disruptive and helped to grow the overall systems integration market.

## Approaching VCs for finance

So Logical Networks was a genuine start-up with access to new technology and a complete and experienced management team. After reviewing directories of venture capital firms, and with the names of suggested firms to approach from Arthur Young (now Ernst & Young) who had been involved at the time of the potential MBO from Data Translation, John approached several VC firms for finance but had detailed talks with just four. Most of these VC firms were demanding a seat on Logical Network's board, which John was not keen on as they clearly wanted to be proactively involved in running the business in a new market that they didn't fully understand. John knew 3i as a main player in the venture capital industry and had approached their Reading office. Hitting it off right away with 3i's new investment director in Reading, John secured an initial investment of £75,000 from 3i for 25% of the equity in addition to a secured loan of £50,000 from 3i and a 3i Loan Guarantee secured loan of £75,000. The management team put in £150,000 for 75% of the equity, with John holding 40%. 3i did not take up their option of a seat on the board.

3i were pleased with the detail and quality of John's business plan. He had the experience of preparing several business plans in the past (including the one which convinced Data Translation to set up in the UK). There was an experienced FD coming on board from day one and there was a quality management team, several of whom had worked together before. John had also got Arthur Young to review the plan and to take part in a rehearsal of his presentation to the VCs, pretending that they were the VCs.

3i's industry specialists carried out technical and financial due diligence. Commercial due diligence was necessarily limited. As noted above, there were no customer contracts in place and only limited market research in the plan in view of the innovative and disruptive business model, so 3i's main risk appears to have been in the market area. John also used the business plan to get his team interested and committed to the new venture. Once 3i had shown their interest in investing the management team came on board.

## Use of ratchet arrangements

As part of the financing deal with 3i, Logical Networks could draw down up to £100,000 more cash from an additional loan facility but this was never taken up. John wanted the option to pay back some of the equity to 3i as growth permitted and reduce 3i's stake in the company. This is in fact what happened as, at the end of the first year of trading, turnover reached £1.5 million and the company broke even, performing ahead of plan. Under the ratchet arrangement, as the company had performed ahead of agreed milestones, 3i reduced its equity stake to 17.5% as the additional £100,000 drawdown facility was not taken up and the company did not have to return any cash to 3i. Four years later the company secured another £500,000 from 3i for additional working capital and 3i's equity stake went back up to 30%.

Shortly after this there was a change in the management team and one of the original members left the company. As the remaining founders were not in a position at the time to purchase the leaver's shares, a business angel investor was invited to do so at a price determined by an independent auditor. However, the business angel did not take a seat on the board and was effectively a silent partner.

## Sale of company at 6× multiple

The company continued to prosper and, with turnover growing to £50 million, was sold in 1997 to South African based Datatec, a global network technology and services group, listed on the Johannesburg Stock Exchange.

During the course of their investment 3i received monthly management accounts. While they did not take up their option of a seat on the board, 3i met with John and the finance director each quarter. Otherwise, as turnover and profits were always better than forecast there was little need for 3i to be proactively involved in the business. A non-executive director had been taken on to assist with an exit strategy but he had to resign because of ill health. John therefore had the dual role of chairman and managing director from start-up to exit.

## Tips for high-growth ventures

John has the following tips for other potentially high-growth venture-backed businesses:

- If you are serious about building a high-growth venture, put together an experienced management team and seek out investment partners that you feel comfortable working with.
- Ensure that the team is well balanced in terms of their skills and personalities.
- Be innovative. Me-too companies create less value and tend to fail during difficult market conditions, which makes them unattractive to outside investors.
- Focus on quality of service for both internal and external customers.
- Demonstrate a strong focus on cash management to your investors and actively restrain cash spend (eg Logical Network's team initially all took reductions in salaries from their previous occupations. Office space was low cost and office furniture, along with John's company car, was all second-hand).
- By all means extend the mortgage on your house to raise finance (as John did) but avoid putting up your house as security.
- Try to get the VC to agree to the use of ratchets if possible to reduce the VC's equity stake if the business performs better than expected.
- Prepare your exit strategy early in order to create maximum value for shareholders.

When trying to raise investment capital for new ventures, both venture capitalists and business angels base their investment decisions on four key criteria: the entrepreneurial team (as opposed to the lone entrepreneur), the product or service being provided, the market dynamics and the financial structure of the business. A recent European study into why venture-capital-backed businesses fail showed that 69% was due to the failure of management while only 14% was due to flawed business models and 17% external shocks, such as war or natural disasters. John believes that this gives a clear indication of where more attention needs to be paid.

www.intermezzo-ventures.com

Make sure the team members and employees are properly rewarded in the long term. While salaries may necessarily have to be restricted in the early years, particularly with a start-up, you can tie in key members of the team, including those responsible for research and development if it's a technology company, with stock options. And don't forget that your business success is dependent on your employees, so do treat them well (see case study 13 on Equiinet where the serial entrepreneur Bob Jones has always created an option pool for his employees with the various companies he has founded).

---

## VC Tip #2

Get good people around you in your team, well balanced in terms of their skills and roles.

---

# MARKET

As we have seen, the quality and experience of your team are one of the key areas that the venture capital firm will be looking at in your investment proposition. On the other hand, if you have an outstanding team, proven technology and excellent products but no market then you are equally sunk – perhaps more so than if it is management that is the weak point (as noted above, VCs can always help fill gaps in the management team or indeed they can oust and replace poor management). You must be able to demonstrate that a large and/or growing market exists for your product or service. You also need to show how you plan to enter and/or address that market, ie what is your strategy to achieve this? What about pressures from existing competitors? Why should customers buy your product or service? How will you sustain competitive advantage?

The areas that you need to consider in addressing the market for your products or services are covered in Chapter 8 when we look at the marketing section of the business plan. The investor will need to understand, and accept, your arguments and evidence of how the market is growing, not just in the short and medium terms but how growth is sustainable in the longer term and how your company will capture its stake in that growing marketplace in terms of both revenues and, more importantly, profits.

While VCs will consider the market risk (ie the risk that the market for the product is not sufficiently growing or large enough for sales of the product, as set out in the business plan, to materialize), they are increasingly looking for more comfort on the market risk than simply adequate market research and analysis and your plans on how to address the market. They are looking for hard evidence of customer contracts in place or even customer revenues being generated. It's a good idea to expose your product or service to as wide a community of potential users as soon as possible, get their feedback and make changes to your product or service if necessary.

Of course, there are some innovative products, usually technology start-ups, which are developed without evidence of a market existing at all, where convincing VCs to invest is even more difficult. 3G in the telecoms industry, SMS messaging and even 'Post-it' notes immediately spring to mind, where the technology was developed (or perhaps happened upon almost by accident in the case of 'Post-it' notes) without there being hard evidence of customer demand, though this obviously materialized in a huge way once the products were available. In fact, when 3M Corporation test marketed 'Post-it' notes in 1977 there was little customer interest and it wasn't until they implemented a massive consumer sampling strategy in 1979 that the 'Post-it' note took off. With 3G it took some time for customers to appreciate the features of the new 3G phones – with access to video calling, faster download speeds and more advanced games. And SMS messaging initially did not appeal to the adult marketplace, which continues to prefer e-mail and voice communication, but has been taken up enthusiastically by the younger members of the population.

Once they see the potential and have invested, the VCs will even support the team in helping to expand the market opportunities. In the case of Media Lario (case study 12), TLcom Capital identified opportunities in the semiconductor equipment industry as the preferred market for repositioning Media Lario's activities and helped validate such markets.

In the case of Cambridge Silicon Radio (case study 11) there was no evidence that there was a market for Bluetooth when 3i first invested in CSR. The timing of the Bluetooth market starting up was unknown. The size of the market was unknown, although analysts' reports were saying that the market was likely to be significant. However, 3i was impressed by the quality of CSR's technology and they were convinced about the technical capabilities of the team and their ability to work together.

# TECHNOLOGY

Of the three areas of people, technology and market it is perhaps the technology that is most important. Indeed it is increasingly taken as a given by many VCs, ie if the technology is not proven, is not supported by a commercial prototype, or does not have protected IP then the VC is not likely to go anywhere near your proposition. But as we will see in the case of Lein Applied Diagnostics (case study 5) you still need to focus on the market need first, not the technology. If you have a great product but nobody wants to buy it then you have wasted your time! And as Jean-Michel Deligny of Go4Venture states in case studies 9 and 18 on Esmertec, the best technology is not always sufficient in a market where price is key (in that case mobile phones) and where customers may prefer a possibly inferior but cheaper technology.

These days most VCs will not take on the technology risk (ie the risk that the technology does not work or is capable of being transferred into a commercially viable product), and will assume only the market risk and then on various conditions as we have seen. And it goes without saying that the product(s) resulting from the technology must itself 'work' and have the competitive edge over other products, or better still results from 'disruptive' technology (see Chapter 4).

The VC will want to understand your product's unique selling point (USP), ie its competitive advantage over other, similar products in the eyes and minds of your potential customers.

'First mover advantage' is not always necessary for success, as we will see in case study 11 on Cambridge Silicon Radio. In fact, learning from competitors' first moves into the market can be a distinct advantage. While first-mover advantage is not necessary, as Dr Phil O'Donovan of CSR states it is important to be one of the first three into the market and to be in the market within a few months of the first entrant.

For a technology company the investors will be looking at the overall industry in which the technology resides and the attractiveness of the applications. Points to consider include:

▌ Barriers to entry: is it easy or difficult for companies to enter the industry?

▌ Supplier power: do suppliers to this industry have the power to set terms and conditions?

▌ Buyer power: do buyers (ie customers) have the power to set terms and conditions?

▌ Threat of substitutes: is it easy or difficult for substitute products to steal the market?

▌ Competitive rivalry: is competitive rivalry intense or more genteel?

The VC will also want to check that your business is, or will be, capable of producing the goods or delivering the services as outlined in your plan and on an increasing scale, and that you have plans and systems in place to develop new or refined products or services to keep up with changes in the marketplace.

## Case study 5

### Lein Applied Diagnostics – putting the market before the technology in an innovative start-up company

By combining expertise in diabetes, ophthalmology and medical devices Lein Applied Diagnostics (Lein), based in Wokingham, UK, is developing a non-invasive glucose meter which will allow people with diabetes to test their blood glucose levels. The technique applies a non-invasive optical measurement principle in a novel way to measure the amount of glucose in the eye. From this measurement, the amount of glucose in the blood can be derived. The glucose meter being developed by Lein will be hand-held, portable and about the size of a mobile phone. The device is held up to the eye in order to take a reading.

Lein has received two tranches of funding from Seven Spires Investments Ltd (Seven Spires), which is an angel investment fund established in 2003 with £25 million of private money. Seven Spires seeks to invest in early-stage, high-tech companies in the UK, such as university and industrial spinouts, start-up ventures etc. This funding is supporting the development of next generation prototypes and detailed clinical testing.

Dan Daly, director and one of Lein's founders, explains how the company first of all researched the market need for medical devices in general, homed in on the issues and problems with current invasive methods for monitoring blood sugar levels and went on to develop their non-invasive meter.

### Background

Lein Applied Diagnostics (Lein) was formed in May 2003 by Dan Daly and Graeme Clark, two former telecoms professionals who had worked at PerkinElmer OptoElectronics and Agilent Technologies. When the telecoms bubble burst in 2002 Dan and Graeme were looking for new opportunities where they could apply their photonics expertise. They decided to explore the medical area, although they had no prior experience in that sector.

Following an extensive review of the market, relevant literature and existing patents, the idea they finally settled on was a portable optical glucose sensor for people with diabetes, because of the huge potential customer market. There are nearly 200 million people with diabetes worldwide and the incidence of diabetes is rising. This translates into a $6.3 billion market for self-administered glucose meters that is growing by 10% each year.

Current control of blood glucose levels is most commonly achieved by taking a blood sample from the finger. The problems for the user associated with the technique are that it is invasive and therefore carries the risk of infection, the continuous pricking of the fingers causes hard skin and nerve damage and the process is not exactly pain free. As a result of inconvenience, social embarrassment and discomfort many people do not test themselves as often as recommended. This increases the likelihood of associated health problems. By removing the need to sample blood directly, Lein's non-invasive meter overcomes these problems.

## Patents awarded

The company built a lab-based prototype using facilities at Reading University and then undertook small-scale patient testing at Manchester University. Lein's first two patents have recently been granted in the UK and the company is now continuing to develop the technology. The third-generation prototypes are undergoing extensive clinical trials in the UK and future generations will be tested first in Europe and then in the United States.

## Seed funding from angels and grants

Initially the concept for this new method for non-invasive testing of blood sugar levels was theoretical only, there was no working prototype, no patented intellectual property, obviously no regulatory approval and certainly no customers. So not an ideal situation for seed/venture capital backing!

The DTI's Business Link network helped to prepare Lein to apply successfully for a DTI SMART Award in 2003. This enabled the founders to work on a feasibility study which demonstrated the viability of the proposed non-invasive glucose measurement method and allowed the production of the first prototype through Reading University. Also, an eminent patent firm was engaged in the UK and two patent applications were filed.

With a business plan prepared by the founders and reviewed by their accountants, Grant Thornton, Lein approached a selection of early-stage venture capital firms for funding later in 2003, drawn from a review of the BVCA's Directory of Members, but the company was too early-stage at that time for the VCs. Lein therefore approached potential business angel investors through such networks as the Thames Valley Investment Network (TVIN) and Library House in Cambridge.

Lein was successful in obtaining funding in February 2004 from Seven Spires, the angel investment fund, which was introduced to Lein through the TVIN. Seven Spires saw the potential of Lein's technology and the quality of the management team, and they believed that Lein had chosen the ultimately winning method to measure blood glucose level. Seven Spires were also impressed with the advances in the prototype devices and the quality of the clinical results obtained. Seven Spires carried out extensive financial and legal due diligence, with technical due diligence being outsourced to a specialist university department.

While the company is obviously not yet generating revenues from the sale of its monitors, it does have revenue income from consultancy and contract research and, as it owns all of its intellectual property and has now been awarded its first two patents, will in the future be licensing its technology to third parties.

The experienced technical and operational team is supplemented with an advisory committee of diabetic and ophthalmic specialists. While the company does not have the need for a finance director as yet, accounting, tax and financial advice is provided by Grant Thornton and a local accounting firm is used for bookkeeping.

In November 2005 Seven Spires put in a second tranche of funding which is enabling Lein to enhance the ergonomics of its prototype glucose meters and again increase the level of clinical testing. This second tranche was conditional upon certain technical milestones being achieved. Seven Spires remains the sole external investor in the company, the other investors being the two founders.

## Latest developments

Since January 2006 Lein has been working with King's College London to test the company's monitoring devices and to evaluate their potential for measuring glucose levels in people with diabetes. The work is being funded partly by the DTI under its Knowledge

Transfer Partnership programme. The clinical research and diabetes-specific expertise at King's will ensure that Lein's optical technology is independently and thoroughly tested over the next two years.

In May 2006 the company was awarded a Grant for Research and Development by the South East England Development Agency (SEEDA). This extra support has accelerated the development of Lein's prototypes and is enabling the company to increase the scale of clinical testing.

Lein plans to approach corporates for potential alliances as a means of funding expansion into global markets. It sees this route as more attractive than seeking a flotation on AIM, for example.

## Dan Daly's tips for entrepreneurs seeking seed capital finance

Dan Daly has the following advice for entrepreneurs seeking seed finance based on his experience with Lein:

- Focus on the market need first – not the technology. If you have a great product but nobody wants to buy it then you have wasted your time!
- Be prepared to take personal risks. If you really believe in yourself and your ideas then you must be prepared to leave the security of full-time employment and set up on your own.

www.lein-ad.com

# THE 'BACK TO BASICS' INVESTMENT APPROACH

The 'back to basics' investment approach of people, markets and technology overturns the approach taken in the dot.com era when investment decisions were based on less than rigorous appraisal analyses, often without any real evidence that a market existed and certainly with propositions put forward by inexperienced (often youthful) management teams. VCs got their fingers burnt during this period of plentiful funds and enormous competition to complete deals and have now returned to the tried and tested ways of appraising investments.

So it is important to present your proposition to the VC investors such that their concerns and questions are appropriately addressed. We will consider the means of doing this in Chapter 8. In the meantime it is worth checking that you have the ingredients for a successful business proposition in place which is likely to attract the interests of VCs.

Case study 6 on Neoss Limited, an investment by Delta Partners, is an example of a company that had all three attributes for VC backing: a strongly defensible product in a very large and rapidly growing market and with a management team that had demonstrated its ability to bring the company from start-up to established sales in multiple countries.

# Case study 6

## Neoss Limited – what an early-stage VC looks for in a start-up life sciences company

Neoss Limited (Neoss), a dental implant company based in Harrogate, UK has not reached an exit as an investment yet, but it exemplifies many of the investment themes that its venture capital investor, Delta Partners, pursues and its history to date captures many of the issues that Delta faces with its portfolio companies.

Delta Partners (Delta) is an early-stage technology (ICT and life sciences) investor. Founded in Dublin in 1994, Delta's third and current fund is €90 million, which was raised in 2000. Delta is typically the first institutional investor in its investee companies and invests in the UK and Ireland.

As with any technology investor, Delta looks for companies with defensible technology in large and growing markets with exceptional management teams. Reality is usually more prosaic and in early-stage investments it is rare to get all three. However, Delta is prepared to back teams or market opportunities and build the rest of the growth platform from there. Motivation and the ability to grow and manage the business are, however, an essential requirement.

Delta's Frank Kenny and Joey Mason explain how Delta came to invest in Neoss back in 2002. Delta initially invested $1 million in Neoss, for a minority stake, along with an angel group which invested $900,000. Delta has subsequently followed on with second-round financing.

### Management, management, management

The Neoss founding team, Neil Meredith and Fredrik Engman, was introduced to Delta in 2002 by MMC Ventures, an angel investor network, soon after the company was established. An academic clinician by training (current Professor of Dentistry at Leeds

University), Neil Meredith, as managing director, was clearly commercially minded, which is unusual for an academic, but very welcome. While he provided the clinical input, Fredrik is a very experienced and inventive engineer, whose background was with Nobel Biocare, one of the world's leading dental implant companies. Together, they had the right mix of clinical and engineering input that is vital in a medical device company.

The company employed some overseas sales people, but neither founder had a strong background in exploiting new commercial products or in growing businesses. This was recognized up front and it was agreed with Delta from the outset that experienced commercial managers would be grafted onto the company over time. This openness to outside influence and willingness to bring in third parties set the team apart from many start-up companies.

## Large market opportunity

The dental implant market is both large and one of the fastest growing in the medical technology sector. In 2002 one million implants were sold, worth more than $900 million. The market was growing by 12–15% per annum, driven by patient awareness, improved aesthetics, ageing populations and dentists' concerns over negligence. Five major players dominated the market, with 80–90% control: Nobel Biocare, Straumann, Centrepulse, Biomet and Dentsply. The first two are pure-play implant companies and are among the most highly rated medtech stocks in the world. The excitement surrounding the market is the sheer number of implants that could be implanted worldwide, with brokers forecasting worldwide sales of $3 billion by 2011.

Typical packs for dental implants contain in excess of 2,000 parts and specialist implantologists have to perform the operation. It is an expensive procedure, typically in the region of $3,000–4,000 per implant. This barrier considerably reduces the pull-through in the market, as GPs perform the vast bulk of dental care. Neoss' solution is a 'stripped-down' version of the dental implant pack. Containing fewer than 100 parts, it provides both experts and GPs with a far reduced, less costly and easier to use set of equipment that provides equal, but much cheaper, clinical and aesthetic results.

Typically, IP is not strongly pursued in the dental market, which is a very conservative market. GPs look to specialists before accepting new technologies and approaches, so the performance of implants over time is the most critical factor in successful adoption. Neoss' implants, which have been suitably patented, are robust and perform very well in the market (to date, no product failures have been recorded and clinical acceptance is excellent). The company believed that GPs would embrace the technology as a way to retain their patients and generate significant profit for the procedure.

## Progress to date

Neoss is performing well. The business has grown its sales by 130% year on year and is penetrating multiple international markets, with the United States its most recent market. In the process, it has had to learn about managing a distributor network and establishing a direct sales channel in its primary markets. This is non-trivial in a market as competitive as dentistry in general and implants in particular.

The board appointed a very experienced and highly regarded non-executive director, Carston Browall, a former VP from Nobel Biocare, who is now chairman. In addition, Denis Tinsley, former head of the healthcare and pharmaceutical practice of McKinsey & Co, was appointed a non-executive director. These two appointments significantly strengthened the board, as the company began to grow. The founding management team remains in place and has successfully developed the business, helped by the addition of a Chief Operating Officer (COO), a financial controller and very experienced international country sales managers.

Testament to Neoss' early success is the fact that a new investor, Medtronic, which was introduced to Neoss by Delta, led the company's $9.5 million second round of finance in December 2005 in which Delta has also invested. The company continues to grow rapidly, while not consuming large amounts of cash, and is now positioned for its next growth phase with a rapidly growing sales line in multiple countries.

## Delta's tips for life sciences entrepreneurs seeking venture capital finance

Frank Kenny and Joey Mason have the following tips for life sciences entrepreneurs seeking venture capital finance:

- A well-thought-out brief presentation prepared by yourselves in order to attract start-up financing is preferable to a huge, glossy business plan prepared professionally by someone else. A VC investor will usually help you with the preparation of your business plan for second-round financing.

- Make your own contacts with VCs. If you are an early-stage company, avoid using a paid broker type of intermediary adviser who will not know your business and market better than you do.
- Don't be afraid to tell investors about the 'bad stuff'. Don't hide things from them. They will find out anyway and they hate surprises!
- Be open to advice from your investors on bringing in outside expertise where necessary.
- Remember that once you have an external investor on board, however small, you have started the process of eventually selling your business, be it through a trade sale or flotation.

www.delta.ie

# QUESTIONS INVESTORS ASK TO DETERMINE COMPANY VALUE

Anthony (Tony) Morris, personal computer (PC) industry pioneer, entrepreneur, business angel investor, independent director and consultant with many years' experience in the information technology business on both sides of the Atlantic, has developed six questions that investors ask to determine company value. He states that the answers to these six questions fundamentally determine the investor's perception of the value in a venture before considering specific deal structure and details. They are presented here to allow you to check whether you have what investors are looking for in a potential investee company.

---

### The six (just six!) questions investors ask to determine company value

Investors ask many questions in order to develop an understanding of a potential venture investment, even more when they are looking to defer an investment decision. But, in fact, just about all investor questions that are not specifically related to the structure of a particular deal can be clustered into one of six question categories.

Obviously, the better and more clearly that company management or others seeking capital can provide answers to these six questions, the more likely they (and the investors) are to create the conditions for a successful deal!

The six questions are:

1. Are you solving a *big problem*, preferably one that is worth a *lot of money* and is recognized or recognizable *today*?
2. Is your solution *differentiated, compelling*, and *sustainable*?
3. Does your venture have an *understandable and relevant business model* given your solution and the problem it addresses?
4. Have you assembled a *team and partners* with *distinctly relevant experience* to make the business happen?
5. Do you have a *reasonable and believable strategy* for getting to market and building a potentially *sizable* and *market-leading* business reasonably *quickly*?
6. What kind of *momentum* has already been established in the business and in the marketplace (especially with customers)?

The six questions are presented above in roughly the order they are likely to appeal to an investor. That is, the magnitude and nature of the problem being addressed are typically the primary attention-getters for the investor.

There is some debate over the importance of the team. Some would argue that the team is the most important element in a deal, but the real question is what the team is assembled to accomplish; hence, the need to present the problem and the solution as a precondition for being able to assess the relevance and value of the team.

Whatever the order, the answers to these six questions need to be presented or signalled appropriately in each of the three key documents aimed at prospective investors: the business plan, the executive summary of the plan, and the investor presentation.

The answers to these six questions fundamentally determine the investor's perception of the value in a venture before considering specific deal structure and details. Better answers (that are also believable!) typically yield higher values – a simple equation that is challenging to solve, but potentially quite rewarding!

In terms of other areas that venture capital firms might be looking for from potential investee companies, it is worth checking out the websites or firm literature of the VC firms themselves to see what they specify. Often they will refer to the key areas covered above, but there may be specifics. They may also state whether they prefer you to send them your full business plan or executive summary or both.

# 6

# Sources of finance

Cash is the No 1 concern of most companies, perhaps more so than such issues as pricing policies, beating the competition, employment issues, succession planning etc. Most entrepreneurs and owner managers are worried about cash, eg not enough of it, how to control it, where to find it. Cash is especially important with early-stage and growing companies.

## THE STAGES OF GROWTH OF A COMPANY

Churchill and Lewis came up with five stages of growth in their paper in the *Harvard Business Review* in 1983 (Figure 6.1):

1.  At the *existence* stage the company's founders are usually technically orientated. Their physical and mental energies are absorbed almost entirely in designing and making a product. The company is run by the owner, who performs nearly all the managerial functions using largely subjective and unsophisticated measures of performance. The company is simply trying to get its foot in the door of the market.
2.  At the *survival* stage the company is aggressively seeking new customers, has a wider but possibly standardized product line than at the existence stage and the owner is beginning to spend more time on managerial functions.
3.  At the *success* stage the company's credibility and product technical feasibility have been well established. Successful companies in this stage usually concentrate on introducing economies of scale and improving their internal reporting systems and financial controls.

The company may be diversified to some extent but still obtaining most of its revenues from a single business.

One of the decisions facing owners at this stage is whether to exploit the company's accomplishments and expand the business (the *success–growth* stage) or to keep the company stable and profitable, providing a base for alternative owner activities (the *success–disengagement* stage).

4. At the *take-off* stage the company will have multiple product lines and channels of distribution. Measurement control systems will become increasingly systematic and orientated towards results.

5. At the *resource maturity* stage the owner and the business have become quite separate both financially and operationally. Planning procedures are well established and regularly reviewed.

As your business moves through these various growth stages you need to know what is going to be critical to your company from one stage to the next. Cash can be a key concern at many of the stages.

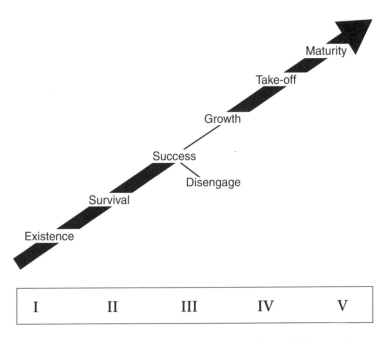

Source: The Five Stages of Small Business Growth – Churchill & Lewis, *Harvard Business Review*

**Figure 6.1**  The five stages of small business growth

# Venture Capital & Banking Alternative

Are you looking to raise £1m to £50m in bank or equity finance?

Frustrated with traditional sources of finance?

Talk to ECS – Eureka Corporate Services. We have access to a vast range of fundraising opportunities and a track record of generating millions in investment.

With our bespoke fund raising services we review your requirements and then work with you to generate the most appropriate funding, from a list of resources including but not limited to:

- Major City Banks
- Venture Capital companies & VCTs
- Invoice Discounting
- Stock Brokers
- High Net Worth Individuals and other investors
- Business Angel Networks and Private Equity
- Flotations on AIM
- Acquisitions

Intrigued? Talk to some of the people we've raised money for –

Optical Partners, Crash Test Munkii, East European Properties, PPE Total Power Solutions and many others – or

**call Ron G Holland on 0208 699 0001**

Eureka Corporate Services Ltd.
Creative Funding Resources from the Top Business Guru.

# HOW TO GET THE FINANCE YOU NEED
## By Top Biz Guru – Ron G Holland

**Ron G. Holland's Top 10 tips for Raising Money for Business**

1. Remember Banks and Venture Capitalists are not the only places to source capital. Don't waste time visiting a multitude of banks and VC's, a business consultant can tell you in 5 minutes whether a business is a suitable Venture Capital target.

2. Sourcing private investors can be a more lucrative method to secure capital. If possible, make sure you bring on board "intelligent money" – that is someone who can also help you to develop the business.

3. The best way to source private investors is by utilising all the contacts that you have.

4. When meeting private investors for the first time, make sure that you are aware of the key selling points and research your "business story".

5. Early investors will be taking the biggest risk and should be rewarded the most. Hire a Corporate Finance Adviser who can create an equity share structure for your company.

6. With one investment of £50K (say 5,000,000 1p shares to the first investor/s) a business can get started and be on the look out for the next investor – who will hopefully buy shares at a higher price - for example, 5p per share. It is important to remember that without an initial injection of cash there is no business.

7. Instead of an expensive and time intensive business plan, provide potential investors with a 2 page "Executive Summary" including details of the team. Face to face meetings will provide the "real" business plan until the company is more developed.

8. Invest in detailed Market Research (e.g. Gartner, Mintel). Knowing whether your idea will succeed or needs further developing before you take it to market could make or break the business.

9. Don't waste your time employing executives who are not prepared to invest in your start-up – this will ensure that all the people that you work with are as dedicated as you, and have a vested interest in your success.

10. Once the business has had time to develop and has investors who also contribute to the business, then write your own business plan. Don't fall into the trap of being seduced by firms promising a plan that will guarantee you money, you can write it much better than they can.

Many business people seek funds in the wrong place because they are not armed with sufficient information about who is looking to invest in a certain sector or who is prepared to invest in non profitable, early stage or start up companies. All too often those seeking funds make approaches before they have got all their 'ducks in a row.' In our experience you don't get too many bites at the cherry and it is best to go in with your best shot, first time around.

Eureka Corporate Services (ECS) offer a bespoke fund raising service to serious and ambitious entrepreneurs and have a massive network of banks, angels, high net

## VC Tip #3

Plan for the unexpected/anticipate problems – know what is going to be critical as your company moves through its various growth stages.

### The importance of cash at each stage

The key management factors – the owner's own ability, financial resources, people, systems and controls – vary at the various growth stages. The importance of cash changes as the business changes. It is an extremely important resource at the start, becomes somewhat more easily manageable at the success stage and is a main concern again as the organization begins to grow. As growth slows at the end of take-off and maturity cash becomes a manageable factor again. Companies in the success stage need to recognize the financial needs and risks entailed in a move to the take-off stage.

# SOURCES OF FINANCE

There are many potential sources of finance available to growing businesses in Europe, including grants available from the European Union and specific countries, particularly in development areas or to support innovation from the universities, equity backing from wealthy individuals or 'business angels' as they are known, in addition to bank loan and venture capital finance. Accessing them is the issue, both in terms of knowing where to go for advice and to initiate the application procedures, and preparing the applications themselves which can be quite time consuming and complex – this applies whether you are completing application forms for a guaranteed bank loan, a government grant or indeed preparing a business plan in connection with obtaining venture capital finance.

The various sources of finance are summarized in Table 6.1.

Information on government grants and advice on how to obtain business angel finance is given below, and the rest of this book is concerned with how to obtain private equity and venture capital financing.

**Table 6.1**  Sources of finance

| |
|---|
| Improved cash flow management techniques |
| Your own resources |
| Friends, family and, a little unfairly, so-called 'fools'! |
| Your fellow directors and employees |
| Business angels |
| Government sources |
| Strategic partnerships – minority stakes from larger players in your sector |
| Banks – overdrafts, short-, medium- and long-term loans, senior (secured) debt, government guarantee loan schemes |
| Factoring and invoice discounting |
| Leasing and hire purchase |
| Private equity/venture capital |
| Corporate venturers |
| Mezzanine finance (which sits between equity and secured debt) |
| Listing on AIM or other country growth markets or indeed on the main markets |

# MAXIMIZING INTERNAL FINANCIAL RESOURCES

Before you consider approaching external sources of finance, first of all make sure you are making optimal use of your internal financial resources. This, of course, depends on the stage of development of your business, but assuming you have been operating for a period from start-up and are generating revenues as well as incurring costs, or are in the process of pursuing a management buyout, then take the time to review your company's financial systems and procedures. In particular:

- ensure that you have effective cash flow forecasting systems in place;

- give customers incentives to encourage prompt payment;

- adhere to rigorous credit control procedures, including:
  - customer credit checks
  - prompt sales invoicing
  - age analysis of debtors
  - monthly statements to customers
  - reminder letters for non-payment;

- plan payments to suppliers – maybe even delay payment, but within the credit terms that they allow;

- maximize sales revenues – easier said than done, but are you really developing all those sales leads and mining your existing client base effectively?

- carefully control overheads, including premises, plant and equipment, marketing and staff costs;

- consider subcontracting to reduce initial capital requirements (if appropriate);

- assess inventory (stock) levels (if applicable);

- check quality control over your operations to reduce the need for reworking or handling claims, again to save costs.

## VC Tip #4

Remember: 'Cash is king' – take care to manage and control your cash resources with the utmost care.

And controlling your cash resources means being a little frugal on things like office facilities, company cars and even management salaries, as we saw with John Cavill and Logical Networks in case study 4. It is important to demonstrate a strong focus on cash management to your investors.

## FRIENDS AND FAMILY

Having maximized your internal sources of finance, look to your own resources and those of your friends and family and of course your fellow directors and even your staff in return for a share in the business. Please note that I have not referred to the 'fools' category here as I am assuming your business proposition is well researched, backed up with solid projections and is a bona-fide investment opportunity for serious investors. You are unlikely to attract even your closest friends and family to invest if you do not have a workable proposition or the plans and other back-up to support your proposition. And if things go wrong you could soon have some very upset friends and family to deal with – so it is not necessarily an ideal option to pursue. Of course, do look into your own resources first, maybe using personal or family savings or even re-mortgaging your house. You cannot expect a third-party investor such as venture capital firm to take the risk of investing in your business if you are not prepared to risk your own resources in the venture, a point reinforced by serial entrepreneur Bob Jones in the Equiinet case study (case study 13). As a rule of thumb you might have to be prepared to forgo the equivalent of a year's salary to demonstrate your commitment to the business. This varies from VC to VC; some may not require you to sell the shirt off your back first, others may pay no heed to the fact that you might already have incurred considerable expense (not to mention time) in setting up your business.

Please don't get the impression that private equity is a last resort after you have exhausted your own, your friends', your business colleagues' and your bank's resources. There are many advantages to private equity over bank debt. Private equity firms can, of course, work in conjunction with the other external sources as part of an overall financing package.

# BUSINESS ANGELS

Business angels are private investors who invest directly in private companies in return for an equity stake and perhaps a seat on the company's board. Research has shown that business angels generally invest smaller amounts of private equity in earlier-stage companies compared with venture capital firms. Angels typically invest between £20,000 and £200,000 at the seed, start-up and early stage of company development, or they may invest more than this as members of syndicates, possibly up to £1.5 million. However, around 75% of angel investments are under £100,000, with the average investment for a business angel at around £75,000.

A typical business angel in the United States will have started and sold one, two, three or more businesses, usually in the technology sector, and have a net worth of several hundred million dollars. In the UK an angel may have no direct experience in the specific sector being invested in and have a net worth of less than a million pounds. In fact, a high net worth individual in the UK is defined by the Financial Services and Markets Act (FSMA) Financial Promotion Order 2001 as having an annual income of not less than £100,000 or net assets to the value of not less than £250,000. However, there are several general partners in private equity and venture capital firms who are business angels in their personal capacities and who do certainly have the appropriate sector experience and are considerably wealthier than the minimum definition of a UK wealthy individual given above!

---

### Some interesting facts on business angels

I Sun Microsystems co-founder, Andy Bechtolsheim, provided Google founders, Larry Page and Sergey Brin, with $100,000 to start up their business.

I Amazon.com, Apple, Body Shop, Kinko's and Starbucks all got started with the help of angel investors.

I In 2004, 3,000 start-ups in the United States were funded by US VCs but 48,000 start-ups were funded by angels (*Source*: Business 2.0).

I There are an estimated 15,000 to 40,000 business angels in the UK compared to 250,000 angels in the United States.

---

As mentioned above, business angels may invest in groups (syndicates) and in specific industries, eg technology start-ups or early-stage businesses.

Business angels will usually want a 'hands-on' role with the company that they invest in, maybe as an adviser or a non-executive director, or even take on an executive role. They expect to 'add value' to the company and usually have much to offer in terms of practical experience (including dealing with VCs, which will come in helpful at a later stage) and a network of contacts. They are therefore in a good position to introduce entrepreneurs to potential customers, suppliers, advisers, government contacts and alliances as well as having hands-on experience in specific operational areas which can help to fill the gaps in the management team of the investee business. As Tony Morris, serial entrepreneur and business angel investor, states in case study 8 later in this chapter, don't look for 'dumb' money, ie where the business angel is not bringing anything to the venture other than finance. Tony himself gets involved in such activities as mentoring the CEO, recruiting members of the management team, introducing potential customers, bringing rigour and independence to the business, generally opening doors through his network of contacts and/or adding significant value to the enterprise in other ways.

The Massachusetts Institute of Technology (MIT) Entrepreneurship Center has attempted to categorize angel investors into four types based on the angel's relevant industry and entrepreneurial experience. Angels may operate in more than one category depending on the individual investment opportunity (Figure 6.2):

I *Operational expertise angels* are, or have been, senior executives in major companies in the investee company's industry. They usually

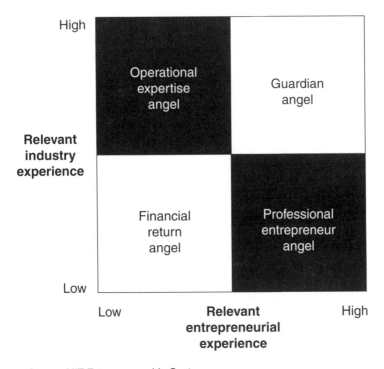

**Figure 6.2** The different types of angel investors

provide active support to the investee company, such as providing industry knowledge and contacts, and later-stage VCs tend to value their involvement.

▌ *Financial return angels* are high net worth investors with little entrepreneurial experience or experience of the industry sector in which they are investing. Their involvement with the company post-investment tends to be passive and limited to financial support and maybe general business advice. Later-stage VCs are less likely to invest in deals that have too many financial return angels in previous rounds.

▌ *Guardian angels* are active investors who guide and coach the management team and help them to grow the company. They have often themselves created a company before, in the same industry sector. They usually take board seats and provide industry contacts and business development support to the investee company. They help recruit members of the management team and next-round VC investors. They are highly valued by VCs.

■ *Professional entrepreneur angels* have usually created a company themselves but may be investing outside their area of expertise and may have limited angel investing experience. Their involvement with the company post-investment is usually limited, though they may assist with market research and help with building the company. They may be valued by VCs. They tend to have a good understanding of start-up milestones and growth stages.

Different types of angel investor are illustrated in the practical real-life example of iBase Systems below.

## Case study 7

### iBase Systems Limited – the many different roles of angel investors

iBase Systems Limited (iBase) is a software and services company operating in the high growth market of mobile working. iBase has developed a suite of software applications called Grip to provide a seamless link between field operations and key business systems. With the addition of visual spatial information such as mapping and integration with the web, powerful user-friendly applications are provided. The principal markets currently served are local government and infrastructure management but there are also significant potential opportunities in aviation. iBase operates out of London, UK and Adelaide, South Australia and has been trading since 1999.

Martin Conder is the chairman of iBase and describes how in early 2006 the company attracted a round of angel financing from three very different types of business angel investor.

### Background

iBase was founded by its current technical director and the systems director. Prior to forming iBase, these co-founders collectively had over 30 years' IT experience within the mining industry.

Up until 2005, iBase had been financed to the extent of around £75,000 by the founders, by direct directors' loans and by deferral of salaries. In addition, the company had raised a £50,000 loan under the DTI Loan Guarantee Scheme. In 2005 Martin Conder, a Chartered Accountant with considerable corporate finance and venture capital experience, came on board as finance director and chairman with the intention to raise some additional external capital and position the business for growth. Key to this process, Martin first reorganized iBase under a new holding company, iBase Group Limited, sorted out the financial records, introduced a monthly management accounting regime and ensured that the IP was suitably protected. Martin provided £75,000 of new equity capital, matched by a further bank loan of £75,000 from Barclays under the Small Firms Loan Guarantee Scheme (SFLGS) as by then the original £50,000 loan had been fully repaid.

## Finance for expansion

The strength of iBase was that it had a fully developed product and had duly established itself as a leader in the provision of mobile business solutions for data capture in the Local Government market. Additional capital of around £250,000 was sought in order to grow the business more aggressively and to build the sales infrastructure.

Martin set about raising the necessary funds. A detailed business plan was prepared, although, as the company's products were at the cutting edge of a new market (ie in terms of mobile data capture), it was not really possible to substantiate the current market size to a potential investor; nevertheless, the opportunities and potential of the market were readily apparent.

Martin approached several VCs but the proposition was too early-stage and below the investment range of most of them. Nevertheless, several expressed interest in looking at the proposal again once iBase had grown further and required a subsequent round of finance. He also approached various angel networks and made presentations at networking events, such as the UK Technology Innovation & Growth Forum. These networks all provided good contacts for the future.

He also contacted previous business colleagues and friends on an informal basis, without directly promoting the investment proposition.

## Three very different styles of business angel investors

A former work colleague, currently active in the venture capital industry, expressed interest and personally injected £125,000 equity into iBase. This angel (Angel No 1) is a passive angel, taking no active role in the business at all.

A further £75,000 was injected by another contact of Martin's who had previously started up and exited from a successful software design and consultancy company (Angel No 2). Martin had originally wanted him involved as a non-executive director as he felt the company required more expertise on the board with strong software contract and licensing experience. Angel No 2 duly came onto the board of directors as a non-executive and is a highly active angel investor.

The third business angel (Angel No 3) came across iBase himself following a period working abroad and became employed by iBase as project manager. He has extensive experience of large-scale IT system implementation in the financial services sector and managed the delivery of new contracts for iBase. Angel No 3 invested £25,000.

All three angels got together before investing in iBase. They jointly submitted a list of detailed questions. Angel No 2 led the legal aspects on behalf of all three angels in conjunction with an external lawyer.

The angels did not perform extensive financial due diligence, basing their investment decision on the business plan and the fact that Martin Conder was himself involved with iBase as an angel investor. They were, however, able to see evidence of the initial success in winning Local Authority customers and in particular a newly won major contract with Transport for London (TfL) under which iBase were installing their product into every London Borough. iBase was also making progress in marketing its products to the aviation sector at this time.

The angels invested into the same class of ordinary shares of iBase as had been taken by the other shareholders. They were thereby able to take advantage of the Enterprise Investment Scheme.

## Martin Conder's tips for entrepreneurs seeking early-stage angel or VC funding

Martin Conder has the following tips for entrepreneurs seeking early-stage angel or VC funding:

- Keep as many irons in the fire as possible in terms of potential sources of finance – keep all your options open and maintain contact with VCs and others you have met who have shown interest in getting involved when the company has grown sufficiently.
- In view of his own expertise in VC finance, Martin did not use an intermediary to help him locate and negotiate equity capital for iBase. However, Martin believes that intermediaries could be useful if an entrepreneur does not understand the process well or has few relevant contacts. Intermediaries can also manage the entire fundraising process, which takes some of the pressure off a busy entrepreneur or management team.

- Investors may show an interest in investing but to guide them through the whole process until they actually commit and then get their cheque book out takes considerable effort – don't underestimate the time involved. In the case of iBase it took around four months to get the three angel investors on board. Do get legal help.

www.ibasesystems.co.uk

## Attracting business angel capital

To attract business angel capital you need to take much the same approach as attracting venture capital finance, ie you will need a business plan which sets out your proposition in detail (see Chapter 8), including an assessment of how you expect the angel investor will make a return on his or her investment in due course commensurate with the amount of investment and the risk inherent in the proposition, a working prototype (for a technology company) and references from potential customers to confirm they will buy your product or service at the price you plan to charge. Get as many testimonials from potential customers as you can.

Make sure you cover the six questions investors ask to determine company value set out in Chapter 5. These have been prepared by an experienced business angel investor and until you have addressed these areas effectively in your proposition it is not worth approaching a potential investor.

What is different between a business angel and a venture capitalist is in the approach and the extent of due diligence carried out by these investors when they come to assess your proposition before proceeding with an investment. Business angels will almost certainly carry out their own due diligence personally and may go more on 'gut feel', their own assessment of your capabilities and of the market potential and the personal chemistry between themselves and you. They will want to be satisfied that they will be able to work closely with you on a day-to-day basis. Of course, the VC will also want to be satisfied on these areas but will most likely engage external consultants to cover aspects of the due diligence, as set out in Chapter 9, and will altogether adopt a more formal approach to the proceedings.

In terms of the equity stake that an angel will require in your business, this will depend on the amount of investment and the risk assessment. You may want to give up no more than a 15% equity stake in the case of a start-up venture seeking £150,000 angel financing. The business angel may want as much as 25% after assessing your proposition. Of course, this is all negotiable. Other areas that the business angel will be concerned with include:

▌ agreeing that management salaries are dependent on management's ability to meet the projections in the business plan;

▌ setting up preference arrangements in the event of a liquidation;

▌ agreeing ratchet mechanisms tied to performance milestones;

▌ anti-dilution agreements to protect angel investment (pre-emption rights);

▌ the entrepreneur personally guaranteeing any bank loans;

▌ protecting intellectual property and patents;

▌ locking in, and protecting, key staff through contracts, stock options and vesting arrangements and key person insurance.

Business angels are particularly concerned about getting their equity stakes diluted if and when a venture capital firm or other investor comes in on a subsequent round of financing. Hence the need to protect their investment through pre-emption rights, ie when the company proposes to issue new shares, existing shareholders have the right to be offered a pro-rata part of any new shares before they are offered to a new shareholder. The rights are contained either in the Articles of Association or imposed by Section 89 of the UK Companies Act 1985. These pre-emption rights may be disapplied either generally or in relation to a particular new issue by a provision in the Articles of Association or a special resolution. With regard to sales of existing shares, similar rights require a shareholder wishing to sell shares to offer them first to existing shareholders before being able to transfer to outside investors. These rights are common for private companies and would be found in the Articles of Association.

Tony Morris, the business angel investor referred to earlier, only gets involved as a business angel investor with other investors and well-known VC firms as part of a 'friendly' group of investors. He avoids getting diluted in subsequent rounds (a common issue for business angel investors) by insisting on investing through preferred stock.

## Where to find these elusive business angels

Many companies find business angels through informal contacts, but for others, finding a business angel may be more difficult, as the details of individual business angels are not always available.

## Business angel organizations

There are many business angel organizations in the UK and continental Europe. The following is just a very small selection, including umbrella organizations in UK, Europe and North America:

■ British Business Angels Association (BBAA) – this evolved from the previous National Business Angel Network (NBAN) and is the national trade association for the business angel networks in the UK. The BBAA is backed by the UK Department of Trade and Industry (DTI) and sponsored by Nesta and Kingston Smith. The BBAA promotes the recognition of business angel networks and organized angel groups. It has a number of roles, ranging from highlighting the contribution business angels make to the entrepreneurial culture, to supporting its members and lobbying government, to encouraging the exchange of best practice, experiences and ideas between its members. It specifically does not promote investment opportunities to investors or to advisers but lists its members on its website (www.bbaa.org.uk) who do pursue investment opportunities, so this is a good place to start to help you find business angel investor networks in the UK.

■ Beer & Partners (www.beerandpartners.com) states that it is the leading source of venture capital and business angel investment for growing SME businesses in the UK and that its contacts with business angels, high net worth private investors and secured lenders are 'second to none'.

■ EBAN, the European Business Angel Network, was established by the European Association of Development Agencies (EURADA) with the support of the European Commission in 1999. It is a non-profit association which has the purpose of:
   – encouraging the exchange of experience among business angel networks and encouraging 'best practice';
   – promoting recognition of business angel networks;
   – contributing to working out and carrying out local, regional and national programmes of assistance to the creation and development of a positive environment for business angels activities.
   EBAN publishes an extensive Directory of Business Angel Networks in Europe covering over 230 separate networks in 24 European countries, including non-EU members: Norway, Russia, Switzerland and Turkey (www.eban.org).

■ The Angel Capital Association (www.angelcapitalassociation.org) is North America's professional alliance of angel groups. This association brings together the 200 or so angel organizations in the United

States and Canada to share best practices, network, and help develop data about the field of angel investing. Its website has a listing of angel groups, as well as a listing of national organizations that have directories of investors and that provide matching services for entrepreneurs and angels.

## Case study 8

### Tony Morris and Nexagent – a leading business angel's approach to investing in high-tech ventures

Anthony (Tony) Morris is a personal computer (PC) industry pioneer, entrepreneur, business angel investor in emerging IT and internet ventures, independent director and consultant with many years' experience in the information technology business on both sides of the Atlantic. Tony is the founder and CEO of Morris Company (UK) which works with promising UK and European IT and internet companies and their investors on venture development in local markets and in the United States.

In Chapter 5 we saw the six questions that Tony has developed that investors ask to determine company value. As we saw, Tony believes that the answers to these six questions fundamentally determine the investor's perception of the value in a venture before they start considering the specific deal structure and details of the investment proposition.

Tony Morris has invested in 24 technology ventures as an angel investor. In twelve of these investments he invested before the first VC financing round, in four he invested with the first VC round and in eight he invested after the first VC round. He is also a limited partner in several well-known venture capital firms in Europe and the United States.

### Nexagent

One of Tony's investments is Nexagent, which is the pioneer and market leader in centralized management software and hardware for interconnecting next-generation telecom networks. One of Nexagent's founders is Charlie Muirhead, who was formerly the founder and CEO of Orchestream, the market leader in IP service activation software for MPLS-VPNs. Orchestream was listed on both the London Stock Exchange and NASDAQ in 2000, valued at over £1billion, and was acquired in 2003 by another NASDAQ-listed software company, Metasolv. Tony knew Charlie from his Orchestream days and Charlie invited Tony onto the board of Nexagent.

Tony helped Nexagent develop its business model as well as the business plan and investor presentations. Tony has subsequently helped Nexagent with its market positioning and sales.

Early-stage funding for Nexagent of £3 million in 2001 was led by iGabriel's angel investment fund (founded by Charlie Muirhead in 2002 and subsequently merged with Pi-Capital) and included angel financing from Tony Morris and other angel investors.

In early 2002 Nexagent completed its Series A £10.3 million funding round, co-led by Atlas Venture (who has also invested in Orchestream) and Benchmark Capital with further participation from Quester Capital and Lago Ventures.

In mid-2003 Nexagent closed a Series B round of £15 million led by Apax Partners. This round included follow-on investments from Atlas, Benchmark, Quester, and Lago Ventures.

When Nexagent was looking for VC finance, no revenues had been generated. Tony's assistance with the market projection and analysis was helpful in working towards a consistent, under-standable and believable story. In all, 12 presentations were made to potential VCs investors, which was the total number approached. This 100% hit rate was achieved as Charlie Muirhead was well known to the potential investors through Orchestream.

## Tony Morris's tips for business angels and entrepreneurs

There are some common traits in all of Tony Morris's investments and these are offered below as tips for budding business angel investors. All of them are clearly present in Tony's involvement with Nexagent:

- All the businesses in which Tony has invested were 'game changers'. They were all trying to do something different. They could in fact be classed as 'disruptive', ie involving a new techno-logical innovation, product, or service that overturns the existing dominant technology or product in the marketplace.
- The businesses were potentially large enough to attract financing from a VC firm, either just after the business angel financing or along with the business angel financing. It is important for the business angel to have the VCs as friends when a subsequent financing round is being negotiated.

- At some point in the life of the business, Tony, as the business angel investor, was key to its development other than by simply providing some of the financing, either in terms of mentoring the CEO (rarely matchable by VCs), recruiting members of the management team, introducing potential customers, bringing rigour and independence to the business, generally opening doors through his network of contacts and/or adding significant value to the enterprise in other ways.
- In all cases Tony not only respected the management team, he actually got on with the key members of the team, ie the personal chemistry between the angel and the team is very important.

Tony strongly cautions against investing in a venture where the business angel cannot add value. He also cautions against investing as a lone angel; as noted above, it is better to invest as part of a 'friendly' group of investors.

Likewise, for the entrepreneur seeking business angel financing he strongly recommends against looking for 'dumb' money, ie where the business angel is not bringing anything to the venture other than finance. It is also essential to make your venture understandable to a potential investor, especially if it is in a highly technical, specialized area. And don't complicate deals with terms that can make it difficult for subsequent financing rounds or cause management to focus all their efforts on meeting ratchet terms, for example, rather than focusing on the business.

Tony only gets involved as a business angel investor with other investors and well-known VC firms. He avoids getting diluted in subsequent rounds (a common issue for business angel investors) by insisting on preferred stock (17 of his 24 investments have been through preferred stock only).

Generally he doesn't issue a term sheet as an angel investor, deciding on whether to invest on the basis of the term sheet issued by the company or more usually the lead VC. He carries out his own extensive due diligence on the company, financials, strategy and market – especially the market potential. The company must have a reasonable and believable strategy for getting to market and building a potentially sizable and market-leading business reasonably quickly (the fifth question in Tony's six questions that investors ask to determine company value). He also aligns himself closely with the technology due diligence.

tonymorris@mindspring.com

# INVESTMENT FORUMS AND NETWORKING ORGANIZATIONS

In addition to business angel networks, you can also find angel investors (and venture capitalists) at the various investment forums that are organized in Europe. Typically, at these events entrepreneurs seeking capital get to present their propositions to an audience of VCs, angels, corporate investors and advisers. Presenters have around 10 to 15 minutes to make their presentation (a sort of extended 'elevator pitch'). Depending on the prestige and size of the event, there may be a selection process to decide which companies get to make presentations and payment may or may not be required. Some of these events are put on by the larger conference organizers, others are organized by universities and business schools and networking clubs. Usually, in addition to the company presentations, there will be one or more plenary sessions from invited guest speakers, including successful entrepreneurs on topical issues. Examples include:

▌ UK Technology Innovation and Growth Forum – an annual event, usually held in February in London, organized by the European Technology Forum with PricewaterhouseCoopers as platinum sponsor (www.innovationandgrowthforum.com).

▌ Cityzone (www.city-zone.com) is an enterprise network that helps entrepreneurs, investors and professional advisers to find opportunities and expertise through its networking events held in London, Cambridge and Reading in the UK.

▌ As an example of a regional network, because it happens to be where I am located, the Thames Valley Investment Network (TVIN) (www.tvin.co.uk) links investors to companies with high growth potential who are seeking funding from £50,000 to £500,000 in early-stage ventures within the Thames Valley region of the UK.

▌ European Tech Tour Association (ETT) (www.techtour.com) organizes around four tours each year to different European countries or emerging regions where the invited delegates of international and local venture capital firms and advisers meet with young, innovative high-tech companies with global market potential – see below.

▌ Europe Unlimited (www.e-unlimited.com) helps European entrepreneurs to innovate, raise investment, partner, grow and internationalize – see below.

## European Tech Tour Association

The European Tech Tour Association (ETT) was founded in Geneva in 1998 in response to growing interest in visiting emerging technology companies in various European regions.

ETT is an independent, non-profit organization, which aims to provide a platform that allows interactions between the three main groups, entrepreneurs, venture capital investors and alliance partners, with the aim of facilitating or funding local high-technology companies looking to expand internationally. The association recognizes that continued prosperity in Europe lies in its ability to transform today's innovative projects into tomorrow's global technology leaders.

Although some European regions show a higher density of innovative projects and expertise than others, extraordinary competence, entrepreneurship and dynamism can be found throughout Europe. Each region is hiding a handful of raw gems deserving more attention and requiring guidance to quickly achieve global success. ETT's goal is to bring more transparency to Europe's regional markets and to build a stronger relationship between its members and each region.

Up to four tours are organized per year in different countries where ETT has identified a particular interest among its delegates and where it believes that innovative young high-tech companies with global market potential can be found.

The ETT local country representative and the executive committee of ETT identify the most promising companies in a selected region through their combined networks. An open competition or 'call for applications' is also made in each region at least three months before each Tech Tour takes place.

Contact:
Sven Lingjaerde, President, sven@techtour.com
www.techtour.com
6, Rue de la Croix d'Or CH-1204 Geneva, Switzerland
Tel: +41 22 544 60 90

### Europe Unlimited

Europe Unlimited helps European entrepreneurs to innovate, raise investment, partner, grow and internationalize. Europe Unlimited believes that more dynamic entrepreneurship will bring sustainable innovation, economic growth and value to our societies. It achieves its mission by:

- match-making some 250 ICT and life sciences companies with venture capital and corporate investors and partners through six major proprietary venture events;
- organizing programmes which help regional governments or European initiatives to provide high-tech start-ups and growth companies with better perspectives on, and opportunities for, funding, partnering, growth, innovation and internationalization; and
- putting on business owner summits where selected dynamic entrepreneurs can exchange best practice and meet each other.

Europe Unlimited events have a proven formula and track record: out of the 430 companies that presented at the first 10 editions of the European Tech Investment Forum, 80 companies are known by the European Commission to have raised in excess of €300 million following their participation.

A more recent study in June 2006 in association with Ernst & Young, comparing the companies presenting at the Nordic Venture Summit with data on venture investments in the Nordic countries, shows that of the 64 companies that presented in the 2003 or 2004 editions, 39 or 58% managed to close new investments following the Summit. For life sciences companies, the percentage was even higher at 62%.

Europe Unlimited is based in Brussels and its multilingual and multinational staff of 20 works with a team of senior strategic advisors.

Contact:
William Stevens, founder & chairman
william@e-unlimited.com
Europe Unlimited SA – www.e-unlimited.com
Place Flagey 7, B – 1050 Brussels, Belgium
Tel: + 32 2 / 644 6580

# GOVERNMENT GRANTS AND ASSISTANCE – UK AND EUROPE

If you are looking for finance at the lower end of the so-called 'equity gap', say up to £250,000 or £500,000 in the UK, then there are various government sources that may be available to you, together with advice on setting up and running your business. The 'equity gap' itself is widely regarded as being between £250,000 and £2 million, where it is very difficult to secure venture capital finance simply because of the amount of time and effort required by a venture capital firm to appraise an investment proposition. For smaller amounts of finance it is simply not worth their while, unless there will be further financing rounds required later.

More recently the UK has addressed the range of financing towards the upper end of the equity gap with the new Enterprise Capital Funds (ECFs) – see below – that can provide up to £2 million of financing.

Government sources of grants for SMEs and growing businesses in the UK include the following.

## Small Firms Loan Guarantee Scheme

The Small Firms Loan Guarantee Scheme allows businesses without sufficient security for commercial bank lending to obtain loans from participating banks that are guaranteed by the UK government. The Small Business Service (SBS) guarantees 70% of the loan (85% if a business has been trading for more than two years). Borrowers pay a 2% premium on the outstanding balance. The scheme is available to UK businesses with an annual turnover of up to £3 million – for manufacturers up to £5 million. The maximum loan for businesses trading for more than two years is £250,000 or £100,000 for newer businesses.

## Regional Venture Capital Funds

The Regional Venture Capital Funds (RVCFs) are one element of the £180 million Enterprise Fund that was created in 1998 through the SBS to stimulate more finance for small businesses in the UK and address market weaknesses in the provision of that finance.

The RVCFs were set up to address SMEs seeking relatively small-scale investment, up to £500,000 in two tranches, and which demonstrate growth potential. The funds are managed by experienced venture capital professionals, are commercially focused and aim to make commercial returns. The funds cover the North East, North West, London, Yorkshire and the Humber, South East and South West, East Midlands, West

Midlands and East of England regions of the UK. The business has to comply with the European Union's definition of a small- and medium-sized enterprise (SME) and there are various ownership and sector exclusions, as well as geographic requirements. An SME is currently defined as a business with fewer than 250 employees and either has a turnover of less than €40 million (approximately £24 million) or a balance sheet total of less than €27 million.

RVCFs can invest up to £250,000 in equity or debt into any qualifying business, be it a start-up, early stage, requiring development capital either for an acquisition or for organic growth, or even a management buyout. All decisions as to whether or not to invest in any proposal will be made by the fund manager based on commercial viability. The RVCFs are allowed to make follow-on investments of up to a further £250,000 or in exceptional circumstances possibly more than this. The follow-on investments are not permitted within a six-month period starting from the date of the original investment.

## Selective Finance for Investment in England

A new product, Selective Finance for Investment in England, has replaced the former Regional Selective Assistance Scheme and is provided by the Regional Development Agencies. Funding of up to 10–15% of a project's total eligible capital expenditure may be obtained. The scheme is designed for businesses that are looking at the possibility of investing in an area of high deprivation but need financial help to go ahead. It is awarded as a percentage of eligible project expenditure and is provided as a grant towards capital costs such as fixed assets, land, property and machinery. It can be used for start-ups, modernizing through introducing technological improvements, expanding an existing business, or taking a new product/service/process from the development stage to production.

## Early growth funds

Early growth funds are regional and national funds provided through the SBS. They can provide up to £100,000 for innovative and knowledge-intensive start-up and early-stage businesses as well as other growth businesses. In most cases they must be matched by at least the same amount of private sector investment.

## University Challenge Seed Funds

The aim of the UK government's University Challenge Seed Fund Scheme is to fill a funding gap in the UK in the provision of finance for bringing university research initiatives in science and engineering to the point where their commercial viability can be demonstrated. Certain charities and the government have contributed around £50 million to the scheme. These funds are divided into 15 University Challenge Seed Funds that have been donated to individual universities or consortia and each one of these has to provide 25% of the total fund from its own resources. If you are looking into the commercialization of research at a UK university which is in receipt of a fund, contact your university administration to enquire about the application process. Follow-on finance may be provided by business angels, corporate venturers and private equity firms.

## Enterprise Capital Funds

Enterprise Capital Funds (ECFs) are a new UK government initiative aimed at bridging the finance gap by improving access to growth capital for small- and medium-sized enterprises by applying a modified US Small Business Investment Company (SBIC) model to the UK, a difference being that with the UK scheme the government has downside protection with a priority return of 4.5% per annum plus a minor profit share.

Equity investments of up to £2 million per deal can be made. ECFs will be privately managed and will use a limited partnership model with two variants: 1) a professional FSA-authorized fund manager who acts on behalf of passive investors; 2) an active investor model (eg business angels) who invest and manage their own funds through ECFs (maybe without authorization).

Six funds have been awarded ECF status in the pathfinder round. They are:

■ *The IQ Capital Fund* – a £25 million fund which will operate across the Cambridge, Oxford and Bristol areas, but will have the ability to invest anywhere in the UK. It will focus on technology-based SMEs and will make investments of up to £1.5 million.

■ *21st Century Sustainable Technology Growth Fund* – a £30 million fund which will operate across the UK and focus on high growth companies employing leading-edge, sustainable technology. E-Synergy Limited, which has close links with the UK's research community and expertise in selecting and backing strong technology in early-stage companies, will manage the Fund.

■ *The Seraphim Capital Fund* – a £30 million generalist co-investment fund that will invest alongside leading business angels and other private investors drawing on the deal flow and investment experience afforded by the funds' diverse investor base. The fund will be managed by a coalition of business angel networks and will focus on investments in companies throughout the UK, predominantly in the early stages of development.

▌ *The Amadeus Enterprise Capital Fund* – a £10 million fund that will focus on seed technology investments throughout the UK. The Fund will be managed by Amadeus Capital Partners, a venture capital firm specializing in high-technology investments in Europe.

▌ *The Dawn Capital Fund* – a £37.5 million fund, which includes £25 million of government funding, which has been created by a group of successful entrepreneurs and experienced fund managers. The Fund will invest throughout the UK with an investment focus on traditional industries where pioneering companies are able to adopt innovative technology to improve products and services.

▌ *The Midlands Enterprise Capital Fund* – a £30 million generalist fund, which includes £18 million of government funding, which will focus on investments in the Midlands region in the UK, but will consider UK-wide opportunities.

ECFs receive their funding from the UK government and private sources. UK government funding of an individual ECF will not exceed £25 million, which will be no more than twice the private capital contribution. To avoid the problems of dilution experienced by many early-stage investors, ECFs will be allowed to invest more than £2 million in a single company if not to do so as part of a subsequent funding round would dilute their existing stake in the company.

## Other grants

There are several other grants available to SMEs and growing businesses in the UK, including:

▌ Grants for Research & Development – these replace the former DTI 'SMART' scheme. They aim to help start-ups and SMEs carry out research and development work on technologically innovative products and processes. From April 2005 the English Regional Development Agencies became responsible for delivering the Grants for R&D.

▌ Various regional 'Accelerator' funds, such as the Finance South East (FSE) Accelerator Fund which is a £10 million loan fund which supports small- and medium-sized companies in the South East with the potential for significant growth (early-stage or established companies). The FSE Accelerator Fund can lend from £25,000 to

£100,000. An additional £100,000 can be made available after a period of 9 months.

For further information on the above UK government grants and others available, visit the website of the Small Business Service (SBS) at www.sbs.gov.uk or the Business Links at www.businesslink.gov.uk.

Business Links are part of the SBS and, in addition to providing advice on the various grants available to small businesses, provide advice, help and an entry point to the various schemes run by the Department of Trade and Industry (DTI). New businesses (particularly those using new technology) can get help with premises and management from the various Business Incubation Centres in the UK or from one of the UK Science Parks. You may also be eligible for EU grants if you are in an innovative business sector or are planning to operate in a deprived area of the UK or a region zoned for regeneration. Apart from Business Links, your local Chamber of Commerce and town hall should have lists of grants and available property.

Case study 5 on Lein Applied Diagnostics illustrates how Business Link helped this start-up company to apply successfully for a SMART award, how the company worked through various angel networks to find their initial seed financing and later obtained a grant for research and development.

Two other UK government incentives include:

▌ The Enterprise Investment Scheme (EIS), which was set up by the UK government to replace the Business Expansion Scheme (BES) and to encourage business angels to invest in certain types of smaller unquoted UK companies. If a company meets the EIS criteria, it may be more attractive to business angels, as tax incentives are available on their investments. Under the EIS, individuals not previously connected with a qualifying unlisted trading company (including shares traded on the Alternative Investment Market (AIM)) can make investments of up to £400,000 (previously £200,000) in any tax year and receive tax relief at 20% on new subscriptions for ordinary shares in the company, and relief from capital gains tax (CGT) on disposal, provided the investment is held for three years.

▌ Venture Capital Trusts (VCTs), which are quoted vehicles to encourage investment in smaller unlisted (unquoted and AIM quoted) UK companies. Investors receive 30% income tax relief on VCT investment (previously 40%) on a maximum investment amount of £200,000 each tax year and no CGT, provided the investment is held for five years (previously three years).

# EUROPEAN GRANTS

Your nearest Euro Info Centre (EIC) will have information on both national and EU financial support. EICs inform, advise and assist businesses on Community issues. They also provide feedback to the European Commission about Community matters affecting SMEs. There are more than 300 EICs across more than 45 countries. To find an EIC near you, go to the weblink: http://ec.europa.eu/enterprise/networks/eic/eic-geo-cover_en.html.

Information on EU funding opportunities is also available in the EU publication: 'An overview of the main funding opportunities available for SMEs in 2005: EU support programmes for SMEs'.

Funding opportunities available to SMEs directly from the EU include those with specific objectives in the areas of environment and energy, innovation and research, and education and training. For technology companies, the Community Research and Development Innovation Service (CORDIS) may be of particular interest. CORDIS (www.cordis.lu) covers all aspects of EU research and innovation policy, including: 'Financing innovation: part of the EC's Innovation/SME programme' (http://www.cordis.lu/finance/src/schemes.htm) and 'SME Tech Web, the website for technology-oriented SMEs, especially those wishing to innovate and internationalize' (http://sme.cordis.lu/ home/index.cfm).

Support is also available to SMEs through the EU's Structural Funds. These are implemented and managed at national and regional level and not available directly from the EU. The structural funds address three objectives:

- development of the least favoured regions: developing and strengthening SME support structures;

- conversion of regions facing difficulties: promoting entrepreneurship and creating alternative job opportunities where large-scale traditional industries have declined;

- modernizing systems of training and promoting employment: promoting the development of human resources.

## European Investment Fund (EIF)

The EIF's activity is centred upon two areas, venture capital and guarantees:

- EIF's venture capital instruments consist of equity investments in venture capital funds and business incubators that support SMEs, particularly those that are early-stage and technology-oriented.

▌ EIF's guarantee instruments consist of providing guarantees to financial institutions that cover credits to SMEs.

The EIF does not invest directly in SMEs but instead always works through financial intermediaries. SMEs in search of finance should contact an EIF intermediary in their country or region for information on eligibility criteria and application procedures. You should check the 'List of investments' (for venture capital) or 'List of deals' (for guarantee instruments) to find out the names and websites of the intermediaries in your region.

### Gate2Growth

Assistance to SMEs is also available through the Gate2Growth initiative which is supported by the European Commission under its Innovation/SMEs programme (see www.gate2growth.com).

The prime objective of the Gate2Growth initiative is to create contact between entrepreneurs (private individuals, management teams and companies) with business ideas and investors (private individuals, companies and funds) in the EU and associated countries and between these advisers and innovation professionals (companies and individuals providing services to entrepreneurs and investors). Gate2Growth fosters networking and the exchange of experience and good practice at the European level between early-stage technology venture capital investors, managers of technology incubators, managers of industrial liaison and technology transfer offices linked to universities and research centres and academics in entrepreneurship, finance research and teaching.

## LACK OF GOVERNMENT SPENDING WITH GROWTH BUSINESSES

While there are a number of government initiatives to support SMEs with early-stage financing, advice on setting up and running SMEs and growth businesses and training programmes in business and finance skills, there is little support to entrepreneurs in terms of revenue generation from being awarded government contracts. Procurement of government contracts tends to go the way of large, established companies in the UK and in most of continental Europe. It's the 'nobody ever got fired for buying from IBM' syndrome. To really support enterprise, government needs to channel a reasonable percentage of its business needs to smaller businesses. In the United States growth companies have benefited from a much more tolerant approach from government procurement, which is backed up by a legal requirement, set out in the US Small Business Act, which requires the US government to set aside 23% of direct contracts and 40% of subcontracts for SMEs. In addition, the Smaller Business Innovation Research Program (SBIR) requires US government agencies to set aside at least 2½% of their research and development budgets for SMEs.

It is not just the risk-averse nature of public procurement agencies, however. Smaller businesses are less visible to the procurers and, for the entrepreneurs, the tender process can take up onerous amounts of management time. In the United States the tender process is much more user friendly.

Lobbying is under way to introduce a US-style process in Europe. In France the 'SME Pact' was set up in late 2004. This allows procurement officials to identify appropriate SMEs and has mechanisms whereby the risks taken in contracting with an early-stage company are lessened. However, in Europe governments are not able to give SMEs preferred supplier status due to the World Trade Organization Agreement on Public Procurement. The US government was able to circumvent this agreement as the Small Business Act was already in force when the WTO agreement came in. In the UK, the government has been able to commit to a target of a minimum of 2½% research and development spending with SMEs.

# PRIVATE EQUITY NOT NECESSARILY A 'LAST RESORT'

Do speak to friends, business contacts and advisers as well as your local Business Link in the UK or other government growing-business advice agency in continental Europe. Do obtain as much information as possible to ensure that you can realistically assess the most suitable finance for your needs and your company's success. And please don't get the impression that private equity is necessarily a last resort after you have exhausted your own, your friends', your business colleagues', government and your bank's resources. There are many advantages to private equity over bank debt, for example, as we saw in Chapter 1. Private equity firms can, of course, work in conjunction with the other external sources as part of an overall financing package.

# 7

# Sources of private equity and selecting a private equity firm

## DIFFERENT TYPES OF PRIVATE EQUITY FIRMS

There are around 1,600 private equity firms in Europe. They vary in many ways, in terms of size of operation and numbers of investment executives, ownership structure, geographical coverage, focus on industry sectors, stages of investment that they will consider, size of investment and whether they adopt a 'hands-on' (as most do these days) or 'hands-off' approach. With this plethora of firms a concern for the entrepreneur, owner manager or management buyout team looking for investment is therefore knowing how to, and which firm(s) to, approach. Then there are more personal considerations such as the background and experience of individual investment executives, such as whether they have hands-on experience working in particular industry sectors, whether they have a financial, technical or marketing background, how long they have been working in the private equity industry or at the particular firm, what is their style of doing business in terms of an informal or formal approach (there will, of course, always be formalities around term sheets, warranties and other agreements but approaches to business plans, presentations, meetings and written or verbal communications may differ) and, very importantly, the personal chemistry between the investment executive and the entrepreneur.

Unless you are in the fortunate position of knowing the investment executive personally, these 'softer' elements won't really apply at the initial selection stage. Rather, these will become important later when you have made your approach to the private equity firm and are hopefully attending your initial meeting. Then you will be able to assess issues such as the 'chemistry' between you and the investment executive. Needless to say, for a long-term relationship such as that between a private equity investment executive and a business owner, you must be able to get on with each other, so if the chemistry is not right, ask to deal with another executive or move on to another firm. As Bernard Vogel of the venture capital firm Endeavour states in case study 16 on Tagsys, you need to be very selective in choosing your lead investor, even take references on them. They are going to be your partners for many years and you need full trust and understanding.

We saw in Chapter 1 that the vast majority of private equity funds are set up as independent limited liability partnerships. Others are captive funds which are owned by a financial institution, such as a bank or pension fund, and receive their funds for investment as required from the parent. Others are semi-captive funds which raise some of their finance from external investors with the remainder coming from the parent.

Does the ownership and funding structure matter at all to the person(s) seeking private equity or venture capital finance? Most people seeking finance from private equity firms would probably assume that the firms have a ready supply of capital to invest. As we have seen in Chapter 2, in the European context as a whole there are plenty of funds available, particularly for buyouts, less so for technology ventures, though there is not what might be called a 'wall' of money available. In the individual fund context though, the availability of finance depends on the stage in the fund's life and whether the fund and its managers have the successful track record to be able to raise a new fund. While a fund may be in a position to make an initial investment of the required amount in an enterprise, it may not be in a position to make a follow-on investment further down the line if it is not successful in raising a new fund.

Funds structured as limited partnerships usually have a fixed life of 10 years. Within this period the funds invest the money committed to them and by the end of the 10 years they will have had to return the investors' original money, plus any additional returns made. This generally requires the investments to be sold, or to be in the form of quoted shares, before the end of the fund, so the point at which you approach the fund for investment is important. You don't want to be too near the end of a fund's life. Some funds are structured as quoted Venture and Development Capital Investment Trusts (VCITs) and some types of unquoted funds may be able to offer companies a longer investment horizon.

So do ask about the stage of the fund's life, enquire to what extent the firm is allocating potential follow-on financing to the venture from the existing fund and gather views on the success of the existing fund.

## Selecting a private equity firm

You should only approach those private equity firms whose investment preferences match your requirements. So do your research thoroughly, as private equity firms appreciate it when they are approached after careful consideration. How you actually go about selecting the private equity firm and how you approach them is covered later in this chapter.

The key considerations are to address:

▐ the **stage** of your company's development or the **type** of private equity investment required;

▐ the **industry** sector in which your business operates;

▐ the **amount** of finance your company needs;

▐ the **geographical location** of your business operations.

# STAGE/TYPE OF INVESTMENT

The terms that most private equity firms use to define the stage of a company's development are determined by the purpose for which the financing is required.

## Seed

Financing provided to research, assess and develop a business concept, perhaps involving the production of a business plan and prototypes, prior to bringing a product to market and commencing large-scale manufacturing.

Only a few seed financings are undertaken each year by private equity firms. There were just over 400 seed investments in the whole of Europe in 2005 (4% of the total number of European investments), according to the EVCA/Thomson Financial/PwC data. Many seed financings are too small and require too much hands-on support from the private equity firm to make them economically viable as investments. There are, however, some specialist private equity firms which are worth approaching, subject to the company meeting their other investment preferences. Business angels should also be considered for seed financing (see Chapter 6). With business angel capital on a company's board, it may be more attractive to private equity firms when later-stage funds are required.

## Start-up

Financing provided to companies for product development and initial marketing. Companies may be in the process of being set up or may have been in business for a short time, but not have sold their product commercially.

Although many start-ups are typically smaller companies, there are an increasing number of companies that start up with several millions of euros. While many venture capital firms, but not generally the mid to large buyout specialists, will consider high quality and generally larger start-up propositions, there are those who specialize in this stage, subject to the company seeking investment meeting the firm's other investment preferences.

## Other early stage

Financing provided to companies that have completed their product development stage and require further funds to initiate commercial manufacturing and sales. They will not yet be generating a profit.

There were over 3,000 start-up and other early-stage investments in Europe in 2005, representing 29% of the total number of investments, and the average financing per deal was €0.8 million.

## Expansion

Financing provided for the growth and expansion of an operating company, which may or may not be breaking even or trading profitably. Capital may be used to finance increased production capacity, market or product development, and/or to provide additional working capital. Also known as 'development' or 'growth' capital.

More European companies at this stage of development receive private equity than any other. Expansion stage investments represented over 40% of total European investments by number in 2005.

## Management buyout (MBO)

Financing provided to enable current operating management and investors to acquire a significant shareholding in the product line or business they manage.

MBOs range from the acquisition of relatively small formerly family-owned businesses to buyouts of €100 million and much more which may arise from the sale of a subsidiary company of a large corporate, taking a publicly quoted company private and sale by financial shareholders. The amounts concerned tend to be larger than other types of financing, as they involve the acquisition of an entire business.

### Management buy-in (MBI)

Financing provided to enable a manager or group of managers from outside a company to buy into the company with the support of private equity investors.

### Buy-in management buyout (BIMBO)

To enable a company's management to acquire the business they manage with the assistance of some incoming management.

### Institutional buyout (IBO)

To enable a private equity firm to acquire a company, following which the incumbent and/or incoming management will be given or acquire a stake in the business.

This is a relatively new term and is an increasingly used method of buyout. It is a method often preferred by vendors, as it reduces the number of parties with whom they have to negotiate.

Buyouts and buy-ins as a whole represented 22% of total European investments by number in 2005, with an average deal size of €13.5 million.

### Secondary purchase

The purchase of existing shares in a company from another private equity firm or from another shareholder or shareholders.

### Replacement equity

Financing to enable existing non-private equity investors to buy back or redeem part, or all, of another investor's shareholding.

### Rescue/turnaround

Financing made available to an existing business which has experienced trading difficulties with a view to re-establishing prosperity or to rescue it from receivership.

### Refinancing bank debt

To reduce a company's level of gearing.

### Bridge financing

Short-term financing made available to a company in the period of transition from being privately owned to being publicly quoted, ie generally planning to float within a year.

# INDUSTRY SECTOR

Many private equity firms will consider investing in a range of industry sectors – if your requirements meet their other investment preferences. Some firms specialize in specific industry sectors, such as biotechnology, computer-related and other technology areas. Others may actively avoid sectors such as property or film production.

# AMOUNT OF INVESTMENT

The process for private equity investment is similar, whether the amount of capital required is €100,000 or €10 million or more, in terms of the amount of time and effort private equity firms have to spend in appraising the business proposal prior to investment, carrying out financial and commercial due diligence, negotiating terms and dealing with the legal documentation. This makes the medium- to larger-sized investments more attractive for private equity investment, as the total size of the return (rather than the percentage) is likely to be greater than for smaller investments where even the initial appraisal costs might not be covered.

The average size of investment at the key stages was given above. For example, the average financing per deal at the early stage, including start-up, was €0.8 million in 2005. Despite my comments in the preceding paragraph on the willingness or otherwise of venture capital firms to consider smaller investments, it is a common misconception that the focus of the industry is only on the much larger private equity investments. For example, in the UK in 2005 one-third of all companies backed at all stages received sums of less than £200,000. There are a number of private equity firms who will consider investing amounts of venture capital of under £100,000. These tend to include specialist, eg seed capital, and regionally orientated firms in the UK. However, companies initially seeking smaller amounts of private equity are more attractive to private equity firms if there is an opportunity for further rounds of private equity investment later on.

As we have seen in Chapter 6, business angels are perhaps the largest source of smaller amounts of equity finance, often investing amounts ranging between £10,000 and £100,000 in early-stage and smaller expanding companies with the average investment for a business angel at around £75,000.

# GEOGRAPHICAL LOCATION

Many private equity firms in Europe focus specifically on the country where they are based for the purpose of sourcing and making investments. In fact in 2005, according to the EVCA data, 86% of total investments by number were made in the same country of management as that of the private equity firm. Ten per cent were made in other European countries and 4% were made outside Europe. This may be overstating the situation somewhat, as the EVCA data, under the office approach on which the country tables are based, classifies an investment in a company in country 'A' made by a private equity firm headquartered in country 'B' as an investment in country 'B' unless the private equity firm has a local office in country 'A' where the decision to invest is made.

Nevertheless, particularly with smaller private equity firms, there is an emphasis in investing in the country where the private equity firm is based. This is largely for practical reasons, not unconnected with risk. First of all, VCs obviously understand the culture of their own country, the ways of doing business, the industry and marketplace and the legal and tax environment. They have their sources of deals, as we saw in Chapter 5, and their network of VCs, intermediaries and other business contacts.

The relative geographical proximity of the potential investee company makes it easier to meet with management, visit company premises and undertake due diligence and subsequently, post-investment, to be near to the company for monitoring purposes, board meetings and to be on hand to deal with any issues or disasters that might arise. If VCs invest outside their own country, in the absence of a network of local offices, then they have all the issues of different markets, cultures, tax and legal regimes and so on to deal with, not to mention the need for considerable additional time and expense incurred in travelling to the company and its management team. While many VCs might specify in their literature and in private equity association member directories that they invest across Europe or in certain countries, in practice this might not be the case and, all other things being equal, they would prefer an investment that they can keep a close eye on.

Several of the larger, and specialist industry sector, private equity and venture capital firms in Europe do have offices outside their country where they are headquartered, many of these with a network of offices in key European cities and outside Europe, such as the United States. Increasingly firms are opening offices in India, Hong Kong and China and the Middle East, establishing relationships with associated offices in these countries or becoming investors in the private equity funds run by native VC firms. Or these larger firms have a sufficient number of investment executives who can afford the time to appraise and monitor investments.

Specialist private equity and venture capital firms operating in the technology sector (several of which I have listed in Chapter 4) adopt a pan-European approach though with a focus on specific countries, and often cover Europe and elsewhere from a relatively small number of offices, maybe even a single office, perhaps based in key technology centres. They may well look outside their office locations to source interesting deals and to compete with rival firms. If the deal flow is strong locally then there is less incentive to do this. The more specialized a firm, the fewer deals that will be sourced for them to appraise and hence the need to look at a wider international area for deals.

So if your company already has operations in several countries or is looking to do business internationally, maybe expanding into the United States and then into Asia Pacific, or indeed is addressing a global marketplace, you should approach a VC firm that you will be able to work with that has offices in the key countries where you are, or plan to conduct business, or has investment executives who proactively cover these countries.

# CORPORATE VENTURE CAPITAL COMPANIES

Corporate venture capital companies are another possible source of equity finance and their approach can be very similar to private equity firms. They are generally part of larger corporate groups, eg Intel Capital which is the world's largest corporate venture investor and part of Intel Corporation. In its literature, Intel Capital states that it 'seeks out and invests in promising technology companies worldwide. We focus on both established and new technologies that help to develop industry standard solutions, drive global Internet growth, facilitate new usage models, and advance the computing and communications platforms.'

Direct corporate venturing occurs where a corporation takes a direct minority stake in an unquoted company operating in a particular industry or sector that is of strategic interest to the corporate or simply as an investment purely for financial gain. Indirect corporate venturing is where a corporation invests in private equity funds managed by an independent private equity firm. Corporate venturers raise their funds from their parent organizations and/or from external sources.

Corporate venturing developed quite rapidly in the period 1999 to 2001, when many companies joined the dot.com bandwagon. Many fell away in the downturn following this period of excessive enthusiasm, with their portfolio companies either insolvent or sold on to a secondary private equity fund. The established corporate venturers continue to invest proactively in innovative and growth businesses but corporate venturing represents only a small fraction when compared to private equity investment activity. According to EVCA research, *Corporate Venturing 2005 – European Activity Update*, published in October 2006, showed that independent fundraising by European corporates grew to €263 million in 2005, a level exceeded only by the 2000 fundraising boom. European direct corporate venturing investment amounted to €430 million in 2005, a 16% increase compared to 2004, with a 33% increase in the number of investments made. Direct corporate venturing activity is defined as when a corporation takes a direct minority stake in an unquoted company, as distinct from indirect corporate venturing where a corporation invests in private equity funds managed by an independent venture capitalist.

An advantage to the growing technology business of having an active corporate venturer on board in the same or similar industry sector is that you will have access to the large corporate's business, engineering and technology resources and expertise as well as possible introductions to potential customers and suppliers. Many corporate venture capital firms work closely with traditional private equity and venture capital firms, often in syndicated deals, so you can get the best of both worlds.

## HOW TO SELECT AND TARGET PRIVATE EQUITY FIRMS

The most effective way of raising private equity is to select just a few private equity firms to target with your business proposition. Choose those where your business meets their preferences for stage, industry, amount and geographical location.

To help you narrow down your selection of private equity firms to approach, access the EVCA Directory (of member private equity and venture capital firms) and the directories of members of the national private equity and venture capital association for your country. Most of the larger or established corporate venture capital companies are also members of these associations.

The EVCA Directory (Figure 7.1) specifies members' investment preferences (stage of investment or financing stage with the range of investment that they will usually consider, industry sectors and geographical preferences). It also includes details on the type of firm (eg independent or captive), the total amount of capital under management (ie the amount of capital available to a management team for making investments), the size of individual funds with their vintage years (the year of the fund's first closing, ie the year in which a fund has raised an initial sum of money with which to commence its investment programme) and the focus of investment of the fund (eg buyout, early-stage). Additional details such as office locations or number of staff may also be given.

National association directories may give additional information. For example, the BVCA Directory of Members, in addition to showing the total funds managed, also shows how much of those funds has already been invested (Figure 7.2). It also shows how many investments are already in the firm's portfolio of investments and lists a selection of companies where the firm has made investments as lead investor. Average current investment size is also given.

Copies of these directories are usually available free of charge to those seeking private equity investment by telephoning the associations or requesting copies via the website. Searchable versions of the directories are also available. See www.evca.com (for details on members of the European Private Equity and Venture Capital Association) and www.bvca.co.uk (for details on members of the BVCA), for example.

The inclusion of companies in which investments have actually been made can be extremely helpful as it allows you to see if the VC firm is actually making investments in your industry sector and not just saying that it will invest in the sector. Avoid those firms who say they consider all industry sectors, all stages of investment, all locations. Unless they are one of the larger, truly international firms it is unlikely that they will invest in all these different areas of focus. Even the larger firms these days tend to focus on buyouts and not so much on early-stage where you need to approach the specialist venture firms.

The EVCA and BVCA directories also list financial organizations, such as mezzanine firms, fund of funds managers and professional advisers, such as accountants and lawyers, who are experienced in the private equity field.

Do view the websites of the private equity and venture capital firms to narrow down your selection further. The websites usually give much more information than the association directories on investment focus, specialist sector teams and descriptions of portfolio company investments.

As discussed below, professional advisers, such as your accountant or lawyer, may be able to introduce you to their private equity contacts and assist you in selecting the right private equity firm. If they do not have

## Sofinnova Partners

| | |
|---|---|
| • Address | 17 rue de Surène, FR – 75008 Paris |
| • Telephone | 33 1/53.05.41.00 |
| • Fax | 33 1/53.05.41.29 |
| • Email | info@sofinnova.fr |
| • Website | www.sofinnova.fr |
| • Staff Size | 25 (Local Staff) |

| | |
|---|---|
| • Contact | Mr. Jean-Bernard Schmidt |
| • Partners | Mr. Jean-Bernard Schmidt |
| | Mr. Denis Lucquin |
| | Mr. Oliver Protard |
| | Mr. Antoine Papiernik |
| | Mr. Jean Schmitt |
| | Mrs. Monique Saulnier |
| • Type of firm | GP — Independent (no parent) |
| • Capital managed/advised | EUR 900,000,000 |

| | |
|---|---|
| • Financing stages | Seed, Start-up, Other early-stage |
| • Type of financing | Majority Equity |
| • Industry sectors | Biotechnology, Computer: semiconductors, Computer: Software, Electronics, Medical, Telecoms: hardware, Internet technology, Nanotechnology |
| • Geographical preferences | Belgium, France, Germany, Switzerland, United Kingdom, United States of America, Denmark, Italy, Netherlands, Norway |

| | |
|---|---|
| • Fund managed/advised | Sofinnova Capital V |
| • Fund capital | EUR 385,000,000 |
| • Vintage year | 2005 |
| • Fund investment focus | Early-stage fund |

| | |
|---|---|
| • Fund managed/advised | Sofinnova Capital IV |
| • Fund capital | EUR 330,000,000 |
| • Vintage year | 2000 |
| • Fund investment focus | Early-stage fund |

| | |
|---|---|
| • Fund managed/advised | Sofinnova Capital III |
| • Fund capital | EUR 121,000,000 |
| • Vintage year | 1999 |
| • Fund investment focus | Early-stage fund |
| • Contact IT | Mr. Oliver Protard |
| • Contact life sciences | Mr. Denis Lucquin |

| | |
|---|---|
| • Remarks | Sofinnova Partners is an independent venture capital company based in Paris. We invest primarily in early-stage projects in information technology and life sciences, in France and in other European countries. Other members of our investment team: Alain Rodermann (Partner IT); Rafaele Tordjman (Partner LS). We have special relations with Sofinnova Ventures, our sister firm based in San Francisco, USA. |

Source: EVCA Directory 2006

**Figure 7.1**  Example of EVCA Directory entry

## Amadeus Capital Partners Limited

---

Mount Pleasant House, 2 Mount Pleasant,
Cambridge, CB3 0RN
Tel: 01223-707 000
Fax: 01223-707 070
Email: info@amadeuscapital.com
Website: www.amadeus capital.com

---

**Investment executives:** 15 (UK)

**Total funds invested:** £229 million (UK)

**Total funds managed/advised:** £288 million (UK)

**Current portfolio size:** 21 (UK), 7 (Continental Europe),
7 (Outside Europe)

**Investment as lead investor:** Clearswift Systems Ltd,
Optos plc, AePONA Group Ltd, PacketFront AB, Agilic Aps

**Minimum investment:** £1 million (Amadeus II)
No minimum (AMSF)

**Maximum Investment:** £20 million

**Stages of investment:** Seed, Start-up, Other early stage,
Expansion/Development, Bridge finance, Secondary
purchase/Replacement capital, Rescue/Turnaround, MBI

**Industry preferences:** Medical/Health related,
Chemicals and materials, Communications, Media and
photography, Information technology hardware, Software
and computer services, Internet technology, Electronics,
Nanotechnology

**Geographical preferences:** UK and Western Europe,
Near/Middle East

**Contacts:** Richard Anton, Shantanu Bhagwat, Alastair
Breward, Simon Cornwell, Will Dawson, Bill Earner,
Anne Glover, Hermann Hauser, Laurence John, Andrey
Kessel, Barak Maoz, Roy Merritt, Edward Snow, Andrea
Traversone, Jeppe Zink

**Other UK Offices:** London

Source: BVCA Directory 2006/7

**Figure 7.2**  Example of BVCA Directory entry

suitable contacts or cannot assist you in seeking private equity, obtain a copy of the EVCA and/or national association directories and refer to the professional advisers listed in the 'Associate Members' section.

## Avoid the scattergun approach

## VC Tip #5

Be selective in which VCs you contact – avoid the scattergun approach!

In Chapter 5 we saw that private equity firms obtain their deal flow from a variety of sources, including 'cold' or unsolicited approaches direct from entrepreneurs and others seeking finance, perhaps having researched the entries in the directories of members of the private equity associations, introductions from intermediaries, such as accountants and lawyers, referrals from their own portfolio company managers and introductions from other VC firms, maybe as part of a proposed syndicated investment.

The private equity firms weight varying degrees of importance to these sources, with perhaps the least importance ascribed to cold approaches from unknown entrepreneurs and management teams. A business plan, or even a synopsis thereof, received cold without any introduction is not likely to receive even the most cursory of reviews by a busy investment executive; it is unlikely even to be scanned over, assuming it gets to the right person after someone has opened the mail. Therefore the worst thing you can do, having carried out your research into appropriate firms whose investment criteria are likely to match your proposition, is to send copies of your proposition to a whole range of venture capital firms all at one go. Far better to find someone who has a good relationship with the venture capital firm who can make an introduction on your behalf.

An introduction from a member of the management team of one of the VC's existing or previous successful portfolio companies is the best way in. Otherwise a knowledgeable adviser, such as an accountant or lawyer experienced in the industry and known to and respected by the VC, could make an introduction on your behalf. An adviser with good contacts in the private equity industry, who regularly works on deals with the private equity firms or maybe provides them with audit, accounting or tax advice, should not only have additional valuable information on which firms to approach but is also more likely to be able to effect a receptive audience for you than if you approach the VC firms cold. Provided the adviser has regular contact with the VC firm he or she should have up-to-date information on their specific investment preferences, eg maybe they are overexposed in a particular industry sector and are not considering additional investments in that area or maybe they have recently taken on a new investment executive with experience in a new sector of specialism for the firm. Such advisers are likely to be associate members of the European or national private equity and venture capital associations.

The VC firm should appreciate that the adviser is likely to have carried out some initial work on the proposition, at least having met with the entrepreneur or management team to understand the elements of the investment proposal and formed his or her own opinion on the quality of the proposal and its proponents. However, beware of advisers who offer to make introductions and find finance for you who don't really have a depth of working contacts in the industry. And as Frank Kenny and Joey Mason of Delta Partners warn in case study 6 on Neoss Limited, if you are an early-stage company avoid using a paid broker type of intermediary adviser if he or she does not know your business and market better than you do and who will make a hefty charge for his or her services. In other situations an adviser can add considerable value, guide and assist you throughout the finance-raising process, provide credibility and ensure that the process is as efficient as possible. The adviser will also ensure that all possible, appropriate sources of finance are considered. Look at how Go4Venture helped Esmertec to raise finance in very difficult conditions in case study 9 below.

In order to meet and develop contacts with the VCs and these potential introducers you need to be active in the marketplace, attending industry events and networking groups such as investment forums, entrepreneur and growing-business conferences and seminars.

If you do not have an adviser or other introducer to make the initial approach to the VC on your behalf then you have no other course but to contact the VC yourself. Do ensure that you write to a specific investment director, the one you have researched from the venture capital firm website or other information who is most likely to be interested in your proposition because it is in the industry sector in which he or she specializes, the geographic area he or she covers or whatever. Do not send your plan cold, addressed simply to the VC firm without addressing a named individual at the firm or it will certainly end up in the wastepaper basket!

# Case study 9

## Esmertec (part one) – how a specialist technology advisory firm assisted with the finance-raising process

Go4Venture is a London-based corporate finance advisory firm focused on providing European technology entrepreneurs and their investors with independent advice to help them develop and execute growth strategies. Go4Venture provides a range of services including capital raising, M&A and strategic advisory.

In 2003 Go4Venture assisted Esmertec AG with its €23 million finance-raising process. Esmertec is a leading provider of world-class software solutions and services for the telecommunications, interactive multimedia and consumer electronics markets and is headquartered in Zurich, Switzerland.

Jean-Michel Deligny, managing director of Go4Venture, gives his perspectives on the challenges of the finance-raising project.

## Everything in place for attracting VC funding – theoretically

At the start of the finance-raising process in late 2002 Esmertec management and shareholders had every reason to believe that they had all the elements in place for attracting venture capital finance.

The company had been established in 1999, had revenues of around €5 million by 2002/3 and was expecting a substantial increase in revenues to €23 million in 2004 on the basis of filling backlog orders. The company had a unique technology, suitably IP protected, and was the only company in the world able to install Java on any phone, including the mass market phones with small processors and little memory. All market studies pointed to a strong target market for mobile phones, driven by exploding demand in developing countries. In addition, analysts agreed that Java was becoming essential in the mobile phone industry as it allows operators to provide sophisticated applications regardless of the underlying hardware platforms.

Management approached VC investors at the end of 2002 seeking €15–18 million using the existing relationships that Esmertec board members had with VCs. The existing investors were Partners Group, a large Swiss asset management firm with a few direct private equity investments, Earlybird, a Munich-based early-stage fund, and Sofinnova Partners, one of Europe's leading VCs managed out of Paris, France. Altogether the financial investors owned just short of 70% of Esmertec. While the VC investors were clearly interested in Esmertec's proposition, no offers of finance were forthcoming. This was perhaps due to the more cautious mood of investors at that time (immediately following the dot.com debacle) and the difficulty of ascribing a value to a company whose revenues were increasing exponentially.

## Specialist adviser brought in to assist with the finance raising

Owing to the difficulties that management were experiencing in raising VC finance, the Esmertec board decided to bring in an adviser to assist with the process. They considered advisers ranging from large investment banks (in view of a potential IPO) to one-person consultancies. They chose Go4Venture on the basis of the firm's mix of investment banking skills, specialist equity private placement skills, specialist sector expertise and the close attention that they could expect from a boutique adviser such as Go4Venture.

## Challenges faced in the finance-raising process

As Go4Venture got to work on the finance raising it became evident that there were several challenges:

- Too narrow a selection of VCs had been approached: the board and existing investors had been helpful in introducing Esmertec to various VCs but many other, and more suitable, VCs had not been considered. Go4Venture ensured that all relevant VCs in Europe, the United States and Asia were considered: a total pool of over 80 potential investors.
- Revenues had not been substantiated by management: while the revenue projections provided to potential investors were impressive, they were not backed up with substantiating documentation. Go4Venture's financial-modelling specialist led the production, with Esmertec's team, of detailed and credible bottom-up financial projections.
- Insufficient evidence to support the target valuation: Go4Venture put considerable effort into documenting the valuation of the company included in the placing documentation. Go4Venture's work consisted of assembling a detailed set of comparables (both M&A and publicly quoted comparables), as well as

producing a discounted cash flow based on the financial projections of the company, together with a detailed discussion of how qualitative factors may influence the results of these various approaches. In addition, data from other similar private equity financings was provided to potential investors in order to substantiate the point that, although demanding, the valuation was in line with other comparable private equity transactions. In all, the valuation document was 55 pages long, with data appendices close to 100 pages.

- Keeping existing investors satisfied: some of the fundraising objectives were not necessarily to the advantage of existing shareholders, eg maximizing the valuation of the company while keeping the term sheet acceptable to existing investors. Go4Venture put in place a process which explained to existing investors the trade-offs between the terms of the deal and the valuation that the market at large was prepared to offer. This proved essential in closing the deal.

With the detailed business plan, financial projections and valuation document now all prepared, potential investors were able to decide quickly whether Esmertec was a suitable investment proposition with a risk/reward profile that they were prepared to underwrite.

## Innovative approach to valuation

However, many of the VCs approached now started to force Esmertec into a deal at a low valuation in what they saw as a buyers' market. Go4Venture knew that the existing investors in Esmertec had said they would be prepared to underwrite the financing required by the company but they were obviously keen to get a third party to price the transaction. Armed with that information, and the appreciation of what was a fair market price for the company that had been gathered during the extensive discussion process with the previous set of potential VCs, Go4Venture decided on a highly innovative approach. A term sheet was issued with a pre-money valuation which increased over time, with offers invited from VCs on a first committed, first served basis.

This had the desired effect and the financing round was oversubscribed, with Esmertec raising €23 million instead of the €15–18 million originally envisaged and with five new investors joining the original VC investors.

## Jean-Michel Deligny's tips for entrepreneurs

Jean-Michel Deligny has the following tips for entrepreneurs who are seeking venture capital based on the lessons learned from the Esmertec case:

- Use your discussions with VCs to get a feel as to what is a fair market price for the business (pre-money valuation).
- Keep your finger on the pulse of the market to know what cycle it is in. As the market picks up so should the valuation, so keep an eye on recent deals.
- Make sure you have people on your team who have the resource to ensure that full and complete documentation is prepared for the investors to consider and the experience to know exactly what investors want included in the documentation.
- Orchestrate some competition among the potential investors in order to get the best deal. This may not necessarily be in terms of the price (as by that stage in the process you should already have an idea of the fair market price) but more in respect of all the other terms of a deal.
- Have someone in the team who is in charge of coordinating all the negotiating positions across the various options.
- Consider appointing an adviser to guide and assist you throughout the finance-raising process, to provide credibility and to ensure that the process is as efficient as possible. After all, you would not even consider completing an M&A transaction without an adviser – why should you go through a financing on your own?

In Esmertec part two (case study 18) we will look at the issues that the company faced as it went through an IPO and post the IPO.

www.go4venture.com

# APPROACHING VCS WITH YOUR PROPOSITION

Avoid contacting or sending your business plan to a whole range of VCs at the same time. Far better to obtain feedback from two or three VCs initially on your proposition so that you can make any changes to the plan before sending it to the next set of VCs on your list. Most VCs who have taken the time to review your plan, or more likely just the executive summary at this early stage in the process, should be prepared to provide you or your introducer with a least some feedback on what changes need to be made or additional information provided if they are interested in proceeding further, or to give brief reasons why they are not interested in proceeding further. You can then incorporate any recommendations, if you agree with them of course, before approaching other VCs. Culturally, European VCs are likely to be less forthcoming with the real reasons why they do not wish to invest than US VCs who tend to spell things out, especially if it is to do with personal chemistry. So you may have to draw them out or use your adviser to act as an intermediary on the debriefing.

Of course, this approach all takes time, so do allow several weeks for getting the VCs interested in your proposition.

## VC Tip #6

Get feedback on your business plan from one or two VCs before sending it to others on your list.

It is better not to send your entire business plan to the venture capital firm at this initial stage in the process when you are simply checking out those VCs who might be interested in hearing more about your proposition. Send them the executive summary to your plan, as long as this covers all the key areas set out below, or a short synopsis of the business plan, around 3 to 5 pages in length. It should not be much longer than this if you want the VC to read it, and it needs its own 'hook' in the first page, ie the reason for the VC to read further, eg your elevator pitch, amount of money being sought and the return that you think might be achievable. This short document needs to cover certain key areas. It is essentially a sales pitch, the purpose of which is to get you a meeting with the VC at which point you will have the opportunity to set out your proposition in detail. The VC may request to see the full business plan before meeting with you or may prefer you to outline your investment proposal at the meeting and then study the plan in detail. For the 'sales pitch' document, include a description of your 'big idea' and its USP, the business model as to how revenues and profits will be generated, the key qualities of the management team and ideally their experience of growing and running successful businesses before, and, very importantly, how you believe the VC will make a handsome return on his or her investment. Revisit the 'Six questions investors ask to determine company value' set out in Chapter 5 and make sure that these are covered in your short 'sales pitch' document.

Incidentally, all these areas need to be covered in the executive summary to the full business plan, but there is more on business plans in Chapter 8. At the end of the day you want to be in the position where between 10 and 20 VCs are actively reviewing your full business plan, having already expressed interest in your proposition from your introductory calls, executive summary and/or 'sales pitch' document or, better still, you have obtained initial meetings with them. For those who are reading the business plan first, aim to obtain initial meetings with half of this group. Eventually aim to negotiate a deal with between two and five VCs. It will help your negotiations if there is an element of competition in the deal.

## 'ELEVATOR' PITCHES

When you are approaching a VC or other investor, or indeed any business contact, for the first time you need to be able to describe in a few, brief words what your business, or investment proposal, is all about. You should be able to describe your company, its products or services and what makes it different from its competitors (ie its unique selling point (USP)) in roughly the time it would take to ride up with someone in a lift, ie around 30 seconds. In many business situations this is all the time you will have with a contact to get your point across. This so-called 'elevator pitch' needs to be concise, carefully planned and well rehearsed. It must be delivered with passion and in terms that anyone can understand. It needs to have a 'hook' for the listener so that he or she is sufficiently interested to want to follow up with you when there is more time to talk (if not at that point in time). In the general business context the elevator pitch should include a brief overview of what your business does, what your main market is, what value or benefits you provide to your customers and your competitive advantage – all in two or three sentences at the most! In the VC context the pitch is similar but should include why you are looking for investment and what's in it for the VC.

## VC Tip #7

Practise your 'elevator pitch': a 60-second pitch about your business that *anyone* can understand. Must have a 'hook', USP and be delivered with passion and don't forget to follow up.

Getting your elevator pitch across to a whole range of potential business contacts is just a part of the whole networking process that you will need to keep going all the time. But don't expect a cold contact to warm immediately to you and your idea just because you've given them your elevator pitch. Building up a good business relationship takes time and the need to build trust and confidence between both parties. Don't oversell to them at the first meeting. Take time to enquire about their business and interests, be a good listener, ask questions and generally show interest. Don't get straight into the details of your business right at the start.

Here is my own personal elevator pitch, which covers a variety of my own situations, as an example:

> Hello. My name is Keith Arundale and I am a speaker, author and visiting university lecturer in venture capital and entrepreneurship. My company, Arundale Consulting Limited, provides business planning and finance-raising advice and support for high-growth ventures and marketing and business development advice for venture capital and professional services firms. I was with PricewaterhouseCoopers for many years where latterly I led the venture capital and business development programmes for PwC's Global Technology Industry Group in Europe. I helped to grow the group into the leading player in the industry in terms of listed company audit appointments and growth company clients in Europe. You can benefit from my knowledge, experience and wide range of contacts in the venture capital industry as you go about your finance-raising exercise.

This might be suitable for an elevator ride up the Empire State Building! Of course, in real life I would tailor it down to fit in with the particular service I was interested in promoting, be it helping an entrepreneur or team with finance raising, assisting a VC firm with due diligence on a potential investment or working with VCs and a professional services firm on their marketing and business development.

The whole point of an elevator pitch in the VC context is to get the opportunity to meet with a VC to explain your proposition further, either via an intermediary or directly. Usually the VC will want to see your business plan, or executive summary, before he or she meets with you, but not necessarily. The whole point of the business plan, from the point of view of attracting investment, is to get the opportunity to meet with a VC. So the first meeting you have with a VC is key and probably your only opportunity to really pitch your proposition to him or her. You are unlikely to get another chance. The process is not dissimilar from applying for employment with a company. You write in to a named individual at the company after having carried out your research into the company and who exactly to approach. The cover letter to your CV, which itself is tailored to the position, relevant and succinct, needs to be sufficiently attractive, interesting and different to get you noticed. You are then hopefully invited to an interview.

When you meet with a potential VC or introducer for the first time, remember the old adage that 'you never get a second chance to make a first impression'. First impressions count, so practise your elevator pitch, look the part and act professionally

## VC Tip #8

Network vigorously with VCs and other potential sources of finance, follow up your contacts and keep your contacts live.

---

### Tips for high-growth ventures

Karl Feilder, a successful serial entrepreneur and CEO of a number of VC-backed businesses, and former angel investor in the UK, has the following tips for technology entrepreneurs looking for VC financing:

- Ask yourself and your team if you are the right people to pursue a high-growth start-up business in terms of stamina, motivation and enthusiasm.
- You must have real passion to succeed, faith in yourself and the team must have faith in their leader.
- Talk to VCs a lot; build your networks with VCs to help in securing finance.
- Don't produce a huge 100-page business plan; a 25-slide presentation may suit your audience well (backed up with financial spreadsheets and appendices as necessary).
- Before that, send a 'tease' letter to the VCs to 'hook' them and get their interest in meeting you.
- Ensure you can justify and back up, if possible, the assumptions you have made in your plan and projections.
- When the VCs are on board, ensure effective and frequent communication with the VC investor.
- Look the part when you meet with investors – first impressions and appearances do count!

We will cover how to approach the initial meeting with the venture capital firm in Chapter 9.

This chapter has been all about how you as the entrepreneur or management team should set about selecting and targeting a private equity firm. In some cases the private equity firm may just target you, as we see in the following case study on Azzurri Communications.

# Case study 10

## Azzurri Communications – an unusual acquisitive start-up/management buy-in

Azzurri Communications (Azzurri) was founded in June 2000 with the aim of creating the first independent national voice and data consultancy company in the UK to fill the gap between the small telecoms dealers and international companies.

3i, a world leader in private equity and venture capital investing focusing on buyouts, growth capital and venture capital, and funds managed by 3i invested £25 million for a majority stake in the company on Azzurri's formation. Working closely alongside the management team, 3i helped the company achieve its first phase of development involving 15 strategic acquisitions.

Julian Davison, a partner in 3i's European Buyouts business, led the Azzurri deal and commented as follows on how 3i worked closely with Azzurri in developing the business concept and model and adding value during the life of 3i's investment.

The Azzurri story is very much a case of the VC seeking out the entrepreneur rather than the other way around as is usually the case.

## Background

3i was looking for highly experienced managers as buy-in candidates for suitable businesses. Through its People Programmes network 3i met Martin St Quinton, the former CEO of Danka plc's international operations. 3i presented him with an interesting proposition: 'If we give you £100 million, what would you do with it?' Working closely together, 3i's telecoms sector specialists, Martin and Julian Davison decided to create a buy-and-build vehicle for the telecoms reseller market focused on small- to medium-sized businesses. They developed a clear strategy of growth through acquisition and fleshed out a business plan together. Steve Dalton joined Azzurri as CFO and they made their first acquisition in the first six months of trading.

## Growth through acquisition

Two more acquisitions followed in the first year and then 12 more. 3i invested equity to support the first few acquisitions, with later purchases funded from cash flow and new debt facilities. The intention was to create a platform capable of generating strong organic growth without the need for further acquisitions.

## How 3i added value to the acquisitions process

3i introduced an experienced private equity chairman, Alan Cornish, to the management team of Azzurri in 2002. He had previously been deputy chairman of another successful 3i investment, the market research company MORI, and chairman of 3i-backed Local Press and was also a non-executive director of TeleCity plc. Alan Cornish built up a management structure that was appropriate for a rapidly growing business, acted as a sounding board for the CEO and led the board's thinking on strategic development.

3i worked closely with Azzurri's chief executive and the management team over a six-year period to help them acquire businesses which would in turn create a platform capable of generating strong organic growth. 3i added further value for Azzurri by introducing the company to several of its portfolio companies, including Target Express, MORI and NCP, leading to highly lucrative contracts. Julian himself provided 3i's board-level input, playing a key part in helping to implement the acquisition strategy, integrate the acquired businesses and drive strong organic growth.

The management team and all of the staff were incentivized with a total of 25% of the equity, with 3i holding 75%.

## Exit

3i ran a highly competitive exit process, running a proposed AIM listing alongside sale discussions with trade buyers and private equity houses. In June 2006 3i sold its 75% stake in Azzurri, to a secondary buyout vehicle backed by Prudential Ventures (PPM) in a deal valuing the company at £182.5 million. 3i's proceeds from the sale of £115 million represented an IRR of 38% and a money multiple of almost 5 times its initial investment.

Azzurri Communications is now one of the largest converged voice, data, and managed service companies in the UK. It's annualized turnover in 2006 was in excess of £100 million. There are around 800 employees nationwide. Partnering with leading manufacturers and networks, Azzurri provides solutions that include voice, data, networking, digital print and mobile. Azzurri also provides consultancy such as in-depth communications audits for large corporations and comprehensive telecoms management services.

Azzurri was a classic private equity deal for 3i having a great management team, a good market opportunity and with management having a real focus on building value for shareholders.

www.3i.com

# 8

# The keys to a successful business plan

## PURPOSE OF THE BUSINESS PLAN

If you are setting up a new business, growing an existing business either organically or through acquisitions, or undertaking a management buyout you need a business plan. It is an essential document for the entrepreneur, owner managers and management teams to formally assess the market needs and the competition, review the business's strengths and weaknesses, identify its critical success factors and what strategy, tactics and actions must be carried out in order to achieve profitable growth. It can be used to agree and set targets for you and your management team and address any gaps in the team, help plan for succession, review and help streamline or reorganize your existing operations and maximize internal financial resources. It is an important practical working document which should be reviewed regularly by you and your team and updated.

A business plan should therefore not just be prepared for the purpose of raising finance. However, in many situations this is when a business plan is first prepared. In the context of raising finance the business plan's main purpose is to market your business proposal to the providers of finance, including the private equity investors. It should show potential investors that if they invest in your business, you and your team will give them a unique opportunity to participate in making an excellent return on their investment.

In the finance-raising context the business plan is likely to follow on from a shorter document in terms of the process of approaching private equity firms, either the executive summary of the plan itself or a 'sales pitch' document, as we saw in the previous chapter, whose purpose is to capture the initial interest of a VC in terms of them asking to see the full plan or setting up an initial meeting to hear the entrepreneur or management team outline their business proposition. However, it is the business plan itself which should be thought out in full, researched and prepared first, with the other, shorter documents effectively being derivatives of the full plan.

## Management team should prepare plan

The entrepreneur or company's management should prepare the business plan. It should not be written by people external to the team, for example by advisers or people who offer a business plan writing service. Private equity investors want to learn what you and your management are planning to do, not see how well others can write for you.

## VC Tip #9

Write the business plan yourself – investors want to learn what you and your team are planning to do, not see how well others can write for you!

Allow plenty of time for writing the plan. Its production frequently takes far longer than management expects. The entrepreneur, owner or managing director of the business should be the one who takes responsibility for its production, but it should be 'owned' and accepted by the management team as a whole and be seen to set challenging but achievable goals that they are committed to meeting. It will probably require several off-site 'away days' to debate strategy and tactics with your team members, days of research on market analysis, channels to market, production and other operational aspects and hours of writing and rewriting before you have a finished product that all your key team members are happy with. It is worth putting the effort into creating a plan that you are proud of and that you are confident will assure an investor why your business will be successful, convey what is so unique about your business and convince him or her to commit the required finance to your venture. Not only should the business plan be prepared to a high standard, it must also be capable of verification. Statements made in the plan need to be defensible with facts, since the business plan is the document against which due diligence will be carried out.

## Business plan must be realistic

While you will naturally want to 'sell' your ideas to the reader, don't oversell things, for example by overstating the potential market for your product or service on purpose, or being over-optimistic in preparing the financial projections – just be realistic. Set out any areas of uncertainty or other concerns in the plan. Private equity firms will appreciate your honesty here and they won't then think that you are trying to pull the wool over their eyes in other areas. But do have ideas to put to them as to how you plan to address these gaps. And if there are flaws in the technology you are presenting it will be best to wait until these have been satisfactorily addressed and resolved. As we saw in Chapter 5, venture capital firms are not keen to take on technology risks in an investment proposition.

The business plan should never remain static. Both as an operational document and as a means to secure funding it needs to be kept up to date. As you receive feedback from potential investors and others on your business proposition, the business model and the plan itself, or as you come across new market data or technological and production advances, incorporate what you have learnt and other changes into the plan. Use the plan to monitor progress with the company's own milestones and targets, and those set by your investors in due course.

Professional advisers can provide a vital role in critically reviewing the draft plan, acting as 'devil's advocate' and helping to give the plan the appropriate focus. However, it is you who must write the plan. As Frank Kenny and Joey Mason of Delta Partners stated in case study 6 on Neoss Limited a well-thought-out brief presentation prepared by yourselves in order to attract start-up financing is preferable to a huge, glossy business plan prepared professionally by someone else. An existing VC investor may even help you with the preparation of your business plan for second-round financing.

# VALID BUSINESS PROPOSITION

Before you put pen to paper you should first of all ensure that you have a valid business proposition. As Phil O'Donovan states in case study 11 on Cambridge Silicon Radio, you need to get the business model right and for a technology company you need a solid product with its own IP that can rapidly gain a major share in a global market.

In his book *The New Business Road Test*, Professor John Mullins of London Business School sets out what entrepreneurs should do before writing a business plan. He says that fewer than 1% of the business plans submitted to venture capitalists will be successful in raising money because of fundamental flaws in the business ideas therein.

John Mullins recommends that before you write your business plan you should:

1. Come up with an idea that you think might fly, one that solves genuine customer problems or needs.
2. Assess and shape the idea, using the seven domains framework (see below). To do this requires lots of data, from secondary sources such as trade and other business publications, government reports etc and from primary sources such as interviews, focus groups or surveys of prospective customers and/or industry participants.
3. Write a customer-driven feasibility study which is effectively a memo to yourself that lays out the conclusions you have reached from your data and analysis and the conclusions of the seven domains road test (see below).

If you take these steps John believes that you will be well prepared to write a 'truly great business plan, one that acknowledges the merits and shortcomings of your opportunity, develops a strategy and shows that your team is the right one to pursue it'.

John cautions against confusing market and industry attractiveness. If they are both important they should be addressed separately: 'judgements about the attractiveness of the market one proposes to serve may be very different from judgements about the industry in which one would compete'.

John Mullins' seven domains framework (Figure 8.1) is made up of four market and industry domains (at the macro (broad, market-wide) level: market attractiveness and industry attractiveness; at the micro (particularly to a specific segment) level: target segment benefits and attractiveness and sustainable advantage) and three additional domains related to the entrepreneurial team (mission, aspirations and propensity for risk; ability to execute on critical success factors; connectedness up, down and across the value chain). His book shows how the seven domains framework can be used to spot flaws in your business idea and work out how they can be fixed.

From his research John also points out five common traps to avoid in an investment proposition and offers the following advice to entrepreneurs:

1. *The large market fallacy* – the problem with large markets, especially large markets that are growing fast, is that others (ie your competitors) like them too. For new ventures serving large markets it's generally far better to pursue a large share of a small but care-

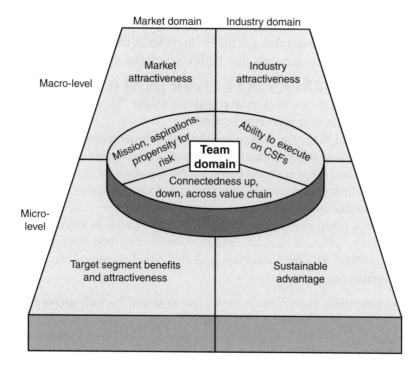

Source: *The New Business Road Test* by John W Mullins – FT Prentice Hall 2003

**Figure 8.1**  The New Business Road Test Seven Domains Framework

fully targeted segment rather than a small share of the overall market.

2. *The better mousetrap fallacy* – better technology (a better mousetrap) does not necessarily equal a better solution for the customer. Entrepreneurial success is not about you and your technology. It's about identifying the right customers and using technology to satisfy their needs.

3. *The no sustainable business model trap* – the benefits for which a group of target customers are willing to pay and a cost structure that makes the intended product or service economically viable must be sustainable.

4. *The me-too trap* – the combination of low barriers to entry and a lack of sustainable advantage should be a red flag to would-be entrepreneurs. Stop before you start!

5. *The hubris trap* – even previously successful serial entrepreneurs can stumble. Having done it before is a great advantage when it comes to fundraising but it does not obviate the need for attention to John's seven domains.

I recommend that you take the 'New Business Road Test'. John's book is well worth a read before you start writing your business plan.

## ESSENTIAL AREAS TO COVER IN THE BUSINESS PLAN

A business plan (Figure 8.2) covering the following areas should be prepared before a private equity firm is approached:

▌ executive summary;

▌ the market;

▌ the technology and product or service;

▌ the management team;

▌ business operations;

▌ financial projections;

▌ amount and use of finance required and exit opportunities.

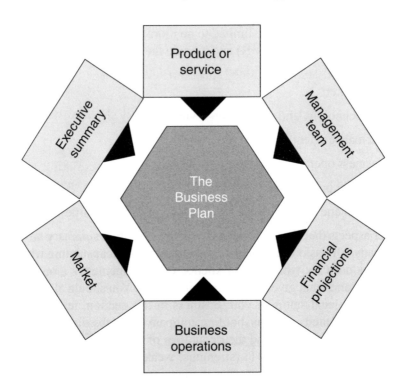

**Figure 8.2**  The business plan

# EXECUTIVE SUMMARY

This is the most important section and is best written last. It summarizes your business plan and is placed at the front of the document. It is vital to give this summary significant thought and time, as it may well determine the amount of consideration the private equity investor will give to your detailed proposal. It should be clearly written and powerfully persuasive, yet balance 'sales talk' with realism in order to be convincing. It needs to be convincing in conveying your company's growth and profit potential and management's prior relevant experience. It needs to clearly encapsulate your company's USP (ie its unique selling point – why people should buy your product or service as distinct from your competitors').

The executive summary of the business plan is rather like the 'sales pitch' document referred to in Chapter 7 and in some cases may well substitute for this other document. The executive summary should be used as 'bait' to get a potential investor hooked and interested to learn more about the opportunity, either by continuing to delve into the rest of the business plan if he or she has it already, requesting to see the full plan or, even better, setting up an initial meeting to discuss the opportunity with the entrepreneur or management team.

The summary should be limited to no more than two to three pages (ie around 1,000 to 1,500 words) and include the key elements from all the sections below:

- the market;
- the technology and product or service;
- the management team;
- business operations;
- financial projections;
- amount and use of finance required and exit opportunities.

Other aspects that should be included in the executive summary are your company's 'mission statement' – a few sentences encapsulating what the business does for what type of clients, the management's aims for the company and what gives it its competitive edge. You should also explain the current legal status of your business in this section, ie its incorporation as a limited company, holding company and subsidiary companies structure, if applicable, and their countries of incorporation. You should include an overall 'SWOT' (strengths, weaknesses, opportunities and threats) analysis that summarizes the key strengths of your proposition and its weaknesses and the opportunities for your business in the marketplace and its competitive threats.

# THE MARKET

You need to convince the private equity firm that there is a real commercial opportunity for the business and its products and services in a large and expanding marketplace. You will need to provide evidence of how the market is growing, not just in the short and medium terms but how growth is sustainable in the longer term and how your company will capture its stake in that growing marketplace in terms of both revenues and, more importantly, profits.

This requires a careful analysis of the market potential for your products or services and how you plan to develop and penetrate the market, ie what is your strategy to achieve this. What about pressures from existing competitors? Why should customers buy your product or service? How will you sustain competitive advantage? If you are looking for finance to fund a technology start-up or spinout company you will need to convince investors of the commercial potential for applications of your technology.

Even if your business plan is documented with market data VCs may still want hard evidence of customer contracts in place or even customer revenues being generated.

## VC Tip #10

Go overboard on the marketing section of the plan: it's often the most deficient part of the investment proposition.

## Market analysis

This section of the business plan will be scrutinized carefully; market analysis should therefore be as specific as possible, focusing on believable, verifiable data. Include under market research a thorough analysis of your company's industry and potential customers. Include data on the size of the market, growth rates, recent technical advances, government regulations and trends – is the market as a whole developing, growing, mature, or declining? Include details on the number of potential customers, the purchase rate per customer, and a profile of the typical decision-maker who will decide whether to purchase your product or service. This information drives the sales forecast and pricing strategy in your plan. Finally, comment on the percentage of the target market your company plans to capture, with justification in the marketing section of the plan.

Existing data on the market, if available, can be obtained from government sources, business libraries, including such organizations as the British Library and Institute of Directors in the UK, the press, IDC and Gartner research studies, company literature and the internet. In the case of a specific new technology, existing market data may not be readily available and you may need to carry out, or commission, original research into its likely acceptance by potential customers. There is no point in developing a fantastic cutting-edge technology product if no one wants to buy it, though this has been severely underestimated on occasions:

> *'There is no reason anyone would want a computer in their home.' Ken Olson, President, Chairman and Founder of Digital Equipment Corporation, 1977*

> *'I think there is a world market for maybe five computers.' Thomas Watson, Chairman of IBM, 1943*

## Marketing plan

The primary purpose of the marketing section of the business plan is for you to convince the private equity firm that the market can be developed and penetrated. The sales projections that you make will drive the rest of the business plan by estimating the rate of growth of operations and the financing required. Explain your plans for the development of the business and how you are going to achieve those goals. Avoid using generalized extrapolations from overall market statistics.

In your plan don't forget to focus on the customer – no matter how good or disruptive the technology. The plan should also include an outline of plans for pricing, distribution channels and promotion as follows.

## Pricing

How you plan to price a product or service provides an investor with insight for evaluating your overall strategy. Explain the key components of the pricing decision – ie image, competitive advantages, supplier costs and gross margins, and the discount structure for each distribution channel. Address to what extent suppliers can control the cost of key components or services, and to what extent customers' attitudes can influence the selling price.

For a technology company the extent of your leadership in the field with a new, especially disruptive, technology will impact on the pricing decision. The pricing strategy should also involve consideration of future product releases.

The potential VC investor is likely to take a very close look at the marketing section of your plan, so don't underestimate the time required to prepare it properly. The VC may want to telephone, or even to meet with, your prospective customers to check that they will be buying your product or service and how they prioritize your offering over other purchases they have budgeted.

## Distribution channels

If you are a manufacturer, your business plan should clearly identify the distribution channels that will get the product to the end-user. If you are a service provider, the distribution channels are not as important as are the means of promotion. Distribution options for a manufacturer may include:

∎ distributors;

∎ wholesalers;

∎ retailers (including online);

∎ direct sales – such as mail order and ordering over the web, direct contact through salespeople and telemarketing;

∎ original equipment manufacturers (OEM) and integration of the product into other manufacturers' products.

Each of these methods has its own advantages, disadvantages and financial impact, and these should be clarified in the business plan. For example, assume your company decides to use direct sales because of the expertise required in selling the product. A direct sales force increases control, but it requires a significant investment. An investor will look to your expertise as a salesperson, or to the plans to hire, train and compensate an expert sales force. If more than one distribution channel is used, they should all be compatible. For example, using both direct sales and wholesalers can create channel conflict if not managed well.

Fully explain the reasons for selecting these distribution approaches and the financial benefits they will provide. The explanation should include a schedule of projected prices, with appropriate discounts and commissions as part of the projected sales estimates. These estimates of profit margin and pricing policy will provide support for the investment decision.

## Promotion

The marketing promotion section of the business plan should include plans for product sheets, potential advertising plans, internet strategy, trade show schedules, and any other promotional materials. The private equity firm must be convinced that the company has the expertise to move the product to market. A well-thought-out promotional approach will help to set your business plan apart from your competitors.

It is important to explain the thought process behind the selected sources of promotion and the reasons for those not selected.

## Competition

A discussion of the competition is an essential part of the business plan. Every product or service has competition; even if your company is first-to-market, you must explain how the market's need is currently being met and how the new product will compete against the existing solution. The investor will be looking to see how and why your company can beat the competition. The business plan should analyse the competition (who are they, how many are there, what proportion of the market do they account for?). Give their strengths and weaknesses relative to your product.

Attempt to anticipate likely competitive responses to your product. Include, if possible, a direct product comparison based on price, quality, warranties, product updates, features, distribution strategies, and other means of comparison. Document the sources used in this analysis.

All the aspects included in the market section of your business plan must be rigorously supported by as much verifiable evidence as possible. In addition to carrying out market research and discussions with your management team, customers and potential customers, you may need input from outside marketing consultants.

# THE TECHNOLOGY AND PRODUCT OR SERVICE

Explain the company's product or service in plain English. If the product or service is technically orientated this is essential, as even if the plan is being reviewed by a specialist technology venture capital executive there may be non-specialists who may need to see it who are less technically qualified.

You will clearly need to set out the product or service's competitive edge or USP. For example, is it:

- a new product?

- totally at the leading edge without any direct competitors?

- available at a lower price than competing products?

▌ of higher technical specifications?

▌ of higher quality?

▌ of greater durability?

▌ faster to operate?

▌ smaller in size?

▌ easier to service and maintain?

▌ offering additional support products or services?

With technology companies where the product or service is new, there has to be a clear 'world class' opportunity to balance the higher risks involved. Address whether it is vulnerable to technological advances being made elsewhere. Include a brief summary of these advances globally, without getting into too much technical detail. Explain how you plan to keep the technology ahead of other developments.

If relevant, explain what legal protection you have on the product, such as patents attained, pending or required. Assess the impact of legal protection on the marketability of the product.

You also need to cover, of course, the price and cost of the product or service.

If the technology product is still under development, the plan should list all the major achievements to date as well as remaining milestones. State whether a working prototype is available or, better still, if trials of the actual product have been carried out such that manufacturing costs are better understood and potential customers have actually sampled and tested the product. State how you have tackled various hurdles and that you are aware of remaining hurdles and how to surmount them. Specific mention should be made in the business plan of the results of alpha (internal) and beta (external) product testing.

For a technology company the legal protection on the product, such as patents attained, pending or required, must be documented. Take care not to disclose any information to the public before a patent application is filed. Investors will assess the impact of legal protection on the marketability of the product and will always ask the following:

▌ Who owns the IP?

▌ In the case of a spinout company, is the IP owned by the university or by other academic organizations or by industrial companies?

▌ How is ownership of the IP to be transferred to the spinout company?

▌ Is the IP licensed to the company in return for a share of royalties or assigned to the company in return for an equity stake in the company?

▌ What happens if the company becomes insolvent – does the IP revert to a university (in the case of a spinout) or other organization or does it remain as an asset for the investors?

Single-product companies can be a concern for investors. It is beneficial to include ideas and plans for a 'second generation' product or even other viable products or services to demonstrate the opportunities for business growth.

# THE MANAGEMENT TEAM

Private equity firms invest in people – people who have run or who are likely to run successful operations. Potential investors will look closely at you and the members of your management team. This section of the plan should introduce the management team and what you all bring to the business. Include your experience, and success, in running businesses before and how you have learnt from not so successful businesses. You need to demonstrate that the company has the quality of management to be able to turn the business plan into reality. After all, investors will be relying on the management team to execute the business plan successfully.

As we saw in Chapter 5, the senior management team ideally should be experienced in complementary areas, such as the technical side, strategy, finance and marketing, and their roles should be specified. The prior experience and special abilities each member brings to the venture should be explained. This is particularly the case with technology companies where it will be the combination of technological and business skills that will be important to the backers. If some members have particular flair and dynamism, this needs to be balanced by those who can ensure that this occurs in a controlled environment.

A concise curriculum vitae should be included for each team member, highlighting their previous track records in running, or being involved with, successful businesses.

Identify the current and potential skills gaps and explain how you aim to fill them. Private equity firms will sometimes assist in locating experienced managers where an important post is unfilled – provided they are convinced about the other aspects of your plan.

In the case of a start-up company or spinout a key consideration will be whether to bring in an external CEO to run the company, leaving the founder to focus on technology and product developments, and maybe technical support for the company, and at what stage in the company's life cycle to bring in the CEO. Certain areas could also be to outsource certain areas to external consultants, for example to help with marketing campaigns or deal with patents. A member of the management board will need to accept responsibility for any outsourced areas.

The business plan should address how the management team and any other key employees will be incentivized. Bringing in people from outside, especially into a start-up, can be difficult, as potential new recruits will be taking a risk in joining the company, maybe even leaving the relative security of possibly well-paid, long-term employment. They need to be compensated for this, usually in terms of stock option plans.

The business plan should include an explanation of what performance measures will be implemented to review the performance of management and employees.

The appointment of a non-executive director (NED) should be seriously considered. NEDs can add significant value to the companies with which they are involved. Many private equity firms at the time of their investment will wish to appoint one of their own executives or an independent expert to your board as an NED. Most private equity executives have previously worked in industry or in finance and all will have a wide experience of companies going through a rapid period of growth and development.

In the case of an early-stage technology company or spinout, you might wish to consider using an advisory board in addition to the legal board of directors. The advisory board may even be set up ahead of the main management team to provide initial guidance to the founder at the earliest stages of looking at the commercialization of the technology.

Auditors, lawyers, bankers and other advisers should also be listed in the plan.

# BUSINESS OPERATIONS

This section of the business plan should explain how the company will carry out its operations, including:

▌ how applications of the technology and/or products will be developed;

▌ how these will be manufactured;

▌ how they will be delivered to customers or end-users;

▌ the company's approach to ongoing research and development.

In the case of a start-up company or spinout the steps needed and the time taken to produce a working prototype and develop a final product should not be underestimated. Many technically orientated founders, and in particular university researchers, naturally focus on the technical aspects of the product. They do not consider in sufficient depth how a new technology will be transformed into commercial reality from both the marketing and operational viewpoints. Bringing in an engineering director experienced in product development at an early stage could be highly beneficial.

The business operations section of the plan should include:

- a timetable and budget for completion of a prototype and the final product;
- the location and size of the planned manufacturing, production and research facilities;
- the availability of labour;
- whether any aspect of the manufacturing is to be outsourced;
- accessibility of materials;
- proximity to distribution channels;
- availability of government grants and tax incentives;
- the equipment used or needed and cost;
- flexibility and efficiency of the facilities;
- applicable safety and employment laws;
- quality control of production;
- requirements for information technology systems.

If more equipment is required in response to production demands, include plans for financing. If your company needs international distribution, mention whether the operations facility will provide adequate support. If work will be outsourced to subcontractors, eliminating the need to expand facilities, state that too. The investor will be looking to see if there are inconsistencies in your business plan.

If a prototype has not been developed or there is other uncertainty concerning production, include a budget and timetable for product development.

The private equity firm will also ask such questions as:

- If sales projections predict a growth rate of 25% per year, for example, does the current site allow for expansion?

▌ Are there suppliers who can provide the materials required?

▌ Is there an educated workforce in the area as a source of potential employees?

These and any other operational factors that might be important to the investor should be included.

Allow a contingency in the plan for slippage, ie to allow management to take action if any key aspects of the development or production plans are delayed.

# FINANCIAL PROJECTIONS

Developing a detailed set of financial projections will help to demonstrate to the investor that you have properly thought out the financial implications of your company's growth plans. Private equity firms will use these projections to determine if:

▌ your company offers enough growth potential to deliver the type of return on investment that the investor is seeking;

▌ the projections are realistic enough to give the company a reasonable chance of attaining them.

Investors will expect to see a full set of cohesive financial statements – including a balance sheet, income statement and cash flow statement, for a period of three to five years. It is usual to show monthly income and cash flow statements until the breakeven point is reached, followed by yearly data for the remaining time frame. Ensure that these are easy to update and adjust. Do include notes that explain the major assumptions used to develop the revenue and expense items and explain the research you have undertaken to support these assumptions.

The financial projections section of the business plan is important but it is not necessarily more important than the other sections of the plan. In his *Harvard Business Review* paper 'How to write a great business plan', which I recommend that you read, Professor William Sahlman states that 'most (business plans) waste too much ink on numbers and devote too little to the information that really matters to intelligent investors. As every seasoned investor knows, financial projections for a new company – especially detailed, month-by-month projections that stretch out for more than a year – are an act of imagination'. So do be careful in predicting revenues and costs and how much capital you need to accomplish your objectives.

## Preparation of the projections

The management team should have regard to the following when considering the assumptions in preparing the projections:

∎ *Sales.* The plan should typically state an average selling price per unit along with the projected number of units to be sold each reporting period. Sales prices should be competitive, depending on the 'uniqueness' of the product in the market, and should take into consideration the cost to produce and distribute the product. Do be realistic with your sales projections, don't overestimate revenues.

∎ *Cost of sales.* Investors will expect accurate unit variable cost data, taking into consideration the labour, material and overhead costs to produce each unit. There should be a good grasp on initial product costing so that it is protected against price pressure from competitors. The fixed costs should also be documented.

∎ *Product development.* Product development expenses should be closely tied to product introduction timetables included elsewhere in the plan. These expenses are typically higher in the earlier years and taper off because product-line extensions are less costly to develop. Investors will focus on these assumptions because further rounds of financing may be needed if major products are not introduced on time.

∎ *Other costs and expenses.* A detailed set of expense assumptions should take into consideration headcount, selling and administrative costs, space and major promotions. It is useful to compare final expense projections with industry norms. All expense categories should be considered.

  Don't underestimate costs, especially of those relating to commercial development and achieving consistent quality expectations and standards.

Other areas where care is required in preparing the projections are as follows:

∎ Assess your present and prospective future profit margins in detail, bearing in mind the potential impact of competition.

∎ Realistically assess cash flow and working capital.

∎ Assess the value attributed to the company's net tangible assets at each projected year-end.

∎ State the level of gearing (ie the debt to shareholders' funds ratio). State how much debt is secured on what assets and the current value of those assets.

❚ Include all costs associated with the business. Remember to split sales costs (eg communications to potential and current customers) and marketing costs (eg research into potential sales areas). What are the sale prices or fee-charging structures?

❚ Provide budgets for each area of your company's activities. What controls do you have in place to ensure that you and your management keep within or improve on these budgets?

❚ Present different scenarios for the financial projections of sales, costs and cash flow for both the short and long term. Ask 'what if?' questions to ensure that key factors and their impact on the financings required are carefully and realistically assessed. For example, what if sales decline by 20%, or supplier costs increase by 30%, or both? How does this impact on the profit and cash flow projections?

If it is envisioned that more than one round of financing will be required (often the case with technology-based businesses in particular), identify the likely timing and any associated progress 'milestones' specified by the investor which need to be achieved before additional funding is considered.

You might wish to consider using an external accountant to review the financial projections and act as 'devil's advocate', asking searching questions about the assumptions used to develop the projections and checking that the projections and assumptions tie in with the rest of the business plan, before presenting your plan and projections to a potential investor.

## AMOUNT AND USE OF FINANCE REQUIRED AND EXIT OPPORTUNITIES

The plan should include the management team's best estimate of how much finance is required by the company to complete any prototypes, commence commercial development and set up the manufacturing operations and distribution channels.

The sources from which the finance is hoped to come should be set out (eg the founder and management team members, government grants and regional funds, business angels, venture capital and private equity firms, banks and others).

Explain what the funds will be used for, whether for capital expenditure or working capital. Include an implementation schedule, including capital expenditure, orders and production timetables, for example.

Consider how the private equity or other investors will make a return, ie by realizing their investment in due course, possibly through a stock market flotation or trade sale. It is important that the options are considered and discussed with your investors.

# TIPS ON THE PRESENTATION OF THE BUSINESS PLAN

Bear the following points in mind when you are writing your business plan.

## Readability

- Make the plan readable. Avoid jargon and general position statements.

- Use simple language – especially if you are explaining technical details.

- Aim the plan at non-specialists, emphasizing its financial viability.

- Avoid including unnecessary detail in the main body of the plan which would make it too lengthy. Put detail into appendices.

Make sure you state clearly, in non-technical language, what the company actually does right at the start of the business plan, ie, in simple terms, what it sells and to whom. There is nothing worse than reading through pages and pages of a business plan and wondering exactly what it is that the company is involved in doing – manufacturing, selling etc, what industry it is in and what markets it is serving.

Ask someone outside the company to check your business plan for clarity and 'readability'.

Remember that the readers targeted will be potential investors. They will need to be convinced of the company's commercial viability and competitive edge and will be particularly looking to see the potential for making a good return.

## Length

The length of your business plan depends on individual circumstances. It should be long enough to cover the subject adequately and short enough to maintain interest. For a multi-million-pound technology company with sophisticated research and manufacturing elements, the business plan could be well over 50 pages, excluding appendices. By contrast, a proposal for €200,000 or so to develop an existing product may be too long at 20 pages in total. It is probably best to err on the side of brevity – for if investors are interested they can always call you to ask for additional information. Unless your business requires several million euros of private equity and is highly complex, I would recommend that the body of the business plan should be no longer than 30 to 40 pages, with as much detail as is required in the appendices.

## Appearance

Graphs and charts should be used to illustrate and simplify complicated information. Use titles and sub-titles to divide different subject matters. Ensure that the plan is neatly typed or printed without spelling, typing or grammar mistakes – these have a disproportionately negative impact. Avoid very expensive documentation, eg with respect to binding and cover design, as this might suggest unnecessary waste and extravagance to investors who will be keen to see that you are careful with their money if they invest in your business.

And finally, remember to keep the plan feasible, avoid being over-optimistic and highlight any challenges and show how they will be met.

## Case study 11

### Cambridge Silicon Radio – the importance of the business model

Cambridge Silicon Radio plc (CSR) is one of Europe's technology success stories. CSR (www.csr.com) is a leading designer, developer and manufacturer of single-chip wireless solutions designed to support data and voice communications between a wide range of products over short-range radio links, using the 2.4 GHz Bluetooth personal area networking standard. More recently, CSR has entered the IEEE 802.11 marketplace, a family of wireless standards also referred to as 'Wi-Fi' or 'Wireless LAN', with devices capable of operation in both the 2.4 and 5 GHz frequency bands.

The international private equity firm, 3i, has been involved with CSR right from the time of its formation, through subsequent financing rounds, through the company's flotation on the London Stock Exchange and remains an investor in CSR. For its part, CSR decided to partner with 3i because 3i had a local office in Cambridge and had deep pockets as well as a global network of contacts. It also recognized that 3i had a track record of backing successful semiconductor manufacturers. This case study looks at how 3i helped CSR with its various financing rounds and how it has added value in other areas.

We hear from Laurence Garrett, director of 3i, who served on the board of CSR as a non-executive director in the period up to its flotation (although a different 3i executive was involved when CSR was formed), and from Dr Phil O'Donovan who is a co-founder of CSR.

## Background

CSR was established in Cambridge, England in 1999 by an engineering and marketing team who previously worked at Cambridge Consultants Limited, a technology consulting firm based in Cambridge. The core founding team of CSR had worked together for more than 10 years on integrating digital processing technology and radio frequency applications using standard CMOS wafer fabrication technology.

When CSR was founded assets were transferred from Cambridge Consultants Limited to CSR in exchange for ordinary shares. This transaction included the assignment, and licence on a non-exclusive, royalty-free basis, of various intellectual property rights.

Following its formation in 1999, CSR's unique single chip was launched in 2000 and CSR started to sell Bluetooth development kits in order to help customers design early Bluetooth products. There was a big marketing push to get the brand out into the marketplace and CSR started to win customers initially in the laptop market segment.

Throughout the downturn of 2001 to 2003 CSR continued to execute its strategy without having to cut any of its workforce. CSR ran its operations from Cambridge and Japan and partnered with TSMC in Taiwan and ST Microelectronics in Switzerland.

During 2002/3 evidence finally came through that Bluetooth was going to be a huge market. Nokia, Ericsson and Motorola all had their own solutions for Bluetooth but saw that CSR provided something extra. Nokia, who were using a two-chip solution before CSR came on the scene, is now a key customer of CSR, though, as a relatively unknown start-up, it took two years for CSR to develop its relationship with Nokia. This was achieved through continual dialogue and by encouraging Nokia to try out CSR's product for themselves.

CSR floated on the London Stock Exchange in April 2004, raising over £300 million, and entered the FTSE 250 in July of the same year. The offering was more than 10 times oversubscribed.

Post-IPO, CSR has achieved an impressive 100% growth per annum. The share price rose from £2 per share to £4 per share in the first year of being listed. 3i has stayed involved as an investor post-flotation, although the other VC investors have sold out. The share price now stands at around £12 per share and CSR has a market capitalization of around £1.2 billion.

## 3i's involvement with CSR

Laurence Garrett, director of 3i, described why and how 3i first got involved with CSR.

There was no evidence that there was a market for Bluetooth when 3i first invested in CSR. CSR's presentation to VCs included a marketing section but there were a lot of unknowns. The timing and size of the Bluetooth market were unknown, although analysts' reports were saying that the market was likely to be significant. The extent of the financing needed to set up and grow CSR to penetrate the market was also not really known.

However, 3i was impressed by the quality of CSR's technology; to perform the wireless air interface and the baseband processing on a single CMOS chip meant that CSR would have a very competitive solution in terms of size, power, and cost. Over 30 competitors entered the market at the same time but most of them were two-chip solutions and often not using CMOS. While CSR did not have first-mover advantage, CSR's unique single chip technology provided the least expensive and lowest power solution in the marketplace.

3i also knew the nine founders from Cambridge Consultants well and, while the team did not have manufacturing experience, 3i were convinced about their technical capabilities and their ability to work together as a team.

£10 million was raised in the initial financing round in late 1998 from three venture capital firms, 3i, Gilde and Amadeus, who all put in equal shares. There were no unusual features in the financing structure.

## How the founder VCs added value in the early stages of CSR

The three VCs brought different aspects to the deal: Amadeus with building profile for CSR through the involvement of Amadeus' co-founder Hermann Hauser, himself a serial entrepreneur who has founded or co-founded companies in a wide range of technology sectors, Gilde with commercial introductions and advice on the technology and legal agreements and 3i with networking contacts and the management recruitment process. 3i brought in CSR's first non-executive chairman, sourced from 3i's People Programme, who had considerable financial and venture capital experience although he had not previously been involved in the semiconductor industry.

3i also helped to recruit a CEO who had extensive experience working in the United States and who brought a team with him who had manufacturing and fabrication experience. This filled a key gap in the founder team's experience as none of the founders had been involved in manufacturing. 3i helped to recruit a CFO and a financial controller. Post-flotation one of the new non-executive directors whom 3i introduced, John Scarisbrick, has been made CEO of CSR.

## Subsequent funding rounds and deals

3i backed CSR through three subsequent funding rounds, along with other VCs, and negotiated a shareholder agreement with Intel Capital in which Intel invested £10 million. In December 2000, 3i underwrote £15 million in a £42 million fundraising exercise with CSFB and Merrill Lynch, although this was not needed in the end.

3i has helped CSR expand its business alliances, negotiate heads of terms for a business agreement with Sony and prepare the company for flotation. This included helping to recruit a new chairman and bringing non-executives onto the board prior to flotation for corporate governance purposes. 3i also co-selected advisers and negotiated the terms of engagement for the IPO. On flotation 3i realized an IRR of 60% on its £10 million investment in the company. 3i held 13% of the shares prior to the float.

More recently, in July 2005, 3i sold its stake in UbiNetics to CSR. The deal, at $48m, along with the sale of the UbiNetics' test and measurement business to Aeroflex in May 2005, delivered an 80% IRR for 3i in less than 18 months. As a founding venture capital investor in both businesses, 3i made the initial introductions which led to CSR's acquisition of the UbiNetics business. 3i's knowledge of CSR made it realize that the UbiNetics handset business would be a fantastic fit for CSR and is another example of how a VC investor, such as 3i, can add real value through its network of contacts and specialist knowledge of industry sectors.

## Laurence Garrett's (3i) tips for entrepreneurs

Laurence Garrett's tips for entrepreneurs seeking venture capital finance, drawn from this particular experience with CSR, are:

- If there is money on the table, take it! It may not be available later.
- First-mover advantage is not always necessary for success. In fact, learning from competitors' first moves into the market can be a distinct advantage.
- Various VC investors, in a syndicate, can all bring different help to the party (as with Amadeus, Gilde and 3i in CSR's case).
- Bring in experts to beef up the management team if necessary (eg the manufacturing people from the United States in CSR's case).

## CSR's views on 3i's and the other VC's involvement

Dr Phil O'Donovan is co-founder of CSR. Dr O'Donovan served as CSR's managing director and sales director from April 1999 until April 2003. Before co-founding CSR, Phil O'Donovan was the vice president of telecommunications at Cambridge Consultants Limited.

Dr O'Donovan confirmed that 3i played a significant role in the company's board meetings and introduced CSR to its first chairman. He said that 3i also introduced the company to a number of partners and advisers and supported CSR through the IPO process.

Unlike Amadeus and Gilde, 3i did not actually take a seat on the board of CSR at the start, in line with 3i's policy at the time not to have board seats. 3i attended board meetings as an observer, taking a board seat later.

Phil got in touch with a total of 12 VCs when he and his colleagues were setting up CSR. Eight of these were solidly interested in CSR's proposition. Phil wanted to work with VCs local to the Cambridge area, if at all possible. This was how Amadeus and 3i got involved. It was Amadeus who introduced the third initial VC, Gilde, to the deal. Herman Hauser of Amadeus added value by asking questions such as 'have you considered this, have you considered that', sharing his vast experience with starting up companies himself. Gilde added value through various commercial deals, including the introduction of Intel Capital.

CSR received term sheets from all three VCs in December 1998. There was no formal business plan prepared for the VCs' review but CSR's presentation covered the key areas. As noted above, Bluetooth was entirely new and there was no hard evidence of real market potential (other than analysts' reports) at the time that 3i and the two VCs invested. Financial, commercial (such as was possible) and technical due diligence was carried out up to April 1999 at the same time as a full business plan was prepared.

The management team held founders' stock, a percentage of which was vested over five years. There were no stock options. Management didn't want options as they had the founders' stock, even though the VCs were pressing for options to be available. Once the company was more advanced, options would be useful to incentivize key staff members.

There were milestones in place for the drawdown of the initial funds in three tranches. The three initial VC firms and Intel Capital provided the financing for the second round. At the third financing round some 14 corporates were involved.

## Dr Phil O-Donovan's (CSR) tips for entrepreneurs

Phil O'Donovan's tips for entrepreneurs seeking venture capital finance, drawn from his experience with CSR, are:

- Get the business model right – you need a solid product with its own IP that can rapidly gain a major share in a global market.
- While first-mover advantage is not necessary, it's important to be one of the first three and to be in the market within a few months of the first entrant.
- Select a group of VCs and corporate investors who will complement each other.
- Always take finance when it is available.
- Concentrate on a clear focus and execute reliably against the business plan.

www.3i.com

www.csr.com

# LEGAL AND REGULATORY ISSUES

Raising finance is a complex legal and regulatory area and this book is not intended to provide legal advice or substitute for the entrepreneur or management team taking its own professional and/or legal advice. Sending a business plan to, or discussing it with, potential investors is a financial promotion and this may require the management team or other persons involved in the process to be authorized or regulated in certain jurisdictions, such as the UK. There are usually exemptions if the plan is to be communicated to investment professionals, such as private equity and venture capital firms, or to high net worth individuals such as many business angels.

Care needs to be exercised to ensure that there are no misleading statements in documents that are designed to induce or persuade people to enter into investment agreements or to buy or sell shares in companies.

It may be necessary to verify any statement, promise or forecast contained in any communication document, including a business plan, private placement memorandum or other information made available to potential investors. However, if the plan is being sent to an authorized private equity or venture capital firm then it may not be necessary to have the verification process undertaken. Nevertheless, the plan should not contain any misleading statements. In cases of any doubt, if the team is seeking equity or debt finance, other than ordinary banking facilities, you are recommended to obtain legal advice before making any communications (whether written or oral) with potential investors, including the circulation of the business plan.

## Warranties and indemnities

As discussed in Chapter 10, the directors of the company in which the investment is being made will be asked to provide warranties and indemnities to the private equity or venture capital firm. If the information later turns out to be inaccurate, the private equity firm can claim against the providers of the information for any resulting loss incurred. A disclosure letter, containing the key information disclosed by the directors to the private equity firm and on which the investment decision has been based, will be required.

The team must be able to support the assumptions used to prepare the financial projections included in the business plan. Vague or unsustainable statements should not be made in the plan. Statements should be substantiated with underlying data and market information. It's a good idea to state where you got the information from – cite your sources.

The business risks in the company and its industry should also be clearly set out in the plan. Management's credibility can be seriously damaged if existing risks and problems are discovered by outside parties.

Any material contracts, not being contracts in the ordinary course of business, would need to be disclosed, as would any litigation or arbitration proceedings of material importance, actual, pending or threatened.

# Case study 12

## Media Lario – how a technology VC firm recognized the unique business potential of a specialist mirror designer and manufacturer... and helped it develop into a leading supplier of reflective optical components and subsystems for the semiconductor equipment industry

Media Lario Technologies (Media Lario) is the leading supplier of reflective optical components and subsystems used in the next generation of semiconductor lithography, X-ray telescopes and other advanced applications. Reflective optics fabricated using Media Lario's high-precision electroforming process have been successfully applied to the full electromagnetic spectrum ranging from X-rays to radio frequency.

## Background

Media Lario was founded in 1993 specifically to design and develop X-ray mirrors by means of replication technology based on metal electroforming methodology. The company was a key contributor to the success of the European Space Agency's (ESA) cornerstone mission, the XMM-Newton, the most powerful X-ray telescope ever built and launched in 1999. This telescope is still orbiting Earth.

Media Lario continues to develop its core technology – the design and manufacturing of high-accuracy reflective opto-mechanical systems – and continues to lead in its historical domain of aerospace, providing groundbreaking solutions to a variety of customers including ESA and many other governmental, corporate and academic centres of excellence worldwide.

Most recently, Media Lario focused its longstanding expertise in reflective components and systems on the development of semiconductor fabrication equipment for extreme ultraviolet (EUV) lithography. It has further combined its superior electroforming and system engineering capabilities to serve new markets with high-precision optical components and systems in the fields of communication and medical applications. Media Lario operates in Luxembourg and has facilities in Italy and the United States.

In 2004 TLcom Capital LLP (TLcom) completed an investment in Media Lario after working on the investment for almost 18 months. The €12 million financing round was co-led with Draper Fisher

Jurvetson (DFJ), with substantial participation from Intel Capital (Intel). TLcom is a London-based venture capital firm which invests in information and communication technology companies across Europe and Israel. TLcom's investment strategy is to identify, back and assist high-quality entrepreneurs and management teams with disruptive technologies and business models, compelling intellectual property and deep market knowledge, as they move from product development to commercialization.

Giuseppe Curatolo, a General Partner with TLcom, describes how TLcom got involved with Medio Lario and was instrumental, together with DFJ, in recognizing its business potential and helping to build it into the leading supplier of reflective optical components and subsystems that it is today.

## How TLcom got involved

Media Lario was founded and originally managed by Dr Arnoldo Valenzuela, a professor and entrepreneur, internationally known for his achievements in the space and defence sectors.

In early 2003 the company founder engaged the consulting firm of Booz Allen and Hamilton to advise on strategic options to expand the scope of application of the company's core technology to new markets. After a review of potential options the consultants recommended involving a venture capital firm to foster company development and introduced the founders to TLcom.

When the opportunity was presented to TLcom, MLT was little more than a strong technology and manufacturing capability in search of valuable market applications. Its revenues were around €1–2 million. Its revenues were generated on an ad hoc contract basis at that time and provided for limited profitability and business visibility. The company, with financial aid from ESA, had invested over €30 million in its intellectual property and assets over the years.

Over a period of almost 18 months TLcom created a highly attractive investment opportunity for itself and its syndicate members by:

- identifying opportunities in the semiconductor equipment industry as the preferred market for repositioning the company's activities;
- validating such markets with the contribution of Intel Corporation as well as other world-class industry experts;

- involving a first-class US co-investor deemed necessary to the company's development (DFJ);
- leading a recruiting effort to identify and hire a CEO for the business, Mr Giovanni Nocerino, an industry veteran and ex Chief Operating Officer of NASDAQ listed company, Thermawave;
- co-leading a highly complex syndicate, including alongside TLcom and DFJ strategic investor Intel Capital in a €12 million Series A round while simultaneously redesigning the corporate structure and governance of the company;
- facilitating the entrance in the shareholder structure of value-added venture capital firms Polytechnos and Vision Capital via a secondary transaction.

The investment was structured in preferred A shares in a Luxembourg holding company, owning 100% of the capital of Media Lario, based in Lombardy where all manufacturing activities are currently located.

When Mr Nocerino came on board as CEO, Dr Valenzuela, the founder, became chief scientist responsible for the company's technology roadmap as well as supporting the CEO in strategic issues. Mr Nocerino was incentivized with share options which vest over four years and an equity drawdown based on annual performance.

## Growth plans

As TLcom was investigating Media Lario it was apparent that the company had aggressive plans for growth in its traditional space and communications business. It had invested significant R&D to expand its knowledge from X-ray and high-precision telescopes to ground-based radio antennas and optical communications. The company's core intellectual property and manufacturing capabilities had unique applicability in areas well beyond the aerospace and communications domain. In particular, in-depth research showed that the same expertise it had used in manufacturing optical components for its historical customers had an application in next-generation semiconductor equipment, a sector that presented significant market opportunity in the medium and long term.

As the semiconductor industry strives for higher resolution in the manufacturing of integrated circuits, paramount technological challenges arise in the manufacturing process. Possibly the most important of these challenges involves the optical components embedded in the photo lithography equipment at the core of the fabrication process. Media Lario was the only supplier of optical components in the world that has overcome these challenges in the past and proven to meet the technical requirements of EUV (Extreme Ultra Violet) photonics. Thus, it had first-mover advantage to leverage its capabilities and to gain leadership in the $4 billion semiconductor equipment optical component market.

TLcom introduced the founder to Intel who agreed that Media Lario was in the unique position to be able to meet these challenges and to capture the market with its first-mover advantage. Intel validated the market opportunity and came on board as an investor.

## Business plan not used to raise finance

When TLcom got involved there was no business plan as such, no strong management team and no specialist knowledge of the semiconductor industry within the company. Early in the process TLcom brought in DFJ to provide the US focus and backing which was necessary for a business operating in the domain of semiconductor equipment. TLcom and DFJ together brought in a specialist technology and business adviser in the semiconductor equipment industry in the person of Mr David Lam, founder of LAM Research. They also engaged a search firm to recruit a CEO, Mr Nocerino, as noted above.

The new CEO provided considerable input to the business plan which was used mainly to assess the size of the opportunity and not to raise finance as such (as the VC syndicate brought in by TLcom were essentially on board ready to invest subject to the market assessment and the CEO having been brought in).

Media Lario now has around 80 employees and revenues of €11 million. When TLcom first got involved in 2004, there were 40 employees and revenues were around €1–2 million.

## Giuseppe Curatolo's observations and tips

Giuseppe Curatolo has the following observations and tips for entrepreneurs seeking venture capital financing based on the Media Lario experience:

- Venture capital investment opportunities in Europe don't necessarily come in fully developed. VCs shouldn't simply wait for a business plan to come into their offices. There are great opportunities out there in Europe. But they may need more proactive involvement from the investor at the beginning. Media Lario would not exist in the form it is today without the involvement of TLcom, DFJ and Intel.

- Outstanding people can be attracted to a fledgling VC-backed company if they can see an equally outstanding opportunity. DFJ has to travel across the Atlantic to attend board meetings and otherwise monitor their investment (hardly 'zip code' investing) but the opportunity with Media Lario makes it worth their while. The same applies to the CEO of the company, whose family still resides in the United States.

- Top management won't join unambitious companies and investor groups. Clearly the CEO who joined Media Lario from a US quoted company was taking a big risk but the upturn potential was worth it.

- Never compromise on quality of management. While the involvement of TLcom and DFJ was key in the development of Media Lario, its current success is largely attributed to the CEO who is able to see the many market opportunities available to Media Lario and strives to align the company's capabilities and positioning to capitalize on such opportunities.

www.tlcom.co.uk

## A lighter note

On a lighter note, the following signs of extravagance and non-productive company expenditure are likely to discourage a private equity firm from investing and so are best not included in your business plan or its financing requirements:

- flashy, expensive cars;
- company yacht/plane;
- personalized number plate;
- carpets woven with the company logo;
- company flagpole;
- fountain in the forecourt;
- 'International' in your name (unless you are!);
- fish tank in the board room;
- founder's statue in reception.

In fact, the above are common signs of a company about to go 'bust'. As one company liquidator commented: 'the common threads I look for in any administration liquidation are as you drive up to the premises there's a flagpole, when I'm in reception, a fish tank and in between typically I walk past a lot of number plates that are personalized, so if they've got all three, there's no hope of recovery'.

# 9

# The investment process

The whole investment process, from when a private equity or venture firm actively reviews your business plan to when the firm actually invests in your proposition, can take anything from one month to one year. Typically, however, the process takes between three and six months. There are of course exceptions to this and deals can be done in extremely short time frames. Much depends on the attractiveness of your proposition to the potential investor, the competition to do a deal from other private equity firms, the quality of information you provide and make available to the private equity firm and the length of time it takes to carry out the various due diligence procedures.

## VC Tip #11

Be patient: allow six to nine months for the investment process.

In this chapter we go through the entire investment process, stage by stage, highlighting the roles of the private equity firm and of the entrepreneur, owner manager or buyout team at the various stages.

## REACHING THE VC AUDIENCE

Having prepared your business plan, agreed it with your management team and incorporated their comments, ideally had feedback on the plan from an impartial but knowledgeable third party, such as an accountant, law firm contact or other professional adviser, the first step in the investment process is to get your plan, or at least your business proposition, in front of an appropriate venture capital firm (early-stage and expansion finance) or private equity firm (management buyout or buy-in).

We looked at various ways of selecting a private equity firm in Chapter 7. You should select only those private equity firms whose investment preferences match the investment stage, industry sector, location of, and amount of, equity finance required by your business proposition. As we also discussed earlier, for the initial approach, it is worth considering sending only a copy of the executive summary or a 'sales pitch' document to potential investors rather than sending them the full business plan. This should increase the chances of your plan receiving attention. Before communicating your plan to potential investors, you should be aware of the legal and regulatory issues concerning the communication of business plans to potential investors mentioned in Chapter 8.

# CONFIDENTIALITY AND NON-DISCLOSURE AGREEMENTS

From your point of view you may well be concerned about confidentiality and the risk that your ideas may be leaked to interested third parties or passed on to other portfolio companies, particularly if in a non-patent-protected area, or highly competitive industry, or where first-mover advantage is key. The ideas in your business plan cannot be copyrighted but they may be protected by various laws concerning confidentiality, depending on your jurisdiction.

You and your lawyer may wish to draft a confidentiality letter or non-disclosure agreement (NDA) for the private equity investor to sign, before you send him or her any sensitive information or the full business plan. Such an agreement should enable you to keep your ideas secret while sharing them with potential investors and indeed other third parties, including your employees, consultants, suppliers and customers. The agreement prevents these parties from divulging the information to anyone else. NDAs themselves are simply a way to flag to the VC that you are serious and professional and that there is *truly* some confidential information in what you are sending them and therefore they should be careful with it. It is unlikely that you will ever engage in litigation with a VC over confidentiality unless there is a specific piece of information which you can demonstrate could only have come into the open via this particular VC.

But beware; confidentiality is a big issue in the VC world. Bear in mind that some VCs will be affronted at being requested to sign an NDA.

They view as taken for granted that they will take confidentiality seriously and will not share a company's confidential material with anyone outside the firm without their consent. For example, all private equity firms in the UK who are members of the BVCA are bound by the BVCA's 'Code of Conduct'. This states that they must respect confidential information supplied to them by companies looking for private equity capital (or indeed information provided by companies in which they have invested). Also, in view of the vast number of plans that most VCs receive it would be an administrative nightmare to enter into an NDA every time they review a business plan.

Most venture capital firms in the United States simply refuse to sign NDAs and ask you to take them on trust. The risk of litigation is just too great there. In Europe VCs are generally not keen on NDAs but are somewhat more flexible. Of course, this will usually vary with the standing of the firm – the higher profile, the less inclined they are to sign NDAs. It will also depend on how much you've told them before asking them to sign an NDA. If hooked on your proposition, the VC will usually be more inclined to go through the trouble of signing an NDA, usually when you need to start sharing some commercially sensitive information.

The usual argument from the VC's standpoint is that they live by their reputation and therefore any reputable firm should be careful with your information. The reality is a bit more murky. If you give them some information useful to one of their portfolio companies, it is a rare VC who will not share (probably on a no-name basis) that information with their portfolio company. More to the point, at any point in time, VCs look at a number of (sometimes competing) opportunities and will of course use all the information they have to make a decision. In assessing that information they will often test it from one company to another.

If you are still concerned about confidentiality there are various safeguards that you can take. These include:

▊ Checking whether the potential investor has any major conflicts of interest, such as a significant investment in a company which is in competition with yours. If this is the case, you may receive the assurances that you need if your investment is dealt with by a different investment team or executive from the competing portfolio company and proper 'Chinese walls' exist, or you may wish to remove that particular VC firm from your list of prospective investors.

▊ Simply leaving out the more confidential data from your plan or, as in the rest of your business, manage confidentiality by releasing information on a 'need-to-know' basis as you are getting more convinced the party you are sharing the information with is likely to be a good partner for you. Sharing information with VCs is like 'peeling an orange': step by step. In any case VCs will not read or absorb the information all in one go since, as we have seen, at every step of the way, they make their own judgement as to whether they want to spend more time (or not) on your investment situation.

If you still want to use an NDA, make it light and use one from your local VC association. An example of a standard confidentiality letter can be obtained from the BVCA's website (www.bvca.co.uk). The general terms of this letter have been agreed by BVCA members and with your lawyer's advice you can adapt it to meet your own requirements. In many instances, VCs will send you their own version of an NDA. Don't spend too much time on arguing the terms. Remember your primary mission is to get on with your funding.

It is best that you only ask for a confidentiality letter when the potential investor has at least shown some interest in giving your proposal more detailed consideration. If you do manage to obtain an NDA at the stage of providing the business plan, make sure that it protects any future information that you disclose later during the negotiations with the potential investor. Certainly at the stage of the due diligence process where the VC is actively providing your venture's details, including details on proprietary technology which may not be fully IP protected, you should obtain a full confidentiality agreement to protect your interests.

In summary, your best protection is your commercial judgement of what to share, when and with whom. At the end of the process, only two to three VCs should have all the details about your venture. If you would like more information on NDAs, Go4Venture (www.go4venture.com) has produced a technical paper on the subject, part of an occasional series of notes describing various technical aspects of fundraising written with private company entrepreneurs in mind.

## HOW VCS EVALUATE THE PROPOSITION

Once your executive summary or sales pitch document is with a private equity or venture capital firm, you should receive an initial indication from the potential investor as to their level of interest within a week or so. This will be either a prompt 'no', a request for further information (such as the full business plan), or a request for a meeting. If you receive a 'no', try to find out the reasons as you will need to consider incorporating any revisions into your business plan, maybe changing or strengthening your management team or carrying out further market research before you approach other potential investors. That is why it is not a good idea to send your plan to several VCs at the same time.

In evaluating your proposition at this initial stage (Figure 9.1) the venture capital investment executive will be considering several key aspects, including those 'Six questions investors ask to determine company value' that we reviewed in Chapter 5. He or she will be checking to see whether or not:

▌ the product or service appears technically sound and commercially viable;

▌ the business model for the company is understandable and makes sense;

▌ there is an effective strategy for getting to market and building a potentially sizable and market-leading business reasonably quickly;

▌ the company has potential for sustained growth;

▌ the company has already established itself in the marketplace with actual customers and a revenue stream;

▌ the management team appears experienced and has the ability to exploit the business's potential, control the company through the growth phases and make the business plan happen;

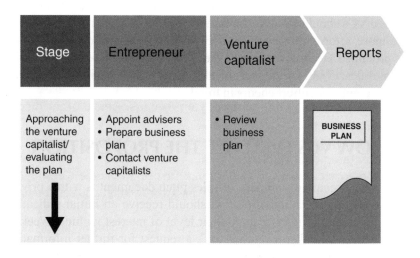

**Figure 9.1** The private equity investment process

▌ the possible reward to the investor justifies the risk he or she is taking in investing;

▌ the potential financial return on the investment meets the venture capital firm's investment criteria.

The answers to the above questions need to be included in the initial documentation sent to the VC. If the venture capital firm is interested in progressing further, they will request the full business plan and/or a meeting with you and your team. The above areas will be checked out thoroughly during the VC's questioning and later enquiries and as part of the due diligence process.

There are various tools that you can use to check the strength of your business proposition and whether you have included all relevant areas in your business plan before you send the summary or the plan to a VC, and two of these are included below: the Go4Venture Business Plan Scoring Tool and the Gauntlet, developed by Library House. First of all, read through Chapter 8 again to ensure that you have addressed all the areas mentioned there.

## Go4Venture Business Plan Scoring Tool

Go4Venture, a corporate finance advisory firm focused on providing European technology entrepreneurs and their investors advice on the development and execution of growth strategies, has developed an interesting diagnostic tool which forces entrepreneurs to go through their business plans with the eyes of a VC. As an adviser to early-stage high-growth technology companies, Go4Venture faces the challenge of identifying the better start-ups which they want to work with, especially in a financing or refinancing exercise. They anticipate which companies VCs may be prepared to back. To help with this exercise they have developed a set of questions and possible answers which they use to benchmark early-stage technology companies. Go4Venture believes that this tool has now been sufficiently tested to share with entrepreneurs so that you can make your own assessment of the merits of your business plan.

To access the Go4Venture Business Plan Scoring Tool go to www.bpscoring.com/BPS/index.html. You will need to provide your name and contact details to Go4Venture first of all via the website and they will send you your user name and password so that you can log onto the system.

For those of you who are relatively new to the VC world, the business plan scoring tool gives good insight into the sort of questions VCs ask when reading a business plan or listening to a pitch. More importantly, the system offers suggested answers which, depending on where you fall, lead to a particular score. These scores reflect the average VC's common wisdom. From the entrepreneur's standpoint, you can take the answers as read, and this will give you a fairly good insight into the way most VCs are going to look at your plan. You can use it as a reality check to measure your chances of getting funding from VCs.

For the more experienced, what you can also do is disregard the proposed score and put your own. But then you should use the free text form to force you to think through why your particular venture should be rated differently. So the business plan scoring system provides a checklist of questions as well as forcing you to think hard about whether your answers stand up to scrutiny.

Also, by submitting your plan to the system, your score is then compared to all the scores of previous business plans at *the same stage* held in the system. This means that you should obviously not look at your 'score' as an absolute but simply as a way to benchmark yourself against others. All information is held in confidence and is not shared with anyone outside the Go4Venture organization without the approval of the provider of the information.

In the future, for the better ventures, Go4Venture will be offering you the option of sharing your information (on a no-name basis) with VCs so that VCs who have a particular expertise in your area can request your details.

## The Gauntlet

Another service that you can use to see if your business is ready for investment is the Gauntlet, developed by Library House, the research group in the UK high-growth company market. The Gauntlet is perhaps more suited to start-ups that have not yet received venture capital investment than the Go4Venture Business Plan Scoring Tool described above, which is intended more for follow-on and expansion capital requirements. The Gauntlet (www.the-gauntlet.com) works like a virtual investor, challenging the entrepreneur and his or her team to answer all of the critical questions potential investors will ask and explaining why they ask these questions. It is based on research by Library House into best practice among successful venture capital firms and, using commercial and academic assessment models, it interrogates innovative companies about 16 investment criteria organized around four key themes: the innovation, the team, the market and the investment. There is a fee for the service, but a personal, confidential report card is provided which assesses the business's investment readiness, with detailed feedback to support the assessment.

# PRESENTING YOUR BUSINESS PLAN TO THE VC FIRM

If, having reviewed your business proposition, a private equity firm is interested in proceeding further, you will be asked to meet with the investment executive to present your proposals in person and answer the questions that the VC will no doubt have on your business. You will need to ensure that you and the key members of your management team are able to present the business proposition convincingly and demonstrate a thorough knowledge and understanding of all aspects of the business, its market, operations and prospects.

## VC Tip #12

Properly prepare for your presentation to the VCs: have roles for all present, work as a team, keep the presentation simple, anticipate questions, don't bluff, and rehearse, rehearse, rehearse!

The primary objective of this initial meeting with the VC and the presentation of your proposition is to interest the VC sufficiently that he or she wants to take the investment process further, ie more than likely to have a further more in-depth meeting with you and your team, to commence discussions regarding the terms of a possible deal with you and to start the due diligence process on the opportunity being presented (Figure 9.2).

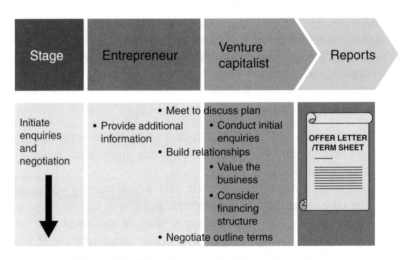

**Figure 9.2**  The private equity investment process

## Things to find out from the VC before the meeting

Find out exactly who will be attending the meeting, their positions in the VC firm and their roles in the meeting. You want to have something in your presentation to interest all of them.

Ideally you want to check that the person you are meeting is the most appropriate investment executive to be considering your proposal, ie in the right industry sector and with the authority to make recommendations to the firm's investment committee. Clearly this needs to be approached with tact, maybe with the help of a knowledgeable intermediary. You may have no control over this and in a large private equity firm the first meeting may be with a more junior person who will almost certainly have to defer to a more senior individual if the process is to be taken further.

Find out when and where the meeting will be held and how much time the VC firm executives are allowing for the meeting, if possible. You should reckon on around an hour or possibly an hour and a half at the most being available to you from European VCs (considerably shorter is allowed in the United States).

Ask the investment executive to whom you sent the business plan about his or her overall impression of the plan. Enquire as to whether there are any areas not covered or where he or she would like further information or clarification. Of course, the investment executive may well have not read it in detail; at best the executive summary will have been read and other sections maybe scanned.

See if you can find out what style of presentation the VC firm prefers: formal or informal, PowerPoint, presentation document or flipchart. Ask what presentation facilities are available (eg litepro projector, flipchart). Arrange to take your own if necessary (useful as backups in any event).

Ask to visit the room to check out the facilities and layout beforehand if possible. This may seem 'over the top' but it will certainly demonstrate your enthusiasm.

## Preparation for the meeting

Pull together any additional information you need to supplement your business plan, particularly those areas already highlighted by the VC as requiring further detail.

Select your team to attend. Decide what key areas you want to cover first and take along the most appropriate persons to talk on those areas. For a start-up or early-stage venture it may be sufficient just for the founder or owner manager to go along to the initial meeting. If you are taking some members of your team, decide on the role of each team member in the presentation and how they will link in to each other.

Draft the presentation – but avoid drafting a full script. Speaking to an outline encourages a more natural and enthusiastic presentation.

Check the timing/length of the presentation. Make sure you allow plenty of time for questions, no less than half the presentation time available.

Anticipate likely questions – this may come from any initial feedback you have had to your business plan from the VC and from your advisers or a colleague's cold reading of your plan. Put yourself in the VC's shoes – what issues and concerns would you have about the business? Also have one or two questions for them (eg what happens next in the process should they decide to proceed?).

Decide on the style of delivery for the presentation. Will you sit opposite the VC and his or her team ('us' and 'them' style) or more casually around the table? Will each of your team stand up or sit down to make their presentations?

Remember to keep visual aids interesting but simple. Don't go overboard on the number of PowerPoint slides, keep them to around 20, don't have too much text, detailed diagrams and charts on each slide, don't read from the slides verbatim but rather expand upon or illustrate the points with examples.

Prepare any handouts you plan to go through with the VC during the presentation or to leave with them for later review.

Plan the setting up of any equipment you need to take to the presentation meeting, such as a litepro projector.

Rehearse, rehearse, rehearse – it is essential to rehearse your presentation with your full team at least two or three times before the real presentation to the VC. Each presentation should be a couple of days or so apart to allow any changes to be made and the individual presenters to get familiar with the changes. Rehearsing will allow you to ensure the key points are coming out of the presentation, the timing is right, the individual team members' presentations link properly together, people get familiar with the visual aids, the team members act as a team, eg when one member is speaking the others are seen to be interested and supportive, and you practise dealing with questions.

Anticipate likely questions. Think of the questions you would least like to be asked. And practise your responses. There will almost certainly be questions concerning exactly what the problem is that you are aiming to solve (if you haven't addressed this adequately), the market potential and how you have conducted your market analysis, the extent of IP protection in any technical areas, the strengths and weaknesses and experience of the key members of the management team, the susceptibility of the production operations to supplier shortages or manufacturing slippage and the sensitivity of the financial projections and cash flow forecasts to various factors.

Invite a colleague, or your adviser, who is not going to be part of the presentation, to sit in on the rehearsals, role-playing the VC, acting as devil's advocate and providing useful feedback on presentation styles etc. You might even consider videoing the rehearsals so that team members get to see their presentation styles and how they deliver the key messages.

## Structure of the presentation

The presentation should not simply be a restatement of the business plan, even if the VCs haven't read it in detail. But it does need to reinforce the key points. All the preparation that you have previously put into the business plan will provide most of the material that you need for the presentation. Copies of the business plan should be taken along in case they need to be briefly referred to or to highlight where additional information can be found in the plan. At the end of the meeting you can leave behind copies of the business plan – if the investors are interested they will read it; if they are not interested they will 'file' it.

## Suggested outline for the presentation

Keep your presentation to about 30 minutes. Allow lots of time for questions. Within this constraint you could structure the presentation as follows:

- Briefly outline your background and introduce the other team members attending, including their roles and responsibilities in the venture.

- Outline the structure/timing of the presentation and how questions will be handled. Ask them for their preference, whether they want to hear all the presentation first and then ask questions or the more informal style of dealing with questions as they arise. The latter will engender a much more interactive and relaxed discussion but you will need to be careful to keep your presentation on track and make sure you leave time to get all your key messages across. It's not really a good sign if the presentation runs without any questions being asked.

- Outline what the company does, in non-technical terms, and what burning problem it is addressing. Describe your solution to this problem and how it meets customers' needs.

▌ Explain the USP (unique selling proposition) of the project, ie its advantage over other similar companies in the same industry. Be prepared to get technical if necessary and if appropriate to the audience's background. Summarize the overall 'SWOTs' (strengths, weaknesses, opportunities and threats), ie the key strengths of your proposition and its weaknesses and the opportunities for your business in the marketplace and its competitive threats.

▌ Without going through the whole business plan, summarize the key aspects on the market, the product or service, the management team and your business operations.

　During this part of the presentation you should be prepared to demonstrate, and be prepared to answer detailed questions on, the following aspects of your proposition:

　– the presence of a large and attractive market, how the timing is right for your product /service, how you have arrived at pricing;

　– what the competition is doing in this area and your USP as above;

　– what customers/revenues you have in place already;

　– what your projected revenues and profits are and how sensitive they are to external factors;

　– that the business model is practical and makes sense;

　– that the management team has the experience and capability to achieve the business plan in practice (be prepared to give references);

　– your detailed tactics to achieve the milestones in your plan over the short and medium term and any issues or obstacles you foresee in achieving the plan over the longer term.

▌ Detail the amount of finance you have in place already (perhaps from the resources of you and your team) and what you are requesting from the VC. Explain how, via your financial projections, you believe they will get their money back and make a handsome return at exit.

▌ Explain the importance to the business project of this particular VC investing and what's in it for the VC.

▌ Conclude by summarizing why you believe the VC firm should invest in the proposition.

During the presentation, or in response to questions, don't 'lecture' the VCs, eg in finance or marketing areas. They may well know far more about all this than you. By all means take the time to explain what the technology is all about.

Do stress the benefits of your products or services, ie what customer needs or problems they are addressing, and not just the features of the products or services.

Do illustrate your presentation with case studies of what you have done, or propose to do, for your customers. This will show the VCs that you actually do have some customers or potential contracts in place. And it will provide evidence that the VCs can check as part of their due diligence procedures.

Don't wash over any glitches in your proposition, in the development of your product or other areas. These will almost certainly come out later if they exist and VCs don't like surprises. Do explain how you are addressing them.

In discussing what finance you are looking for, don't say that you will give them 'x'% of the equity for an investment of €'x'. It is far too early a stage to discuss this. It effectively puts a value on the company and it is up to the VC to make his or her own determination of the company value and not for you to dictate his or her equity stake, although this is negotiable of course. You don't want to get into negotiations at this first meeting. This meeting is more about developing relationships, seeing if the initial chemistry is there, getting the VC hooked on your proposition and dealing with the VC's initial questions. Nevertheless, you should have a rough idea of your company's value (see next section below) so that you can assess the attractiveness or otherwise of the investor's offer and not look totally blank if indeed you are asked by the VC what you think your company is worth.

Do be confident, polished but relaxed in your presentation. But don't come across as overconfident. And 'good luck'!

## VALUING THE BUSINESS

Assuming the venture capital executive is excited by your proposal and you have dealt satisfactorily with their initial questions, the next step in the investment process will be for the VC to arrive at a valuation of your business so that they can arrive at the proposed equity stake they will need in your business to compensate them for their level of perceived risk in the venture and to provide them with their required rate of return over the period of their investment.

There are several ways in which the business can be valued. Two possible ways are discussed here: 1) calculate the value of the company in comparison with the values of similar companies quoted on the stock market; 2) calculate a value for your company that will give the private equity firms their required rate of return over the period they anticipate being shareholders.

Private equity firms may also use other ways of valuing businesses, such as those based on the existing net assets of the business or their realizable value, but these would not be applicable for an early-stage, potentially high-growth technology or service business with limited assets.

## Calculate the value of the company in comparison with the values of similar companies quoted on the stock market

The key to this calculation is to establish an appropriate price/earnings (P/E) ratio for the company. The P/E ratio is the multiple of profits after tax attributed to a company to establish its capital value. P/E ratios for quoted companies are listed in the back pages of the *Financial Times*, and are calculated by dividing the current share price by historic post-tax earnings per share. Quoted companies' P/E ratios will vary according to industry sector (its popularity and prospects), company size, investors' sentiments towards it, its management and its prospects, and can also be affected by the timing of year-end results announcements.

The P/E ratio is calculated as: P/E ratio = Price per share/Earnings per share. The price per share is the market price of a single share of the stock. The earnings per share is the annual profit after interest and tax of the company (ie the profit available to the equity shareholders).

The P/E ratio of a company describes the price of its shares relative to the earnings of the underlying assets. The lower the P/E ratio, the less you have to pay for the company's stock, relative to what you can expect to earn from it. The higher the P/E ratio the more over-valued the stock is. For example, if a company's stock is trading at €16 and the earnings per share for the most recent year is €2 then the P/E ratio is 16/2 = 8. The company is said to have a P/E ratio of 8. Or for every € of earnings you have to pay €8.

An unquoted company's P/E ratio will tend to be lower than a quoted company's P/E ratio for the following reasons:

■ its shares are far less marketable and its shares cannot be bought and sold at will;

■ the unquoted company often has a higher risk profile, as there may be less diversification of products and services and a narrower geographical spread than with a larger quoted company;

■ it generally has a shorter track record and a less experienced management team;

▌ the cost of making and monitoring a private equity investment is much higher than investing in a quoted company.

There are factors that may, however, raise an unquoted company's P/E ratio:

▌ substantially higher than might be expected projected turnover and profits growth;

▌ inclusion in a fashionable sector, or ownership of unique intellectual property (IP) rights;

▌ competition among private equity firms to do a deal.

In using a quoted company P/E ratio discounted in this way to arrive at a P/E ratio for your unquoted company, care needs to be exercised that conditions are similar between the companies, eg that the companies are in the same industry sector, the same country and it is the same time period that is being compared, eg 12 months.

So if you determine that your private company is similar to a quoted company with a P/E ratio of 8 and you discount this by, say, 25% because your company is private, you arrive at a P/E ratio of 6. If you have 1,000 shares in issue and your current annual earnings are €500,000 then your company will be currently valued at €3 million on this basis. Of course, this is a very simplistic calculation, based on a less than ideal comparison with larger, quoted companies and it takes no account of the future earnings potential of the company. You could, of course, apply it to projected future earnings discounted to net present value. Nevertheless, it is essentially what investors do when they place a notional value on the business by investing in the company's shares at what they regard as a market value for the company. It is not likely to be the true value of the business based on future earnings streams.

### Calculate a value for your company that will give the private equity firms their required rate of return over the period they anticipate being shareholders

The second method of valuing the business discussed here bases the valuation on the target overall return that private equity firms expect from their investments. Generally 'return' refers to the annualized internal rate of return (IRR), calculated over the life of the investment and based on the cash flows of money invested by the VC and money returned to the VC through capital redemptions, capital gains (through the eventual 'exit' from the investment or sale of shares), and income through fees and dividends. As mentioned above, the returns required will depend on the perceived risk of the investment – the higher the risk, the higher the return that will be sought – and it will vary considerably according to the sector and stage of the business.

In Chapter 3 we saw the diversity of returns actually achieved by different sectors of the private equity industry. The overall net return per annum to investors in UK private equity funds raised between 1980 and 2005 was 16.4% pa over 10 years measured to 31 December 2005. Many individual firms do better than this and, as a rough guide, you should have in mind that the average return required by the private equity firms you approach will certainly exceed 20% per annum. The higher the risk in your business proposal (as perceived by the VC firm) the higher the return the venture capital firm will expect to make. For an early-stage technology deal they might be looking to achieve a return of over 50% per annum. For a buyout investment the desired return may be nearer 30% and upwards.

The required IRR depends on the following factors:

▮ the risk associated with the business proposal;

▮ the length of time the private equity firm's money will be tied up in the investment;

▮ how easily the private equity firm expects to realize its investment – ie through a trade sale, public flotation, etc;

▮ how many other private equity firms are interested in the deal (ie the competition involved).

Assume an investor requires 30% IRR on an equity investment of €1,175,000.

€1,175,000 becomes:

| At end of: | | | |
|---|---|---|---|
| | Year 1 | plus 30% | 1,527,500 |
| | Year 2 | plus 30% | 1,985,750 |
| | Year 3 | plus 30% | 2,581,475 |
| | Year 4 | plus 30% | 3,355,918 |
| | Year 5 | plus 30% | 4,362,693 |

Therefore the investor needs to receive 3.7 times his or her money after 5 years to justify his or her investment risk, ie an IRR of 30% is equivalent to a multiple of 3.7 times the original investment.

## Pre-money and post-money valuations

As the person seeking private equity finance you will be focused on the value of the company at the point in time that you are offering a stake in the company to the venture capital firm in return for its investment in your company. This is the pre-money valuation, ie the value of the business or company before the particular finance-raising round has been completed.

The post-money valuation is the value of the business after the finance-raising round has been completed, ie after the venture capital firm has made its investment. The VC will be more focused on this than the pre-money valuation as it is the post-money valuation that will be used as the benchmark for any subsequent rounds of financing or indeed for the eventual exit. To achieve his or her required return the VC will be concerned at too high a post-money valuation.

As an example, consider an entrepreneur who owns 100% of a company and is seeking an initial investment of €5 million for his venture. The VC reviews the proposition and offers to invest €5 million in return for a 40% stake in the entrepreneur's company. Based on what the VC is prepared to invest in the company, a 100% shareholding must be worth €12.5 million post-investment. This is the post-money valuation.

The remaining 60% of the shares, held by the entrepreneur, are therefore worth €7.5 million. But before the VC's investment the entrepreneur held 100% of the shares in the company. The VC has therefore valued the business before he or she makes his or her investment at €7.5 million. This is the pre-money valuation.

If the VC is concerned that the post-money valuation is too high, he or she will either put less money into the venture for the same equity stake or indeed increase his or her equity stake.

## How the VC arrives at his or her equity stake

To illustrate how a VC arrives at his or her required equity stake in a company, by way of another example, assume we have a business proposition for an early-stage software venture that is looking for €10 million of investment and is projected to earn €20 million in year 5 which is the year the VC wishes to exit his or her investment. Similar quoted software companies have average P/E ratios of 15. The VC discounts this by 20% to allow for the fact that the company in which he or she proposes to invest is private and a relatively early-stage company and applies this discounted P/E to his or her investment's earnings in year 5 to give a terminal value on exit of €240 million. The VC needs to discount this to present-day value based on his or her target IRR, using the formula:

Present value = Terminal value / (1 + Target IRR)* where * is the number of years of the investment.

The VC sets the target IRR at 50%, commensurate with the risk of investing in this early-stage software venture.

This therefore gives a present-day, or discounted, terminal value of:

€240 million / $(1 + 50\%)^5$ = €31.6 million

The VC's required stake in the venture is therefore his or her investment of €10 million divided by the present-day value of €31.6 million, ie nearly a third of the equity (31.6%).

The deficiencies in using this method to arrive at the investor's required equity stake are that the use of quoted company current P/E ratios may not reflect the state of the market at the time of the VC's exit from the investment in a few years' time and that the discount factor applied to the P/E ratio to reflect that the investee company is not quoted and different in other ways from the larger company is quite subjective. Of course, the VC can play around with different discount factors and required IRRs to see how these affect the required equity stake.

Don't underestimate the amount you request from the VC. As we have seen, small amounts of equity are not worth the VC's time in appraising an investment and carrying out due diligence procedures. So, to the extent possible, work out what finance you will need over the life of the venture and ask for the total package, even if this will be delivered in tranches depending on milestones being met.

## Envy ratio

The envy ratio is used to determine how generous, or not as the case may be, the VCs are being to management. The envy ratio is the ratio between the effective price paid by management and that paid by the VC for their equity stakes in the company. For example, if the VC invests €6 million for 60% equity and management invests €300,000 for 40% equity the envy ratio is:

Envy ratio = (6/60) / (0.3/40) = 13.

The higher the envy ratio the better the deal is for management. The envy ratio depends on how keen the VC is to do the transaction, what competition they are facing and the general economic conditions at the time of doing the deal.

## Personal financial commitment

---

# VC Tip #13

Be prepared to commit yourself financially when the VC invests – the time and money you have spent up to that point is not enough.

---

You and your team must have already invested, or be prepared to invest, some of your own capital in the company to demonstrate a personal financial commitment to the venture. After all, why should a private equity firm risk its money, and its investors', if you are not prepared to risk your own! The proportion of money you and your team should invest depends on what is seen to be 'material' to you, which is very subjective. This could mean re-mortgaging your house, for example (but best to avoid offering your home as security in connection with a bank or other secured loan), or forgoing the equivalent of one year's salary. As serial entrepreneur Bob Jones states in case study 13 below on Equiinet, 'saying "I've put two years of my life into developing this business" is not enough. You need to make a financial commitment too. A rough rule of thumb is to expect to put in the equivalent of your last year's salary. If you can't do that, the VC may expect you to go out and find it' (maybe from family and friends).

# TYPES OF FINANCING STRUCTURE

If you use advisers experienced in the private equity field, they will help you to negotiate the terms of the equity deal. You must be prepared to give up a realistic portion of the equity in your business if you want to secure the financing. There are various ways in which the deal can be financed and these are open to negotiation. The private equity firm will put forward a proposed structure for consideration by you and your advisers that will be tailored to meet the company's needs. The private equity firm may also offer to provide more finance than just pure equity capital, such as debt or mezzanine finance. In any case, should additional capital be required, with private equity on board other forms of finance are often easier to raise.

Whatever percentage of the shares you sell, the day-to-day operations will remain the responsibility of you and your management team. The level of a private equity firm's involvement with your company depends on the general style of the firm and on what you have agreed with them.

The financing structure by the private equity firm may include a package of some or all of the following elements.

## Classes of capital used by private equity firms

The main classes of share and loan capital used to finance companies are shown below.

### Share capital

The structure of share capital that will be developed involves the establishment of certain rights. The private equity firm through these rights will try to balance the risks they are taking with the rewards they are seeking. They will also be aiming to put together a package that best suits your company for future growth. These structures require the assistance of an experienced qualified legal adviser:

▌ *Ordinary shares.* These are equity shares that are entitled to all income and capital after the rights of all other classes of capital and creditors have been satisfied. Ordinary shares have votes. In a private equity deal these are the shares typically held by the management and family shareholders rather than the private equity firm.

▌ *Preferred ordinary shares.* These may also be known as 'A' ordinary shares, cumulative convertible participating preferred ordinary shares or cumulative preferred ordinary shares. These are equity shares with preferred rights. Typically they will rank ahead of the ordinary shares for both income and capital. Once the preferred ordinary share capital has been repaid and then the ordinary share capital has been repaid, the two classes would then rank pari passu in sharing any surplus capital. Their income rights may be defined; they may be entitled to a fixed dividend (a percentage linked to the subscription price, eg 8% fixed) and/or they may have a right to a defined share of the company's profits – known as a participating dividend (eg 5% of profits before tax). Preferred ordinary shares have votes.

▌ *Preference shares.* These are non-equity shares. They rank ahead of all classes of ordinary shares for both income and capital. Their income rights are defined and they are usually entitled to a fixed dividend (eg 10% fixed). The shares may be redeemable on fixed dates or they may be irredeemable. Sometimes they may be redeemable at a fixed premium (eg at 120% of cost). They may be convertible into a class of ordinary shares.

## *Loan capital*

Loan capital ranks ahead of share capital for both income and capital. Loans typically are entitled to interest and are usually, though not necessarily, repayable. Loans may be secured on the company's assets or may be unsecured. A secured loan will rank ahead of unsecured loans and certain other creditors of the company. A loan may be convertible into equity shares. Alternatively, it may have a warrant attached that gives the loan holder the option to subscribe for new equity shares on terms fixed in the warrant. They typically carry a higher rate of interest than bank term loans and rank behind the bank for payment of interest and repayment of capital.

## *Other forms of finance provided in addition to equity*

- *Clearing banks* – principally provide overdrafts and short- to medium-term loans at fixed or, more usually, variable rates of interest.

- *Investment banks* – organize the provision of medium- to longer-term loans, usually for larger amounts than clearing banks. Later they can play an important role in the process of 'going public' by advising on the terms and price of public issues and by arranging underwriting when necessary.

- *Finance houses* – provide various forms of instalment credit, ranging from hire purchase to leasing, often asset based and usually for a fixed term and at fixed interest rates.

- *Factoring companies* – provide finance by buying trade debts at a discount, either on a recourse basis (you retain the credit risk on the debts) or on a non-recourse basis (the factoring company takes over the credit risk).

- *Government and European Commission sources* – provide financial aid to UK companies, ranging from project grants (related to jobs created and safeguarded) to enterprise loans in selective areas. See Chapter 6 for details.

- *Mezzanine firms* – provide loan finance that is halfway between equity and secured debt. These facilities require either a second charge on the company's assets or are unsecured. Because the risk is consequently higher than senior debt, the interest charged by the mezzanine debt provider will be higher than that from the principal lenders and sometimes a modest equity 'up-side' will be required through options or warrants. It is generally most appropriate for larger transactions.

# STRUCTURING A VC DEAL

In terms of structuring the deal the different parties involved have different interests:

▌ management want the highest proportion of equity possible;

▌ VCs want to exit with a high IRR, and the higher the risk they perceive in the investment the higher the IRR they will require;

▌ banks want the company to be able to generate a cash flow adequate to pay the interest and principal repayments on their loans with the appropriate level of security in terms of a first or second charge on the company's assets.

The first step in the process is to determine how much finance is required by your venture as detailed in your cash flow projections. This needs to be the total financing requirement, including fixed asset and working capital requirements, and future cash requirement, costs of doing the deal etc. Ascertain how much of this can be taken as debt as this is a cheaper form of finance than equity. This will depend on the assets in the business that can be used to secure the debt, the cash flow being generated to pay interest and repay amounts borrowed, and the level of interest cover, ie the safety margin that the business has in terms of being able to meet its banking interest obligations from its profits. Then determine how much management can invest in the venture from your own resources and those of family and friends. Include any government sources of finance available to you also.

The balance is then the amount you are seeking from the VC. The private equity finance is normally provided as a mixture or ordinary and preference shares with possibly debt hybrids and variations in classes of shares. How much of the VC's capital is the form of ordinary shares or preference shares is open to negotiation.

Preference shares rank ahead of ordinary shares for both income and capital. The VC investor can attach various rights to the preference shares and these are discussed under the term sheet considerations below. These rights are not available to ordinary shareholders and can include, for example, rights with regard to liquidation preferences, or the right to receive cumulative or non-cumulative dividends or the right to convert their shares into ordinary shares, for example in the event of an IPO, as well as anti-dilution provisions which protect the VC preferred shareholder from dilution resulting from a later issues of shares in connection with a subsequent financing round.

One of the most basic reasons for an investor wanting preference shares in the venture, rather than ordinary shares, is to protect their investment in the event of a liquidation or sale soon after investment. If they hold just ordinary shares along with the founder they will both receive any proceeds in proportion to their ordinary shareholdings, even though the VC investor is likely to have contributed substantially more to the venture, in terms of finance provided, than the founder. By holding preference shares the VC investor gets substantially more of their original investment back out in the event of a liquidation or a sale immediately post-investment (see worked example below).

While preference shares serve to protect the investor and can have various rights attached to them, they do not themselves allow the investor to benefit from the growth and success of the investee company. Therefore the preference shares usually have the ability to be converted into fully participating ordinary shares at any time at the option of the VC investors. As an exit opportunity approaches the VC will convert their preference shares into ordinary shares at the appropriate point when their holding is more valuable to the VC in ordinary shares than in preference shares and participate in the exit opportunity.

Through this combination of ordinary shares and preference shares the VC investor can protect their downside exposure in the event of a liquidation or 'fire sale' while benefiting from the upside potential of the business. Such luxury is not, unfortunately, available to the management team! Also, by having different classes of share, the VC does not have to wait for an exit to enjoy a return. Shares with preferred or participating rights may improve the overall rate of return to the investor by returning cash in the form of dividends rather earlier and at a greater rate than the ordinary shares are able to do.

The following worked example shows how a mixture of ordinary and preference shares can be used to structure a transaction.

---

### Worked example: Structuring the deal

**Venture Limited**

- Requires finance to purchase equipment of €3.0 million and inventory of €0.5 million.
- Completion set for 31 March 2007.
- Also requires €125,000 to cover fundraising expenses, including accountant's and lawyer's fees.

**Financial projections**

| (€'000) | 2007 | 2008 | 2009 | 2010 | 2011 |
|---|---|---|---|---|---|
| Sales | 5,125 | 6,150 | 7,380 | 8,856 | 10,627 |
| Cost of sales | (3,844) | (4,613) | (5,535) | (6,642) | (7,971) |
| Gross profit | 1,281 | 1,537 | 1,845 | 2,214 | 2,656 |
| Overheads | (615) | (677) | (745) | (818) | (901) |
| Profit before interest and tax | 666 | 860 | 1,100 | 1,396 | 1,755 |
| Interest | (345) | (370) | (295) | (235) | (175) |
| Profit before tax | 321 | 490 | 805 | 1,161 | 1,580 |
| Tax | (96) | (147) | (242) | (348) | (474) |
| Profit after tax | 225 | 343 | 563 | 813 | 1,106 |

Note: The interest and tax rates used in the above projections are for illustrative purposes only and are not necessarily representative of rates currently in force or commercially attainable.

**Bank borrowing**

▮ Bank agrees to lend €1.8 million over 4 years, provided this represents 60% of value of the assets and interests costs met even if there is large shortfall in sales projections.
▮ Overdraft facility of €1.0 million also agreed to finance inventory of €0.5 million and future working capital requirements.

**Equity stake**

▮ Leaves €1,325,000 financing gap. Management team can raise €150,000 between them by taking out second mortgages.
▮ Percentage equity required by VC:

| | Amount € | equity % |
|---|---|---|
| Management team | 150,000 | 11% |
| Investors | 1,175,000 | 89% |
| | 1,325,000 | 100% |

▮ Only 11% of equity for management. Not worth risk to management with second mortgages.
▮ Assume VC investors require 30% IRR and company will be sold in 5 years' time.

€1,175,000 becomes:

| At end of: | | |
|---|---|---|
| | Year 1 plus 30% | 1,527,500 |
| | Year 2 plus 30% | 1,985,750 |
| | Year 3 plus 30% | 2,581,475 |
| | Year 4 plus 30% | 3,355,918 |
| | Year 5 plus 30% | 4,362,693 |

▌ Therefore investors need to receive 3.7 times their money after 5 years to justify their investment risk.

**Exit**

▌ Assume investor wants a P/E ratio on exit of 7 (compared with shares in quoted companies in same industrial sector at a discount of 20 to 40%):

▌ In March 2011 Venture Limited will be worth $1,106 \times 7 =$ €7,742,000.

▌ To receive €4,362,693 from sale of Venture Limited for €7,742,000 the investor needs 56% of the company, leaving management with 44%. This can be achieved by issuing ordinary shares as follows:

| €1 ordinary shares | No | Price | Cost | equity % |
|---|---|---|---|---|
| Management team | 110,000 | €1.00 | 110,000 | 44% |
| Investors | 140,000 | €8.68 | 1,215,000 | 56% |
| | 250,000 | | 1,325,000 | 100% |

▌ Shows the effect of 'sweat equity' for management, ie their shares cost €1.00 whereas the investors' shares cost €8.68. The uplift over the nominal share price of €1.00, ie €7.68, is the share premium.

▌ On sale, management would receive €3,406,480 (44% of €7,742,000), more than 30 times their original investment.

▌ Problem for investor – immediately after making their investment, investor owns 56% of company worth €3,000,000 but is also carrying €1,800,000 million debt, which will not be paid off completely for 4 years.

▌ If sold soon after investment, management receives 44% of €1,200,000, ie €528,000, which is an instant profit of €418,000. Investors are left with only €672,000, ie an instant loss of €543,000. Therefore introduce preference shares concept to counteract this.

**Preference shares**

▌ Starting point:

| €1 ordinary shares | No | Price | Cost | equity % |
|---|---|---|---|---|
| Management team | 110,000 | €1.00 | 110,000 | 44% |
| Investors | 140,000 | €1.00 | 140,000 | 56% |
| | 250,000 | | 250,000 | 100% |

▌ Shortfall in finance of €1,325,000 – €250,000, ie €1,075,000. Investor purchases 1,075,000 preference shares at €1.00 each, with prior claim over ordinary shares on company assets.
▌ Company sold after 5 years:

| | € |
|---|---|
| Sale price | 7,742,000 |
| Less: preference shares | (1,075,000) |
| Available to ordinary shareholders | 6,667,000 |
| Management team: 44% | 2,933,480 |
| Investors: 56% | 3,733,520 |

▌ Management receives €473,000 less than under the previous structure (€3,406,480 – €2,933,480).
▌ Investors receive €4,808,520 (ie €1,075,000 for preference shares plus €3,733,520 for ordinary shares), which is more than the €4,362,693 needed for target IRR of 30%. So could amend ordinary share split with more ordinary shares going to management.
▌ Also, if sold soon after investment, investors left with €1,075,000 preference shares and €70,000 from ordinary shares (at 56% of (net assets of €1,200,000 less preference shares of €1,075,000)), ie €1,145,000. This is just €70,000 less than their investment of €1,215,000.

# TWEAKING THE DEAL

In addition to the variations of combinations of ordinary and preference share capital and the different types of preference shares, and the addition of loan capital, including convertible loan and mezzanine capital, referred to above, there are several other components of the deal that the VCs may introduce or indeed that you may wish to negotiate into the deal.

## Dividends

Management usually want as high a percentage of the equity share capital as possible. The VC wants a high IRR. It may be possible to maintain the VC's equity stake at a level acceptable to management by giving the VC a dividend return during the life of the investment as well as a capital gain on exit. This would increase the VC's potential IRR. Of course, this depends on the business being sufficiently cash generative to be in a position to pay dividends.

For example, the dividend terms might be set so that the VC's (or maybe all the) ordinary shares receive an extra dividend that starts at, say, 10% of distributable profits and increases annually by 5% or more. The VC receives a higher IRR through this dividend yield. This also means that some of the potential capital gain will have been taken out before exit by the VC, reducing management's potential capital gain also. So management will be focused on achieving a successful exit as soon as possible before all the profits are stripped out as dividends.

## Ratchets

This is where the proportion of equity held by the management team is altered depending on certain profit levels (or other targets) being achieved. Ratchets may be used when management cannot convince the investors about the potential of the business to generate the level of future revenues and profits as set out in the business plan. This therefore impacts on management's equity stake; management wanting a high percentage of the equity believing that the company will do well and meet its projections.

Ratchets allow the proportion of equity held by management to be varied depending on what levels of profits the company achieves. Ratchets can be set on any other variable, not just profits; basically some milestone or milestones that the company is targeted to achieve either as set out in the business plan or set by the VC.

Ratchets may be positive or negative. A positive ratchet provides the incentive that, should management perform well and meet the requisite profit level or other milestone, their share of the equity will increase. A negative ratchet works the other way and management's equity stake is reduced if they fail to meet their targets.

## Stage finance

Quite a common tactic of VCs to reduce their exposure is not to allow the management team to have immediate access to all the required finance at the initial stage. Instead the finance is released as, and if, certain milestones are met. This is fine if the business plan shows that additional finance is required at certain points of the company's life but not if by restricting access to the finance the company does not have sufficient access to working capital and other requirements to be in a position to grow the business and service customer contracts effectively. Finance could be provided in stages at various milestones to allow for:

▌ product development and market research;

▌ product launch, initial marketing, proof of concept;

▌ launch of major marketing offensive;

▌ turnover growth to break even position;

▌ provision of working capital for continued revenue growth;

▌ finance for geographic expansion and/or product diversification.

In the following case study on Equiinet we see how an injection of £5 million from the private equity firm Schroder Ventures (now Permira) was provided in four tranches against certain milestones being met.

## Case study 13

### Equiinet – 'a roller-coaster ride' of start-up, sale, downturn, buy-back and growth

Equiinet is a secure server appliance specialist offering integrated solutions that give controlled, secure, easy and cost-effective access to the internet and optimize bandwidth over stressed networks. The company is based in Swindon, UK. Chairman Bob Jones is a high-profile serial entrepreneur who has previously headed three successful networking start-ups and subsequently sold them on: Steebek Systems, Mayze Systems and Sonix Communications. Bob has won accolades as 'Venturer of the Year' from the British Venture Capital Association, Cartier and the *Financial Times*, 'Entrepreneur of the Year' in the Real Business CBI Growing Business Awards and 'Technology Entrepreneur of the Year' at the European Technology Forum. He tells the story of Equiinet's formation (his fourth start-up), the sale of the company to its German distributor and his subsequent buy-back of the company from the hands of the receivers.

## Background and initial financing

Equiinet was founded in January 1998 by Bob Jones and Keith Baker (now managing director of Equiinet). Bob and Keith are electronics engineers by background. Keith Baker had previously worked with Bob at Sonix, one of Bob's previous start-ups, and came up with the concept of internet appliances. Equiinet pioneered and is now a leader in the manufacture and supply of extremely secure server appliances.

Equiinet's formation was financed partly out of Bob Jones's own resources and a £5 million injection from Schroder Ventures (now Permira) for around 35% of the equity in a mixture of ordinary shares and loan stock. The company had been run for around nine months prior to the financing and had modest revenues. Bob and his team had prepared the business plan and had it reviewed by PwC, with whom Bob has worked closely in all of his ventures. Bob approached Schroders as they had previously backed one of his previous start-ups, Sonix. The business plan included a detailed market analysis prepared by the management team, including an assessment of Equiinet's competitors strengths and weaknesses.

Schroders carried out full due diligence procedures on Equiinet and came up with a term sheet which was essentially acceptable to Bob without much negotiation. While Schroders held around 35% of the equity, Bob did not control the company on a fully diluted basis as, in common with his previous ventures, he set up a substantial share option pool for his employees.

## Rapid early growth

The £5 million finance from Schroders provided the opportunity to expand the business into Europe. Schroders retained a seat on the board during this period and had the usual veto rights on management appointments, salaries, acquisitions etc.

The £5 million injection from Schroders was provided in tranches against various milestones being met as follows:

- £1.0 million initial drawdown to include all of the equity element;
- £1.5 million loan stock to be drawn down four months later provided an acceptable plan had been completed for the development of the company's Benelux office and a CEO or Sales Director had been appointed (to be agreed with Schroders);

- £1.25 million loan stock one year after the initial investment provided the low-cost version of the company's key product had been completed and that revenues in the preceding two quarters were not less than 70% of those shown in the company's business plan;
- £1.25 million loan stock four months later provided revenues in the previous two quarters were not less than 70% of plan, with gross margins running at 45% or above and an up-to-date forecast had been prepared, acceptable to Schroder's representative on the board, which showed that the business would not require further cash after this last round of finance.

For the next two years the company experienced rapid growth, with around 1,000 units per month being shipped out fairly quickly after formation. Bob and Keith had hired a team of experienced corporate managers to supplement their own entrepreneurial skills and management style.

## Sale to distributor

Dica Technologies (Dica) was the company's distributor in Germany and Bob had noted that Dica appeared to be on a fast track to an IPO. Bob considered that a merger with Dica was a good way of capitalizing on the success that Equiinet was having. After the first two years of trading in which, as noted above, Equiinet had experienced massive growth, Bob was comfortable with relinquishing control to Dica if that meant the business would reach its full potential. Bob recounts that 'every IT business was going for world domination in whatever market they were in in those days (1999 to 2000) and, in order to achieve that, you would have had to raise more money than an early-stage investor would actually be prepared to put into the business. But a lot of these early-stage businesses were actually floating and were making big returns for their investors. It seemed like a good strategy to merge with Dica.'

## Disaster strikes

Schroders went along with Bob's plan and Equiinet was duly sold to Dica in a share-for-share exchange. Unexpectedly, Dica took Bob out of his executive role and put him on the Supervisory Board (more of a non-executive role as this board supervises and advises the Executive Board).

Unfortunately, the dot.com bubble burst at the end of 2000, the Neuer Markt crashed and Dica's attempts at an IPO failed. Dica went into administration and the original Equiinet investors, including Bob and Schroders, lost everything.

## Management buy-back

This turn of events galvanized Bob into action: 'the whole episode made me angry and fuelled my desire to prove everybody wrong'. With Dica in administration, its UK subsidiary, Equiinet, had gone into receivership in the UK. Bob discovered that Dica had not taken up the IP rights in Equiinet into the holding company and the rights remained with Equiinet. Bob put in a bid to the UK receiver to buy Equiinet back over the course of a bank holiday weekend and ended up owning 100% of Equiinet financed entirely by himself. In a matter of weeks he secured funding of £2 million to restart the business from Herald Ventures and private investor, Jon Moulton, whom Bob had known during his Sonix days when Jon Moulton was the managing partner of Schroder Ventures. On a fully diluted basis, the investors held around 30% of the equity, Bob around 31% and the rest held by Equiinet staff and the share option scheme.

Dica had made Equiinet into an R&D and marketing centre so it was necessary to refocus this, bring in new people and transform it back into an operational and sales centre, albeit with the loss of one of its main customers, ie Dica. Sales were split roughly 50/50 between UK and continental Europe but Europe was very diversified, difficult to manage and loss making. Hence Bob refocused efforts back into the UK. Already UK market-leader in internet server appliances, Equiinet had broadened its product range to include dedicated VPN (virtual private networks) and smart caching appliances.

## Expansion into e-learning

Equiinet suffered from the global slowdown in the technology sector following the dot.com crash and 9/11, with the resultant nervousness in the telecoms and networking markets. However, Equiinet adapted, refocused on the UK and developed a niche in the educational sector with transmission devices for the delivery, storage and updating of web-based e-learning material in schools. This now represents some two-thirds of all revenues. Equiinet is now a UK leader in the provision of network and IT security tools to the education market. The company is looking at expanding into continental Europe in this area.

## Bob Jones's tips for entrepreneurs seeking VC finance

Bob Jones has the following tips for entrepreneurs seeking venture capital finance:

- Don't be unreasonable, and certainly not arrogant, in your expectations from and approaches to VCs (this is less of an issue now than it was in the heady days of the dot.com boom).
- Do expect to have to commit yourself financially. You can't expect a VC to invest if you are not prepared to do so. Saying 'I've put two years of my life into developing this business' is not enough. You need to make a financial commitment too. VCs' expectations can vary on this but a rough rule of thumb is to expect to put in the equivalent of your last year's salary. If you can't do that, the VC may expect you to go out and find it (maybe from family or friends). You may have to remortgage your house. The VC will not, however, expect your commitment to threaten your or your family's entire existence but he will want to see some 'pain'.
- Do be generous to your employees. Your business success is dependent on them. Create an option pool.
- Don't expect to control your business in a fully diluted situation post VC investment.

www.equiinet.com

## Stock options

Stock options are the right to acquire ordinary shares at a specified time and price. Stock options are often used to incentivize management and key employees – both to retain key current staff and to attract new senior people.

Getting stock options is not the same thing as getting shares of stock. The option is the right, but not the obligation, to purchase a share at a specific price, at a specific time. Exercising your options will make the employee a shareholder and hopefully provide him or her with an investment with growth potential, ie in your business.

In granting options care is required not to dilute the existing management team shareholders when the option is eventually exercised.

We will now return to the example of Venture Limited and look at how the use of mezzanine finance, dividends and ratchets can impact on deal structuring and can be used to reduce the VC investors' equity stake, thereby increasing the management team's stake.

---

## Venture Limited: Variations to the deal

### Additional bank debt and mezzanine finance

- By shopping around, Venture Limited's team finds an alternative bank which is prepared to provide a larger loan of €2.3 million on Venture Limited's assets of €3 million, the downside being an increased interest rate. This reduces the amount of external equity finance that the management team needs to raise to €675,000. This will enable management to retain a greater share of the company as they are still providing €150,000 of the equity finance but the total amount now required is reduced to €825,000 from €1,325,000 previously. As the VC investors are making a smaller investment they can still earn their required 30% pa IRR with a reduced equity stake.
- But as the company is now paying considerably more in interest costs, this makes the interest cover (profit before interest and tax/total interest charge) rather worse. This serves to increase the risk for the VC investors and the VCs are therefore likely to demand a higher return than the 30% pa IRR to compensate them for their increased exposure.
- If a mezzanine provider can be found instead of the alternative bank but additional to the original bank, the mezzanine provider may accept a lower level of security for its loan, provided it is confident that the company can generate sufficient profits and cash flow to meet the principal and interest repayments on the loan. The original bank provides a €1.8 million loan as before, which ranks ahead of the loan of say €800,000 from the mezzanine provider which itself charges interest at a higher rate than the bank to compensate it for its lack of security on the company's assets.
- With a higher borrowing, now from the original bank and the mezzanine provider combined, the amount of external equity finance required reduces further and the VC investors' stake is again reduced while still giving them their required 30% pa return.

■ But the company's interest cover is now even worse and the mezzanine provider may require options to acquire ordinary shares, as well as charging a higher interest rate, to compensate it for the increased risk of the company defaulting on interest and principal repayments.

### Fixed and participating dividends

■ The management team then decides that the amount of interest that is to be paid is too great based on the company's projected profits and decides to revert to the original financing structure.

■ The more return a VC can take from the company during the period of investment the less the VC needs to take as a capital gain at the time of exit. So, instead of waiting for their investment to be realized on sale or IPO the VC investors take a return from the company during the life of the investment in terms of a fixed dividend of, say, 10% pa on the preference shares. By earning a 10% return during the life of the investment the IRR required on exit reduces from 30% pa to 20% pa.

■ But the fixed yield dividend requirement placed on Venture Limited above is quite onerous because it is not dependent on the level of profits generated by the company. It has to be paid no matter what.

■ It would not be wise to extend this fixed yield too far but it can be supplemented or reduced or even eliminated, if necessary, in the negotiation process by an entitlement which is based on the company's performance, ie its level of profits.

■ The VC could receive a participating yield via a 'twice covered' dividend, for example, on 'A' ordinary shares whereby half the available profits are earmarked for distribution. Twice covered means that the dividend payment is twice covered by profits. The 'A' ordinary shares are differentiated from the management team's ordinary shares which do not carry any right to a participating dividend.

■ While the VC investors will receive their share of this participating dividend, the management team shareholders will not be entitled to receive a dividend until the bulk of the VC's preference shares have been redeemed.

■ Again, by taking more of their return in this way, the VC investors can even further reduce their required share of the

equity in the company, leaving management with a correspond-
ingly larger stake.

### Ratchets

▌ As noted above, ratchets can be set on the company achieving,
or not achieving, basically any milestones. Ratchets may, for
example, be based on profits, valuations on exit or return of
cash to investors.

▌ In the case of Venture Limited it is agreed to adopt a ratchet
based on the sale of the company by 31 March 2011.

▌ The VC investor will purchase 'A' ordinary shares giving it 60%
of the equity. These 'A' ordinary shares will convert into a
number of ordinary shares at the time of exit, in order to give the
VC investor an equity percentage based on the following table:

| (€'000) | 2007 | 2008 | 2009 | 2010 | 2011 |
|---|---|---|---|---|---|
| Company sale price | 7,000 | 7,500 | 8,000 | 8,500 | 9,000 |
| VC's equity % | 64% | 59% | 54% | 50% | 45% |
| (illustrative only) | | | | | |

▌ Under the terms of the deal, the maximum equity holding for
the VC investor is 64%. If the company is sold for less than €7
million, or is not sold at all before 31 March 2011, the 'A'
ordinary shares convert on a one-for-one basis into ordinary
shares. If the company is sold for more than €9 million, the VC
investor's share is not reduced below 45%.

## Additional points to be considered

By discussing a mixture of the various forms of finance discussed above,
making dividend payments, and the use of ratchets and stage finance, a
deal acceptable to both management and the venture capital firm can
hopefully be negotiated. Other negotiating points that may be considered
and which you should bear in mind include:

▌ Whether the venture capital firm requires a seat on the company's
board of directors (usually the investment executive) or wishes to
appoint an independent director from outside the VC firm or from its
monitoring team.

▌ What happens if agreed targets are not met?

▌ What happens if dividend or interest payments are not made by the
company?

▌ How many votes are to be ascribed to the venture capital firm's shares?

▌ The level of warranties and indemnities provided by the directors (see below).

▌ The level of management's salaries being dependent on the ability to meet the profit projections.

▌ Whether there is to be a one-off fee for completing the deal and how much this will be.

▌ Who will bear the costs of the external due diligence process? What if the deal is aborted? Who pays the costs then?

# THE OFFER LETTER OR TERM SHEET

At about this stage in the process but certainly before you and the VC have agreed on all of the above points, depending on where you are with negotiations, how keen the VC is to do the deal and the level of competition there is from different VCs to do a deal with you, the venture capital firm will send you an offer letter or term sheet, which outlines the framework for the final deal, subject to the outcome of the due diligence process and other enquiries and the conclusion of negotiations between you and the VC. The term sheet, without being legally binding on either party, demonstrates the investor's commitment to management's business plan and shows that serious consideration is being given to making an investment. The term sheet represents the VC's preferred terms, not necessarily and indeed, unlikely at this early stage in negotiations, yours.

You should ask a lawyer, experienced in the private equity industry, to review the term sheet and give you his or her views on whether it is reasonable or not and advise you on how to negotiate for better terms. Also ask someone you know who has already gone through the process to have a look at the term sheet and give you his or her opinion and any advice in connection with what you may be able to negotiate.

The VC may change the terms himself as the due diligence process and negotiations progress, eg adjustments to the overall valuation, refinement of ratchets etc.

The terms in the term sheet will be incorporated into the shareholders' agreement at the end of the negotiation process. It is better for the term sheet to be as detailed and unambiguous as possible so that there are no surprises when the eventual shareholders' agreement has been drafted for you to sign. Unfortunately, there are no standard term sheets and the detail and quality of drafting varies from country to country, within countries and from firm to firm, so have your lawyer review the term sheet carefully.

While there are no standard term sheets, you can expect that the term sheet will cover the following areas, all of which are described below:

- amount to be invested, instruments (eg convertible preferred shares), valuation, capital structure;

- liquidation preferences, dividend rights, conversion rights, anti-dilution protection, redemption rights, lock-ups, pre-emption rights;

- board composition, consent rights, information rights;

- warranties, vesting, option pool, milestones;

- confidentiality, exclusivity, fees, conditions precedent.

## Amount to be invested and instruments

The term sheet will set out the amount that the private equity firm is to invest in the company, the format in which the investment is to be made, eg convertible preference shares, and the number and price of the shares.

## Valuation

Valuation is obviously a key element of the term sheet. If you cannot negotiate a mutually acceptable valuation then either the VC or you call off the deal, you accept the VC's valuation or the VC reluctantly agrees to a valuation less acceptable to them. If the latter, watch out for the VC adding in or tweaking a whole mass of other terms which could make the deal far less attractive to you than if you had accepted their preferred valuation in the first place!

Make sure that the valuation (pre-money) has been firmly buttoned down before you sign the term sheet. The pre-money valuation is the value of the business or company before the particular finance-raising round has been completed.

## Capital structure

The capital structure should be shown in the final term sheet both before and after the VC's investment, on a fully diluted basis, including all share options.

## Liquidation preferences

The VC will include their liquidation preferences, ie the right of the VC preference shareholder to receive before any other shareholders cash that is available in the event of the company being liquidated or indeed sold, as in a trade sale, or achieving an IPO. The VC may express that they require a multiple of their original investment in these situations, maybe five times their original investment or even more as was seen at the height of the dot.com boom. Such multiples can be quite unrealistic and you will need to negotiate carefully to get them reduced. Otherwise management could end up with nothing from a trade sale or flotation!

## Dividend rights

The right to receive dividends may be cumulative or non-cumulative. If cumulative, the dividend due to the VC preference shareholder accrues even if the company does not have adequate distributable reserves to be able to pay a dividend when it is due. The accumulated dividends then become payable to the VC in the event of a liquidation occurrence as above. If non-cumulative, there is no problem and the dividends are not accrued if the company does not have distributable reserves to pay them.

## Conversion rights

Preference shareholders usually have the right to convert their shares into ordinary shares, for example in the event of an IPO. They will do this only if it is a 'qualifying' IPO where above a certain minimum amount of capital is raised at above a minimum stock price. This protects preferred shareholders converting from preferred shares to ordinary shares in connection with an IPO that is too small or has no meaningful public market or liquidity for the shareholder.

## Anti-dilution provisions

Anti-dilution provisions protect the VC preferred shareholder from dilution resulting from later issues of shares, in connection with a subsequent financing round, at a lower price than the VC investor originally paid (known as a 'down round'). This could happen, for example, if the company does not meet its targets and the valuation of the company declines from that at which the VC invested. They may decline to invest in the subsequent round or do not purchase sufficient shares in the subsequent financing round pro-rata to their original share holding and get diluted. The anti-dilution provisions in their most aggressive form are set up such that the lower share price of the later share issue is applied to the original, higher-priced shares and the VC's share holding adjusted as if they had invested at this lower price. Of course, this does not apply to the management team shareholders, who end up getting heavily diluted. Even if you successfully negotiate out a VC from having an anti-dilution provision, when it comes to a subsequent financing round the VC may insist on anti-dilution being applied to their original shareholding. A new prospective investor in a subsequent round may similarly not invest unless anti-dilution rights of earlier investors are waived. This can be particularly the case where business angel early-stage investors are in place and a VC comes on board for second- or third-round financing.

## Redemption rights

Redemption rights require the founder or management team to buy back the VC investor's shares by a specific date. These rights are used if the business does not generate the growth required by the VC investor to give them their required capital gain. A multiple of what the VC invested may be required to be paid back to them. If the company does not have the distributable reserves to be able to redeem the VC's shares, this provision may not be legally possible in certain jurisdictions, such as the UK.

## Lock-ups

Lock-ups specify how soon after a flotation the management team and the VCs can sell their shares, which is important in making the shares attractive to public investors at the time of the IPO. It is in your interest that a reasonable lock-up period is included.

## Pre-emption rights

Pre-emption rights apply when a company proposes to issue new shares and existing shareholders, such as the VC investor, have the right to be offered a pro-rata part of the new shares before they are offered to a new shareholder in a way that does not dilute the original VC shareholder. In relation to sales of existing shares, similar rights require a shareholder wishing to sell shares to offer them first to existing shareholders before being able to transfer them to outsiders.

## Board composition

Another aspect of the term sheet concerns the composition of the board. This is the VC's right to have a seat on the board of directors, or maybe two seats if there are two separate VC firm investors.

## Consent rights

Consent rights give VCs the right of veto over a whole range of areas even though the VC does not have a majority of the shares with voting rights. They can therefore have effective control over such areas as the recruitment of new members of the management team, hiring of key staff, purchase of new equipment, corporate mergers and acquisitions, expansion overseas or into new markets, future finance raisings, issue of stock options, borrowing levels and the sale or flotation of the company; a whole range of areas critical to the company but usually outside of the day-to-day business of running the company. The VC may set limits over which they want the right of veto, eg new equipment purchases greater than €100,000 or borrowing limits greater than €250,000.

## Information rights

Information rights will require the company to provide the VC firm with copies of the monthly management accounts (including budget versus actual comparisons and explanation of variances), updated monthly cash flow forecasts, audited annual accounts, annual strategic plan and budget etc.

## Warranties

The term sheet may require the management team to warrant all sorts of information which the VC say they are relying on in arriving at their investment decision. Care needs to be taken that these are not too onerous, eg avoid warranting the financial projections in the case of a young, growing company or even the assumptions on which they are based. Avoid warranting that you won't lose a major customer. But it is reasonable for the VC to ask you to warrant that, for example, you know of no outstanding litigation against the company or that you have the rights to the IP around your new technology and it is not infringing anyone else's IP or patents.

You will need to negotiate, with your lawyer involved, the nature, extent and limit of these warranties and what happens if they are breached in terms of indemnification (if the value of the company is reduced in the event of breach of warranty you may have to compensate the investor for the reduction in value) or contractual damages (if it can be argued that the shareholders have suffered no loss you would not have to pay the VC in connection with the breach). Warranties and indemnities are covered in more detail in Chapter 10.

## Vesting

The VC may require the shareholder founders or management or other key employees to remain working with the company for a minimum term before they can realize the rights over all the options or all the shares ascribed to them. The shares are considered vested when an employee can leave his or her job, yet maintain ownership of the shares or exercise his or her options to obtain the shares with no consequences. Vesting is meant to incentivize these key individuals to remain with the venture in the critical period of early-stage growth. Vesting may occur over a period of between three and five years. The shares may vest to the individuals on a straight-line basis over this designated period, with say 20% vested in year one, a further 20% in year two and so on, or they may vest on any other basis that might be negotiated. There may be an initial period during which no options can be exercised or shares sold at all, known as the 'cliff' period.

This all might seem rather draconian to entrepreneurs who have spent not inconsiderable time and most likely considerable personal funds in developing and growing their business idea and who have equity control of their own limited company. When the VC comes on board they find themselves having to earn the rights to their shares all over again, except for any 'sweat equity', which are equity shares given to the founder in recognition of all the effort (sweat) they have expended in getting the company started up.

If the founder, or a key member of the management team, leaves before the end of the vesting period the VC firm will want to replace them as quickly as possible. Having unvested equity shares or options from the person who has left to attract the replacement will act as a key element of the incentive package to get them on board.

Different vesting terms can be used to reward the founder and members of the management team according to their contribution to the venture. Maybe the founder has expended considerable effort but has not had much of the way of personal financial resources to put into the venture, maybe another person has contributed money but not much time and other effort, someone else may be a brilliant technical expert or star salesperson. By varying the vesting period and the percentage of shares or options these people can be rewarded to recognize their different contributions.

## Options

The percentage of equity shares reserved for new options for existing and future employees should also be set out in the term sheet. This will affect the valuation of the company.

## Milestones

Milestones, as we have seen, are often used to set goals that the management team have to reach before additional tranches are put into the company by the VC, or management salaries are reviewed or share options granted. The term sheet may specify different milestones with regard to technical, production, marketing or financial progress. If they are too onerous, or too geared to incentivization, management may focus all their efforts on meeting the milestones to the detriment of the overall business.

## Confidentiality

The term sheet will also contain a clause on confidentiality, ie that both the investor and the founder/management team will keep the fact that discussions are progressing between them confidential as well as agreeing not to divulge any information supplied.

## Exclusivity

The VC firm may attempt to include an exclusivity clause in the term sheet preventing you from talking with other VC firms about investing in your proposition for a period of say one month or so, usually the period that the various due diligence exercises are carried out. This is not unreasonable but if things fall through or the VC makes the terms of their investment less attractive to you following the due diligence, you don't want to be in the position where you have run out of time to find another VC and are forced to accept the onerous terms of the VC who had exclusivity.

## Fees

The term sheet will set out the basis on which fees are to be paid.

In many cases, the costs of all the professional advisers involved in the deal, including lawyers and accountants, and consultants engaged in the due diligence process will be charged to the company receiving the investment. The private equity firm will usually increase the funding provided to allow for these costs, so you and your team should not be 'out of pocket' as a result, although you may be left with a slightly smaller equity stake. However, there are circumstances where this is not possible, due to contravention of company law, or where it is agreed that each party bears its own costs.

Professional costs incurred by the financial advisers, accountants and lawyers employed by the management team and the private equity firm, like any service, need to be carefully controlled. There is a range of costs that will depend on the complexity of the transaction, but will typically be around 5% of the money being raised.

In addition, some VCs may charge a fee for doing the transaction (deal fee) and, post-investment, some VCs will charge the company for monitoring their own investment by taking a fee for the provision of non-executive directors appointed to the board.

Ensure that you agree the basis of costs as set out in the term sheet before any work commences. In particular, ensure that you have firm agreement as to who is to bear the costs in the event of the negotiations being aborted. Usually in this case the private equity firm will bear the cost of work commissioned by them, eg the external due diligence process, and you will pay the costs of your own professional advisers.

## Conditions precedent

The conditions precedent included in the term sheet include details on what has to happen between the term sheet being signed and the completion of the investment. This of course includes the satisfactory completion of the due diligence process and the completion of the various legal agreements, including the shareholders' agreement and the warranties and indemnities documentation. Conditions precedent may also specify that you must do certain other things during this period, such as secure the contract with the major customer that you have informed the VCs is in process, or bring a key member of the management team on board or reduce overhead costs or even headcount in some way.

All of the above areas included in the term sheet are negotiable. You will want to get heavily onerous terms removed or watered down. But you also don't want to end up with the VC aborting the deal, unless of course you have already decided that you don't want to work with them. You may consider accepting a reduced equity stake or option pool in return for better terms in other areas such as the vesting provisions or exclusivity. It all takes care and excellent negotiating skills.

If you can get term sheets from more than one VC (in order to compare their terms and help with negotiations) so much the better.

Negotiate well – but remember that it is often better to be a smaller part of a potentially large business than a large part of a potentially small business!

If you would like further information on term sheets, the BVCA in the UK has produced *A Guide to Venture Capital Term Sheets* which explains in more detail the terminology typically contained in a term sheet, an example of a term sheet for a Series A round, as well as outlining how investments can be structured and the broader investment process. This is available as a pdf from the BVCA's website, www.bvca.co.uk.

Assuming all is satisfactorily negotiated, both parties will sign the term sheet. Remember though that it is not a legally binding document. The due diligence process has to be successfully completed (see below). The VC may even still have to get the firm's investment committee to formally decide on the investment; that may not take place until nearer the final closing, though the investment executive will hopefully have been discussing the proposed investment with his or her partner colleagues and the investment committee as negotiations progress. The term sheet will go on to form the basis of the final legally binding investment agreements (see Chapter 10).

# SYNDICATION

The term sheet is a useful document when it comes to the VC deciding whether to get other VCs involved in the deal as part of a syndicate. Syndication is where several private equity firms participate in the deal, each putting in part of the total equity package for proportionate amounts of equity, usually with one private equity firm acting as lead investor. Syndication may be considered by a private equity or venture capital firm for various reasons. Maybe the finance being requested is above the maximum investment limit set by the VC and they prefer to bring in other VCs initially rather than the company having to go out to find new investors for a subsequent later round. Maybe the investment is considered to be relatively high risk and the lead VC wants to cap their risk by sharing the overall risk with other firm(s). Maybe the VC needs the specific sector expertise of another VC firm.

Syndication can also have advantages for the entrepreneur as syndication:

▌ avoids any one investor having a major equity share and significant unilateral control over the business;

▌ makes available the combined business experience of all the private equity partners to the benefit of the company;

▌ permits a relatively greater amount of financing than with a single investor;

▌ can offer more sources of additional future financing.

In the case of Cambridge Silicon Radio (case study 11) we saw how the three VCs brought different aspects to the deal: Amadeus with building profile for CSR through the involvement of Amadeus' co-founder Hermann Hauser, himself a serial entrepreneur who has founded or co-founded companies in a wide range of technology sectors, Gilde with commercial introductions and advice on the technology and legal agreements, and 3i with networking contacts and the management recruitment process.

The lead VC will pitch the investment opportunity to the other potential VC investors and give them the signed term sheet to help get them on board. In the absence of a term sheet each other potential investor would have to go through the entire formulation of deal terms, greatly increasing the overall time and costs of doing a syndicated deal.

# THE DUE DILIGENCE PROCESS

Having heard your pitch, considered your investment proposition, reviewed your business plan and met with you and the key members of your management team, if they are still interested in potentially going forward with the investment the VC will start to carry out various elements of due diligence (Figure 9.3). This is the process whereby the VC checks out the details of your business plan and financial projection. It is a necessary process to back up their 'gut feel' and professional experience about investing in your business After all, they are looking after their investors' funds (eg the limited partners who have invested in the private equity or venture capital fund) and cannot afford to risk them on a speculative investment. The VC does not want to pay over the odds for their investment, nor expose themselves to any liabilities that might come out of the woodwork later. On the more positive side, the due diligence process may reveal other revenue channels, operational improvements or other ways in which value can be added.

The due diligence process will cover areas such as the company's trading history, the factual statements included in the business plan, the assumptions on which the financial projections are based, looking into the backgrounds and capabilities of the management team (including taking up references), an appraisal of the technology involved if applicable and the product or service, review of the market potential for the product or service and the production process and operations. It will also cover such areas as unfunded pension obligations, environmental issues and patent protection.

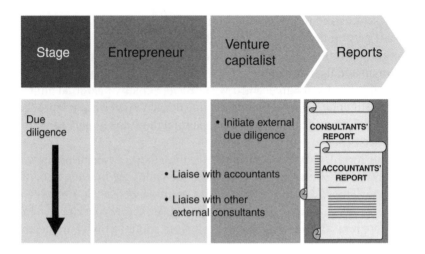

**Figure 9.3** The private equity investment process

As we saw in Chapter 5, and as Nigel Grierson of Doughty Hanson Technology Ventures says in case study 14 below, investors typically list 'the team' as the most important attribute when considering an investment. A VC will carry out extensive due diligence in this area, including assessing whether the relationship with the management team is going to work. After all, the VC is an integral part of the 'team'. Due diligence in the 'soft' areas of relationships, transition from sole ownership to running a business involving external shareholders, communication issues etc is one of the most important aspects, as Nigel describes below. It is also important to get the overall composition of the board correct, which is also discussed in case study 14.

The initial due diligence process will start before the term sheet is drawn up, with the VC meeting with management, asking detailed questions, conducting site visits as appropriate, maybe contacting some of your actual or proposed customers to check that they will be purchasing your (new) product(s) or service(s), tweaking the financial projections, reviewing the assumptions that have been made in the plan and projections, asking their VC firm colleagues and maybe management and technical experts at the firm's existing portfolio companies or external consultants about technical and market feasibility (this is where confidences might be broken, as discussed in the section on non-disclosure agreements above), checking into the company's competitors and assessing the company's SWOTs (strengths, weaknesses, opportunities and threats), identifying risk factors etc.

As a result of these initial enquiries there will be more questions for the management team to answer. The VC investment executive will also be presenting the proposals to his or her internal investment committee to start getting the partners' agreement to making an investment in due course. Assuming all goes well at this initial stage, the term sheet is drawn up and the negotiation process around that commences.

Once it has been agreed who will bear the costs of external advisers and consultants, the final part of the due diligence process will proceed. This is the more extensive, time-consuming and costly part of the due diligence exercise.

If the venture capital firm commissions these external advisers, it usually means that they are seriously considering investing in your business. The due diligence process is used to sift out any skeletons or fundamental problems that may exist. Make the process easier (and therefore less costly) for you and the venture capital firm by not keeping back any information of which you think they should be aware in arriving at a decision. In any event, you will have to warrant such information in due course.

Chartered accountants are often called on to do much of the financial due diligence, such as to report on the financial projections and other financial aspects of the plan. These reports often follow a detailed study, or a one- or two-day overview may be all that is required by the venture capital firm. They will assess and review the following points concerning the company and its management:

- management information systems;
- financial controls and procedures;
- forecasting techniques and accuracy of past forecasting;
- business model and financial projections and the assumptions on which the financial projections are based;
- the latest available management accounts, including the company's cash/debtor positions;
- bank facilities and leasing agreements;
- insurance arrangements, including 'key person' insurance;
- funding of the pensions provisions – large pension fund deficits have been a major issue in several recent M&A deals;
- directors' and employees' service contracts, etc.

This review aims to support or contradict the venture capital firm's own initial impressions of the business formed during the initial enquiries and due diligence stage. References may also be taken up on the company (eg with suppliers, customers, and bankers) and on the individual members of the management team (eg previous employers). The chartered accountancy firm may also be able to provide advice on the key commercial and structural risks facing the business and to carry out assessments on the company's technology base and intellectual property.

Other external consultants are often called in to assess various areas such as the following, although the venture capital firms will always be forming their own views and may themselves carry out extensive due diligence in these areas, especially if they have the appropriately qualified people in-house:

▌ Commercial due diligence: the assessment of the market prospects for the venture by looking at its customers, competitors, its existing market share and projected market share, whether the market is expanding, ability to reach overseas markets etc. Brand due diligence may be carried out on the company's intangible assets and provide an independent opinion and quantification of the strength of the brand and business valuation. Operational due diligence may look at the manufacturing and production process in detail, including the supply chain and any outsourcing arrangements. Patentability, and ownership, of intellectual property will also be covered.

▌ Technical due diligence: the technical feasibility of the product, whether (in conjunction with market due diligence) it is likely to be 'disruptive'. Also covers a review of the company's computer systems, data security and disaster recovery.

▌ Management due diligence: investigating the backgrounds and capabilities of the management team, their priorities and negotiating styles, taking up references from former employers, customers, suppliers, bankers and other finance providers. Psychometric profiling may even be carried out on key team members.

▌ Legal due diligence: this will cover ownership of property and employment contracts, customer, supplier, alliance and other contracts, existence of litigation, etc.

▌ Environmental due diligence: such as environmental liabilities and remediation costs.

# Case study 14

## Two immutable laws of investing – a view from a VC on the role of the CEO and the importance of the interpersonal relationship between the CEO/management team and the investor

*By Nigel Grierson, Co-founder Doughty Hanson Technology Ventures*

### Introduction

One of the most complex, and frequently underestimated, parts of making and managing a venture capital investment is the interpersonal relationships between the various parties involved. If the entrepreneurs, investors and board members get this right it can be a tremendous contributor to creating shareholder value. By contrast, getting it wrong will likely lead to value destruction of the business. In my experience both the investor and the entrepreneur fail to pay enough attention to evaluating these factors prior to investment.

Investors typically list 'the team' as the most important attribute when considering an investment. However, the specificity of what constitutes a great 'team' varies and is subjective to investor opinion. It will typically be some combination of technical skill, prior track record (serial entrepreneurs especially), interpersonal dynamics, management style and character to name but a few.

However, when venture capital investors join the company they also become an integral part of 'the team'. Both the investor and the entrepreneur should ask themselves three questions:

- Can I work with this new, and unknown to me, person efficiently?
- Can the person work with me efficiently?
- What will need to change, on both our parts, to form an optimum relationship?

It is useful to put some context into this question. Research has shown that people do not have to like each other in order to work together professionally. An acrimonious relationship will definitely not help, but then neither will becoming best of family friends. The former is simply a barrier to working together and the latter introduces too many complications that compromise tough conversations.

Research also shows that typically it takes two years for a new relationship to achieve a good performance. That is two years of tolerance, experimentation and learning by all parties.

The second reason that the team is important is that the CEO must be empowered and trusted to manage the business, and the investor needs confidence that the business is in good hands.

## The first immutable law of investing: the amount of time the investor has to involuntarily make available to the business is inversely proportional to the quality of the management team

The relationship breaks down when the investor is experiencing declining confidence and corrects this by more frequent engagement. More frequent engagement often frustrates the CEO, and hence the start of a deteriorating relationship is experienced. Hence, the definition of what constitutes an 'exceptional team' has to be extended to include the investor as well as the CEO and board members.

Frequently this complex situation arises when a business transitions from being a sole-owner business to a shareholder business. The problem is compounded the longer the business has been a sole-owner business.

Consider a successful 10-year-old business, achieving €100 million revenue and managed by a founder/CEO that has demonstrated excellent growth of the business under his or her tenure. The CEO is discussing with investors a straight equity investment to accelerate growth, or perhaps a mixture of growth equity and secondary purchase of a part of the founder shares.

## Due diligence in 'soft' areas

There must be several considerations during the due diligence process prior to investment to understand how easily the founder will transition from the mentality of running a sole-owner business to running a business involving external shareholders. The questions to ask might include: does the founder understand the need to demonstrate accountability to a broader shareholder group than just him/herself? Does the CEO understand what the venture capital investor expects from the relationship? Does the CEO understand the need to apply investor quality corporate governance as part of the grooming for an exit in years to come? What level of communication is required between the CEO and the investor? Does the investor understand that a 10-year relationship between the founder and the organization has effectively set the culture of the business for the future?

I have come across this situation many times in my career. I believe it is essential that both the VC and the entrepreneur voluntarily spend what may seem like a disproportionate amount of time in due diligence evaluating these soft areas. Unless you can be sure that this will be a successful transition then the relationship may not be very sustainable. In one example where I faced this situation I spent quality time explaining to the founder what a typical VC/company relationship looked like. I provided learning and guidance notes from impartial organizations such as the Institute of Directors, EVCA and published books. I also provided unlimited access to founder/CEOs of other investments I had made, and those that I had no investment in, and encouraged him to call as many as possible and gain their perspective. In a normal competitive environment it could be argued I was weakening my negotiating position. In fact, this relationship and building of trust was strengthening it considerably.

## Essential to get composition of the board correct

The constitution of the board is important and its construction can be a critical success factor to managing the relationship. It should be understood that there is a clear demarcation between the role of the investor, as an investor, and the role of the investor as a board director. For the individual concerned, never the two should meet in order to maintain good corporate governance. As a board director, the task is always to act in the best interest of *all* shareholders (except at times of possible insolvency and in Europe where the concept of stakeholder supersedes that of shareholder). The parties should seek for fair representation of shareholders, but always appoint non-executive directors to provide a route to absolute independence in the quality of decisions made. In one investment I made, I ensured there was equal representation of investors and founders with a top-quality non-executive chairman – nominated by the founder and approved by the investor. This provided the parties with an equal and impartial tie-break opinion for the board to truly act in the interests of all investors. I cannot overemphasize the importance of getting the constitution and the membership of the board correct from day one.

My litmus test of the strength of the management/investor relationship is what I call the midnight call. If an unexpected serious problem arises that keeps you awake, can you call your partner at midnight and discuss it without fear of annoyance? If you can, you probably have achieved a relationship of significant strength and value.

## The second immutable law of investing: the CEO only has two tasks in life, ie: to 1) hire and motivate an outstanding management team and 2) to keep the company funded

To keep life simple for the CEO, I frequently condense this to just one objective: hire and motivate an outstanding management team. Outstanding teams solve all other problems and achieve great results. Companies with great results get funded and so it is a self-fulfilling prophecy to hire and motivate outstanding managers.

In my due diligence, I frequently select eight employees at random throughout the organization to ask their impression of what the business is seeking to achieve, explain the culture of the company to me, what constitutes success for the business in one year and three years, and why they are excited about working for the company. If all eight people give similar answers you have an aligned organization. In due diligence, I rarely call the CEO or his or her assistant. I frequently call the switchboard and ask to speak to the CEO in order to experience how the business presents itself to the outside world. The results are frequently very enlightening about the culture of the organization. A company can create stunning PowerPoint slides and compelling spreadsheets when it is time to raise money. Rarely can they change the culture of the organization to suit.

## Organizational due diligence

In an investment I made recently, the CEO was an exceptional business and organization leader. How did I conclude this prior to making the investment? Conventional due diligence reveals the financial and competitive strength of the business and can be a proxy for the skill of the management team. However, even a mediocre management team can deliver great results when favourable market conditions prevail. The technology industry experienced this during the ill-fated internet boom of 1998–2002. Mediocrity is not a long-term sustainable advantage.

The business I refer to had experienced four major market transitions and had navigated all four with precision. Only if you build outstanding organizations can you do this and rapidly attain a leadership position at each transition. Along with the normal monthly indicators that investors ask for, which are typically tactical at best, this relentless focus on the organization is a key indicator that is rarely measured and managed, and yet is perhaps the most important over the long run. In this company, the executive team are rewarded not only for sales and product development, but for how well they are building and continually investing in the team beneath them – the indelible organization.

I recently heard Katherine Corich, founder and chief executive of Sysdoc, present her business. Katherine, like all great business leaders, had worked relentlessly to build a successful business with significant growth still ahead of it. Mid-way through her presentation I was struck by the comment that Katherine decided to 'step out of the business for 12 months on a sabbatical'. She expressed no doubt that she had developed a management team that was perfectly capable of running the business in her absence. On her return her thesis was perfectly correct and the business had continued to exceed expectations. It is another example of an entrepreneur who has consciously invested in building a high-performance organization that can develop shareholder value and not be overly reliant on any single individual. The importance of this to investors cannot be overstated, and is a strong contributor to attracting high-quality investors with high-quality sustainable capital.

## Focus on organization development

In retrospect, this is all so simple. The problem is that these success factors are dependant on efficient interpersonal relationships. Building these relationships is typically difficult, time consuming and a distraction to the immediate tasks at hand for start-ups. I suggest that management, investors and board members consciously construct board meetings to focus on progress in organization development. Separate time at the board meeting into two different agendas, with a break between. Title one as 'urgent' and deal with the business of the day. Title the other as 'important' and deal with organization development.

A focus on both will build an indelible organization that will be more attractive to financiers and hence will have a greater chance of attracting high-quality capital.

www.doughtyhanson.com

If the above due diligence process reveals any 'skeletons in the cupboard' or other negative aspects, in the worst case, it may cause the VC firm to abandon the deal, the valuation may be lowered, indemnities required from management, or the terms of the deal otherwise made more onerous to the founder or management team.

The due diligence process itself can take some considerable time, maybe as much as three months or longer. The entire investment process, from presenting your business plan to an interested VC to completion, can take considerably longer, partly depending on the VC's desire to do the deal and the level of competition they are facing from other investors.

Case study 15 below illustrates the extensive hands-on role of the VC in both the due diligence and the post-acquisition processes.

# Case study 15

## How Rutland Partners turned round H&T Group

Rutland Partners, the UK private equity firm, bought the UK's largest pawnbroker Harvey & Thompson Group (H&T) from Cash America Inc for £49 million in 2004. Rutland tripled its money after floating H&T Group on London's Alternative Investment Market (AIM) in 2006.

A Rutland investment typically involves a UK company that is facing difficult strategic challenges or which may be underperforming, in need of restructuring or entering a period of change. The company will have defensive properties through its market niche, asset underpinning or other forms of competitive advantage and will ideally possess strong operating management. Through the proactive involvement of its team, Rutland seeks to assist operating management to effect a transformation of the prospects for the company.

Paul Cartwright, Rutland managing partner, explains how Rutland executed its typical hands-on operational role in the turn round of H&T.

### Background

H&T is the UK's leading pawnbroker now with over 70 outlets across the UK. The group's core business is pawnbroking but it also retails jewellery and provides cheque cashing and pay-day advance loans.

Rutland acquired H&T in September 2004 from Cash America International Inc on a debt-free/cash-free basis for £49.0 million with Rutland investing £15.4 million and the balance provided by bank acquisition finance.

While H&T was profitable and cash generative, it had flat trading and was underperforming its potential prior to acquisition. Rutland was introduced to the pawnbroking sector by an intermediary contact of Rutland's who was working with Peter Middleton, an experienced leader in financial services with recent sub-prime experience. Rutland's desktop review identified H&T because its value was underpinned by assets, it had a high market share compared to its competitors and a protected brand. However, it was materially underperforming given its market-leading position. Rutland made a direct approach to the group's owners, Cash America, to ascertain their interest in selling the group.

For strategic reasons Cash America was keen to sell H&T and also sold Rutland a £3.0 million controlling investment in Svensk Pantbelaning, Sweden's leading pawnbroker, at the same time. This left Cash America with only US interests.

## Extensive due diligence process

Rutland was able to negotiate exclusivity and carried out extensive due diligence prior to acquiring H&T which lasted from spring 2004 to the purchase from Cash America in September 2004. While Rutland got access to financial information on H&T, there was limited access to H&T management. It was clear to Rutland that the US parent had taken little interest in its subsidiary and the CEO had surrounded himself with a relatively weak, and incomplete, management team.

Financial due diligence was carried out by Deloittes and legal due diligence by Eversheds. Rutland took a particularly hands-on approach to the commercial due diligence process, visiting high-street stores and utilizing OC&C to carry out demographic analysis and run a series of customer focus groups in order to check the group's potential for growth.

## Hands-on operational role by the private equity firm

Post-acquisition, Rutland reshaped the senior management team. Peter Middleton was appointed as executive chairman. One of the chairman's key roles was to act as mentor to the existing CEO. Rutland brought in a commercial director, replaced the finance director with the ex-finance director of Oddbins and recruited externally to fill key roles in marketing and property. Changes were also made to the regional and area management structure of the group. The new team was driven and worked well together. At maximum dilution Rutland was to hold 80% of the shares and the senior management team were to hold 20% which vested over 18 months.

Over the following 18 months, Rutland worked closely with management to improve operational efficiency, develop new products such as the introduction of pre-paid debit cards and accelerate the roll-out of new stores with the addition of 12 outlets.

Prior to acquisition by Rutland, H&T was overstaffed in store on the pawnbroking side of the business and had inconsistent and poor-quality advertising and marketing literature. Other parts of the business, which Rutland helped develop, included third-party cheque cashing (typically for customers who do not have bank accounts or don't want the proceeds to go through a bank account or need the cash right away), the sale of unredeemed pledge stock (mainly gold items which are melted down and sold on through the stores), cash in advance of employer pay-days, unsecured loans to pre-qualified customers at a high annual percentage rate (APR) and pre-paid credit cards.

Paul Cartwright and another Rutland team member were heavily involved in the operational aspects of the business post-acquisition, working in a store to familarize themselves with the operations, gaining an understanding of what the staff were doing all day, and also reviewing the operational and procedural systems and the IT systems. One result of this was a task-orientated analysis to work out how many people each store should ideally be employing. This resulted in 15% staff savings. A more effective IT system, particularly for database management, was also commissioned. Management reporting was improved, with better statistical analysis and a clear focus on key performance indicators (KPIs).

In addition, a university mathematician was contracted to model from historical transaction data the effect on the business of varying the key elements of a pawn loan, such as interest rates and amount of loan. This enabled changes to the proposition to be made with the confidence of how this would impact the business. Another improvement was to re-engineer the process in the business to enable non-redeemed jewellery (representing about 20% of pawned jewellery) to be allocated to stores in the network where it was needed and could be sold effectively, rather than leaving it with the store where it had been pawned in the first place.

## Flotation

Having strengthened the business to become the sector leader, and increased the number of stores to 69, Rutland went on to list H&T on AIM in May 2006. The enterprise value of H&T on flotation was £91.9 million with a market capitalization of £54.2 million. Rutland achieved an 89% IRR, a return of nearly three times its original investment.

Rutland retains its £3.0 million controlling investment in Svensk Pantbelaning made at the same time as the original acquisition of H&T.

## Paul Cartwright's tips for entrepreneurs

Paul Cartwright has the following tips for entrepreneurs seeking venture capital finance:

- Get good people around you; don't feel threatened by people who might be more qualified than you.
- Bring resources on board to cover any gaps in your team.
- Review and control where money is spent regularly – always cut costs where possible.
- Never stop challenging yourself on business.
www.rutlandpartners.com

## Completion

Once all the due diligence is complete, the terms of the deal can be finally negotiated and, once agreed by all parties, the lawyers will draw up Heads of Agreement or Agreement in Principle and then the legally binding completion documents (Figure 9.4). Management should ensure that they take both legal advice and have a firm grasp themselves of all the legalities within the documents. The legal documentation is described in the next chapter.

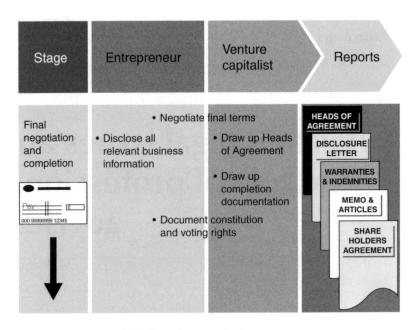

**Figure 9.4** The private equity investment process

# Tax and legal issues and the role of professional advisers

## DIFFERENT TAX AND LEGAL REGIMES AROUND EUROPE

The legal and fiscal environment in which the European private equity industry operates is complex, to say the least. With 25 member states in the European Union in 2006, 5 candidate countries due to join the EU shortly and 16 other European countries, there are 46 countries in all, each with their own, and often quite different, legal and tax environments. This gives rise to considerable legal complexity and high administrative costs in pursuing private equity and venture capital investments in Europe, particularly in connection with funds and deals operating and taking place across different European countries.

As we saw in Chapter 2, the European Union has implemented various incentives for the venture capital industry and entrepreneurs seeking venture capital financing and a number of initiatives such as the Lisbon agenda. However, there is still much further to go in terms of the practical measures to simplify and streamline legal and tax regimes across Europe.

### Lack of pan-European fund structure

EVCA has been lobbying for a pan-European fund structure for some time to facilitate cross-border investment decisions. Currently, private equity and venture capital funds have to structure themselves around the

25 different tax, regulatory and legal systems of the EU member countries. This can lead to many complexities and uncertainties, not to mention increased costs, for private equity and venture capital investors and fund managers. There is currently no suitable tax or legal structure for private equity and venture capital funds that is effective in all situations across Europe. Nor is the principle of tax transparency of a limited partnership structure recognized by all European countries. This can lead to a double charge to tax within the fund. Investors should not be worse off by investing through a fund than if they had invested directly in the underlying companies in the fund. Investors should also be able to claim the benefit of any double tax treaties between themselves and the countries of the underlying investments on any profits from those investments allocated to the investors as if they had held the investments directly.

## EVCA publications on European tax and legal environment

In view of the variety and complexity of the tax and legal regimes in Europe there is not the space to discuss each of them individually here. However, EVCA has produced a number of publications on the European tax and legal environment which may well be of interest to entrepreneurs and others setting up operations and seeking private equity and venture capital financing in or across various European countries. Many of these are available free of charge from the EVCA website: www.evca.com.

In particular, the EVCA publication *Benchmarking European Tax and Legal Environments; Indicators of Tax and Legal Environments favouring the Development of Private Equity, Venture Capital and Entrepreneurship in Europe* sets out a selection of important factors that impact on the private equity and venture capital industry in Europe, focusing on the tax and legal issues relating to both private equity firms and the investors in their funds and to the entrepreneurs. The publication covers, by country, the fund structures used for private equity in each country, merger regulation, investments by pension funds into private equity, company tax and private individual income tax rates, capital gains tax rates for individuals, tax incentives for individuals investing in private equity, taxation of stock options, the entrepreneurial environment, fiscal incentives for research and development, and bankruptcy and insolvency regulations.

Other EVCA papers in this area of interest include:

■ 'Employment Law Issues for European Companies' – this paper outlines key employment law issues for 17 of the countries in the European Union and Switzerland.

■ 'Taxation of Corporate Profits, Dividends and Capital Gains in Europe' – this paper compares the current situation on the taxation of corporate profits, dividends and capital gains in 19 European countries.

■ 'Private Equity and Venture Capital Incentives in Europe' – this paper outlines the tax incentives for private equity and venture capital in relation to 12 European countries and also includes the United States in order to provide a comparative view to set against Europe's initiatives.

■ 'Company Law across Europe' – when structuring a cross-border transaction, all kinds of issues and requirements arising from the diversity of legislations in the different European jurisdictions have to be taken into account and addressed. This paper identifies the relevant company law questions in 18 different countries and gives an overview of the similarities and differences in these jurisdictions.

■ 'Taxation of Stock Options across Europe' – this paper summarizes how stock options are taxed in each country and highlights those countries that have tax provisions that facilitate the granting of options and encourage option holders to become shareholders. Stock options are still usually subject to tax when the option is exercised. Consequently, many managers who have been granted options end up selling their shares, if they can, bearing in mind that the shares are in an unquoted company, as soon as they have exercised the options, in order to meet the tax liability. The tax charge is usually the difference between the market value of the share at the date of the exercise and the exercise price. EVCA considers that the actual sale of the shares is the time when it is appropriate to impose a tax charge and not when the options are exercised. This is necessary in order to attract experienced managers from the relative security of large corporates into entrepreneurial ventures.

## Need for professional advice

In view of the complexity of the tax and legal aspects of completing a private equity or venture capital deal in Europe, you must take professional advice even if you are operating in just one country, but especially if your business or finance raising crosses jurisdictions.

The financial adviser, accountant and lawyer all have important roles to play at many stages of the private equity and venture capital process, both for the management team seeking finance and for the private equity firm.

# THE FINANCIAL ADVISER'S ROLE

The primary role of the financial adviser in a private equity transaction is to provide corporate finance advice either to you and your management team or to the private equity firm sponsoring the transaction. Your financial adviser will provide you with impartial financial advice, independent of the private equity or venture capital firm that you are dealing with and the firm's own advisers.

The exact nature of the financial adviser's role varies from situation to situation but typically includes:

▌ Undertaking an initial appraisal of your business and financing proposition.

▌ Advice on your business plan – critically reviewing and appraising your plan to ensure that it includes all the areas referred to on business plans in Chapter 8 of this book. Ensuring that the business plan covers any specific requirements of the private equity or venture capital firms and is presented in accordance with their requirements.

▌ Advice on valuation of the business and planning for the ultimate sale of the business and realization of management's and the private equity firm's investment.

▌ Carrying out financial modelling, in particular sensitivity analysis on the financial projections to establish that the projections make accounting and commercial sense. Checking that they have been prepared in accordance with reasonable accounting policies and with due regard to publicly available information. Checking that they have been prepared in accordance with the assumptions used in the projections and that the assumptions appear reasonable.

▌ Advice on the most appropriate capital structure to be used to finance your proposal.

▌ Making introductions to appropriate sources of private equity and venture capital with firms whose investment criteria match your business proposition and a business style that should be right for you. If your business is a highly attractive investment opportunity for private equity firms, this may include organizing an 'auction' or a 'beauty parade' of private equity firms to compete for the right to finance your company. The financial adviser will need to ensure that the terms of any legal requirements regarding the communication of an invitation or inducement to engage in investment activity are properly complied with in providing this service, such as the provisions contained in the Financial Services and Markets Act (FSMA) in the UK.

■ Making introductions to appropriate sources of debt and other finance to help to finance the proposition.

■ Reviewing offers of finance – reviewing the terms of the deal offered by the private equity and venture capital firms and any other finance providers and assisting in negotiating the most advantageous terms from those on offer.

■ Assisting in negotiating the terms of the deal with the private equity firms and banks and with the vendor.

■ Project managing the transaction to minimize calls on management time and disruption to the business.

■ Providing other advice, at a later stage if required, on the flotation of the company's shares on a stock exchange or their sale to another commercial organization (trade sale).

# THE ACCOUNTANT'S ROLE

The primary role of the accountant acting on behalf of the private equity or venture capital firm is to undertake investigatory due diligence, such as described in Chapter 9. The precise scope of the accountant's role varies from situation to situation but typically includes:

■ Reporting formally on the projections.

■ Undertaking financial and possibly other types of due diligence, including commercial due diligence (see Chapter 9 for the various types of due diligence). Due diligence is usually a prerequisite to a private equity firm making its investment. The accountant will also be able to make informal opinions on aspects of the plan to the benefit of both the management team and the private equity firm.

■ Undertaking pensions, IT or environmental investigatory work and due diligence.

The management team may also engage an accountant to:

■ Provide audit, accounting and other advisory services.

■ Help you plan your tax efficiently so that management obtains the maximum benefit from the tax system, whether the aim is for a public flotation or to remain independent, and to minimize tax liability on any ultimate sale of equity.

■ Value your company's shares – for tax planning purposes and for negotiation with the appropriate tax authorities.

■ It is often the case that the financial advisory role and the role of the accountant performing investigatory due diligence are performed by different teams within the same organization. Your accountant may therefore also be able to act as your financial adviser.

## THE TAX ADVISER'S ROLE

The tax adviser will also help to ensure that, where possible:

■ Tax relief is available for interest paid on personal borrowings to finance management's equity investment.

■ Potential gains on the sale of equity are taxed as a capital gain and not treated as earned income.

■ Any capital gains taxes are deferred on the sale of equity.

■ Exposure to any inheritance taxes is minimized.

■ Tax relief on professional costs in connection with a management buyout, flotation or other exit is maximized.

■ Corporate funding is structured to maximize tax relief.

■ Tax due diligence procedures are properly carried out.

A very important role of the accountant and/or tax adviser is reviewing the tax indemnities provided by the company directors and shareholders to the private equity firm.

Your tax adviser can also explain the qualifying criteria under which personal investments can be made under various government initiatives, such as the Enterprise Investment Scheme and Venture Capital Trusts in the UK (see Chapter 6).

If you require an accountant or financial adviser with experience in the private equity or venture capital fields, see the Associate Members sections of the various country sections included in the EVCA Directory or your local private equity association directory, such as the BVCA Directory in the UK.

## THE LAWYER'S ROLE

Usually there are at least two sets of lawyers involved in the private equity investment process; one representing the management team and one representing the private equity firm. Other parties, such as bankers and other private equity firms, if acting as a syndicate, will each want their own lawyer involved.

## The private equity firm's lawyer

The private equity firm's lawyer is mainly concerned with ensuring that the private equity firm's investment is adequately protected from a legal standpoint. The lawyer will draw up the various investment agreements, usually including the shareholders' or subscription agreements, warranties and indemnities, loan stock or debenture agreements, directors' service contracts and the disclosure letter as discussed below.

### Shareholders' or subscription agreements

The shareholders' or subscription agreement (or investment agreement as it is often called) documents in detail the terms of the investment, including any continuing obligations of management required by the private equity firm, the warranties and indemnities given by the existing shareholders, penalty clauses and the definition of shareholder rights. The shareholders' agreement will include many of the elements of the term sheet or offer letter produced during the negotiation process and discussed in Chapter 9. As previously noted, it is better for the term sheet to be as detailed and unambiguous as possible so that there are no surprises when the shareholders' agreement has been drafted for you to sign.

### Warranties and indemnities

These are documents that confirm that the information provided by the directors and/or shareholders to the private equity firm, either in writing or spoken, is accurate. If this information turns out later to be inaccurate, the private equity firm can claim against the providers of the information (ie management) for any resulting loss incurred. The disclosure letter (see below) helps to protect management from the onerous nature of the warranties and indemnities.

### Loan stock or debenture agreements

The loan stock and/or debenture agreements set out the terms under which these forms of finance are provided.

### Service contracts

Service contracts formally document the conditions of employment of key members of the management team.

## *Disclosure letter*

The disclosure letter contains all the key information disclosed to the private equity firm on which the investment decision has been based. It is essential that the directors do not omit anything that could have an impact on that decision, so do put everything you think is even remotely important or areas in which you have concerns into the disclosure letter. Once something is documented in the disclosure letter you are deemed to have informed the investors about it (eg your concern as to whether a particular major customer contract will materialize or a concern about some aspect of the manufacturing process). The investors cannot then come after you legally on what you have disclosed to them. The disclosure letter effectively serves to limit the warranties and indemnities.

## The management team's lawyer

The management team's lawyer will review the term sheet or offer letter (also sometimes called the Heads of Agreement) provided by the private equity firm, as detailed in Chapter 9, and, together with your financial adviser, will help you to negotiate acceptable terms. The team's lawyer will also, in due course, negotiate the investment agreements with the private equity firm's lawyer and produce the disclosure letter, as well as negotiating any loan documents with the banker's lawyer.

In the case of a new company, your lawyer can incorporate the company and draw up the documents that govern the constitution of the company, its permitted activities and the powers of its shareholders and directors. These are known as the Memorandum and Articles of Association in the UK, for example. Even in the case of an existing company, a new Memorandum may be required and new Articles almost certainly will be needed to document the dividend and other rights attaching to the company's shares following the private equity investment.

If you need to find a lawyer experienced in private equity and venture capital, refer to the Associate Members section of the various country sections included in the EVCA Directory or your local private equity association directory, such as the BVCA Directory in the UK.

Professional costs incurred by the financial advisers, accountants and lawyers employed by the management team and the private equity firm were discussed in Chapter 9. As a reminder the costs will depend on the complexity of the transaction but will typically be around 5% of the money being raised.

# The ongoing relationship with the investor

## HOW THE VC FIRM CAN HELP THE GROWTH AND SUCCESS OF AN INVESTEE COMPANY

The private equity or venture capital firm's involvement with your company does not end once they have written their investment cheque – at least hopefully not! From the private equity firm's viewpoint they will want to closely monitor their investment and the business's progress in achieving its planned milestones, they will want proactive input into strategic and key operational decisions, including hiring new or replacement members of the management team, firing members of the team for poor performance, expanding overseas, acquiring other businesses, and many other areas, as well as the right to veto certain decisions. In return they will hopefully add value to their investment and the work of the management team in many areas.

### Surveys demonstrate the contribution of private equity

Private equity investment has been demonstrated to contribute significantly to companies' growth. An EVCA survey on 'The Economic and Social Impact of Venture Capital in Europe' carried out in 2002 investigated the function and value of venture capital investments in early-stage and expansion-stage companies. Some 95% of the companies that replied to the survey stated that, without venture capital investment, they could not have existed or would have developed more slowly, and 72% of seed/start-up companies stated that they would have never come into existence without the contribution of venture capital.

While VCs focus on monitoring financial performance of the investee companies and giving financial advice, their input can extend to many other areas, including monitoring operating performance, formulating strategy, acting as a sounding board for management's ideas and helping management to maintain focus. Seed/start-up companies valued venture capitalists most for their strategic advice, followed by networking opportunities and focus and support. Companies receiving investment to fund expansion considered the VC's most important contribution to be the provision of credibility/status and focus and support, followed by strategic and financial advice. More than 90% of all responding companies reported that they had contact with their venture capital backer on a weekly or monthly basis.

This EVCA survey also showed that the post-VC investment period was characterized by large percentage increases in turnover, with, for 90% of respondents, the growth in turnover the same as or greater than that of their competitors. Companies also reported an increase in exporting activities following the venture capital investment and the creation of substantial numbers of new jobs.

EVCA had carried out a survey previously, in 2001, on 'The Economic and Social Impact of Management Buyouts and Buyins in Europe'. Eighty-four per cent of respondents stated that without the buyout they would either have failed to survive or would have had limited growth prospects. Respondents also stated that the contribution of the private equity firm, in both financial and non-financial aspects of company operations, had been crucial to post-buyout success. Two-thirds of respondents reported improvements in competitive position and financial performance that were significantly greater than those achieved by their competitors. More than 60% of respondents declared an increase in the total number of employees post-buyout. And, as with the early-stage and expansion survey, the involvement of the private equity firm was not simply restricted to financial contributions but, for example, extended to acting as a sounding board for management ideas and monitoring operational performance.

Similarly, the BVCA's annual 'Economic Impact of Private Equity in the UK' shows that the vast majority of companies receiving private equity believe that without private equity they would not exist at all or would have developed less rapidly. Furthermore, the report consistently demonstrates that private-equity-backed companies increase their sales, exports, investments and people employed at a considerably higher rate than the national average.

While the growth and success of these companies owe much to private equity investment, enabling them to achieve their full potential, the non-financial input by the private equity firm is also a very important contributor. The private equity firm's involvement generally does not end following the initial investment. Of the private-equity-backed companies analysed in the BVCA survey annually, over three-quarters say that their private equity firms make a major contribution other than the provision of money. Contributions cited by private-equity-backed companies often include private equity firms being used to provide financial advice, guidance on strategic matters, and for management recruitment purposes as well as with their contacts and market information.

Most private equity firms' executives have a wide range of experience. Many have worked in industry and others have a financial background, but what is more important, all have the specialist experience of funding and assisting companies at a time of rapid development and growth. Levels of support vary, however, ranging from 'hands-on' to 'hands-off'.

# HANDS-ON APPROACH

A 'hands-on' or active approach from the investor aims to add value to your company. In addition to advising on strategy and development, the private equity firm will have many useful business connections to share with you, perhaps introducing you to potential customers, suppliers, alliance partners, acquisition candidates, even other VCs. The private equity firm will aim to be a real business partner to you, someone you can approach to bounce off ideas and to discuss strategy and tactics.

A hands-on investor is particularly suited to a company embarking on a period of rapid expansion, perhaps into new markets, overseas or through acquisition. The VC may act as the facilitator to encourage a locally focused entrepreneur to look outside his or her local boundaries and even take the entrepreneur overseas to network and meet with customers and strategic partners, for example in the United States or India or China. The VC may also encourage a technically focused entrepreneur to think more in terms of his or her customers' needs. However, the VC is unlikely to expect or want to get involved in the day-to-day operational control of the business, unless something goes seriously wrong.

In order to provide this hands-on support, most private equity firms will expect to participate through a seat on your board. The director may be an executive from the private equity firm, such as the executive who worked on your investment proposition, or the director may be an external consultant or monitoring director brought in by the private equity firm (Figure 11.1). Fees will need to be paid for the director's services.

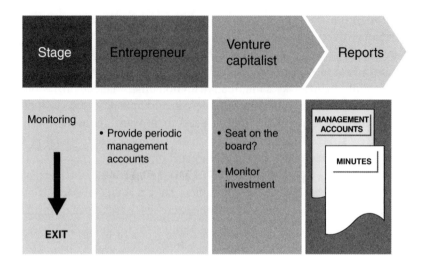

**Figure 11.1** The private equity investment process

In addition, in order to monitor their investment, the private equity firm will expect to:

▌ receive copies of your management accounts, promptly after each month end;

▌ receive copies of the minutes of the board of directors' meetings;

▌ be consulted and involved in, and sometimes have the right to veto (depending on the terms included in the subscription agreement), any important decisions affecting the company's business – this will include major capital purchases, changes in strategic direction, business acquisitions and disposals, appointment of directors, key management and auditors, obtaining additional borrowings, etc.

Case study 16 below illustrates the exceptional hands-on approach taken by venture capital firm Endeavour with its investment Tagsys. Over a period of around 18 months managing partner Bernard Vogel spent at least two-thirds of his time with Tagsys, reshaping the organization with the CEO, talking to potential investors and recruiting members of the management team as well as chairing the board. And we saw in case study 11 on Cambridge Silicon Radio how the three VCs involved had brought different aspects to the deal: helping to build profile, providing commercial introductions, advising on the technology and on legal agreements, providing useful contacts and assisting with the management recruitment process. Rutland Partners in case study 15 spent a huge amount of time working closely with the management team of H&T in improving the operational efficiency of the business, developing new products, accelerating the roll-out of new stores, and getting involved in the operational aspects of the business to the extent of even working in a store to familiarize themselves with the operations, staff activities and procedural and IT systems. In just about all of the case studies that I have included in this book you will see evidence of how the VC investors have added considerable value to their investee companies to both their own and the founder/management team's benefit.

# HANDS-OFF APPROACH

Some investors may take a less active role in the business. A 'hands-off' or passive approach essentially leaves management to run the business without involvement from the private equity firm until it is time to exit. The private equity firm will still, however, expect to receive regular financial information on your company and the board minutes. If your company defaults on payments, does not meet agreed targets or runs into other types of difficulties, a typically hands-off investor is likely to become more closely involved with the management of the company to try to ensure that its prospects are turned around.

## Case study 16

### Tagsys – the VC's (Endeavour's) leading role in securing financing rounds and effecting changes to the management team

TAGSYS (www.tagsysrfid.com) designs, manufactures and integrates end-to-end radio frequency identification (RFID) infrastructure for e-connecting goods. With a global presence of over 40 million RFID tags, 10,000 reader systems and 500 installations worldwide, TAGSYS is a leading provider of RFID solutions in the supply chain for item-level, case-level and pallet-level tracking, tracing, security and anti-counterfeiting measures. TAGSYS RFID solutions are currently being deployed in a range of highly specialized vertical markets that include pharmaceutical, fashion apparel, libraries, and textile rental.

In 2001 Endeavour LP (www.endeavourlp.com), a pan-European venture capital fund investing in early-stage companies within the Information and Communication Technology sector, assisted Tagsys in its spin-off from Gemplus, the world leader in smart card solutions and services.

Bernard Vogel, managing partner of Geneva-based Endeavour and chairman of the board of Tagsys, is the partner responsible for Endeavour's involvement with Tagsys from the MBO from Gemplus up to the present day. Bernard explained how Endeavour worked with Tagsys through five financing rounds to date, bringing a range of VCs on board and effecting many changes in the management team.

## MBO from Gemplus

In 2001, following a strategic review, Gemplus decided to refocus on its core business areas, which at that time were largely SIM cards for mobile phones and 'smart' credit cards. The RFID business of Gemplus, a pioneer in an embryonic market, was to be disposed of. Five of the key managers of the RFID operations prepared a business plan and organized an MBO with US $13.9 million finance provided largely by AXA Private Equity (82%), part of the AXA Group, and also by Endeavour (12%) and Saffron Hill Ventures (6%), a London-based early-stage venture capital fund. Tagsys' USP was its proven technology, protected IP, leading-edge innovation, highly experienced team out of Gemplus at the time and its market-specific RFID tag products fully tailored to the requirements of its customers in several sectors. Today, customers include pharmaceutical companies such as Pfizer and Glaxo, some of the largest libraries in the world, the fashion sector and the textile rental market for such items as uniforms, bedding and linen for hotels.

Tagsys was established with headquarters in Marseille, France. The original MBO team, who have now left Tagsys apart from the technical leaders, were incentivized with options over a percentage of the equity based on the value added for the three private equity investors, but these did not materialize as the company underperformed against its initial targets and timing.

## Subsequent financing rounds

With difficult market conditions post 9/11, Tagsys was burning cash heavily through 2003 and with the strategy agreed to focus on mature markets only and an attempt to break even, a further US $5.7 million was secured in a second round of financing from the existing three VCs and also bringing in FCJE (Joint Investment Fund for Young Enterprises), a French fund which is equally invested by the French state, the European Investment Fund, and France's

Caisse des Dépôts et Consignations. The objective of the FCJE is to take minority interests in French high-tech companies that are less than seven years old, at the request of and alongside investment funds operating in countries in the European Union.

The company was still burning cash into 2004 and was underperforming against the targets agreed by its investors, but with a new focus on growing markets (pharma, fashion, retail) and a strategy to enter more intensely the US marketplace (which was not necessarily welcomed by the French investors) a further finance round of US $8.8 million was secured, again from the same original three shareholders and with Add Partners, a London-based venture capital firm which invests in European IT and communications businesses, now coming in.

Following the closing, Endeavour was instrumental in bringing in an executive chairman, Elie Simon, at this time. Elie Simon joined Tagsys from Sun Microsystems where he was president of the EMEA region, responsible for over $3 billion of sales for the corporation.

## Major changes to the management team

In 2005, now with 40% of the revenues being generated in the United States, Endeavour talked with Elliott Associates, a New-York-based private investment fund with more than US $4 billion of capital under management and an investor in AXA's fund involved in Tagsys. As it happened, Elliott had been watching Tagsys' growth in the United States. Elliott agreed to co-invest in a fourth US $12 million financing round with Endeavour at which point Endeavour and Elliott took control of the company. They changed the board of directors, with three out of four board members now from Endeavour, and several members of the management team, with Endeavour helping to bring a new group CFO, new Head of Marketing, new VP of Operations, new Head of Engineering and several new sales people onto the team. Elie Simon was made President and CEO, the headquarters moved to Cambridge, Massachusetts and the company reincorporated as a Delaware company.

In May 2006 a fifth round was closed with JP Morgan Partners for US $35 million. Cazenove Private Equity was also brought in as an investor following a successful presentation by Tagsys' CEO on the French Tech Tour in October 2005. Elliott, JP Morgan and Cazenove now all sit on the board of directors.

Endeavour has increased its equity stake through all the various financing rounds, while the main original investor, AXA Private Equity, has seen its stake reduced from 82% to nearer 10%.

## Hands-on throughout the process

Endeavour has adopted a very hands-on role throughout its involvement with the company. In the period 2005 to 2006 Bernard Vogel spent at least two-thirds of his time with Tagsys, in particular reshaping the organization with the CEO, talking to potential investors and recruiting members of the management team as well as chairing the board of Tagsys. Elliott has been supportive of Endeavour's efforts, leaving the active role to Endeavour, while keeping fully informed as an investor and attending board and other meetings. Endeavour believes that Tagsys is now well on track for an IPO in two years' time.

## Bernard Vogel's tips for management teams

Bernard Vogel has the following tips for management teams on how to work with the lead private equity investor:

- Be very selective in choosing your lead investor and take references on them! They are going to be your partners for many years and you need full trust and understanding.
- Work in a true partnership with your lead investor: be completely transparent, disclose all news, in particular bad news, and be part of the solution going through the inevitable problems of a growing company.
- Listen carefully to the firm's advice and validate it; VC investors have typically seen many cases of developing companies. They can usually help you in identifying issues ahead of time.
- Together with your lead investor, hire the right talents at the right time for your company.
- Talk to the VC investors regularly, and share your issues and views as often as possible.

www.endeavourlp.com

# HELP TO AVOID PITFALLS

What investors, or indeed your bankers and advisers, do not like at all are surprises. So if you are running into difficulties or see problems looming, do inform your private equity investor and other key providers of finance, whether they are operating a hands-on or a hands-off approach. The private equity investor can help you spot the danger signs of troubled times ahead and avoid business pitfalls. He or she might even be able to help you avoid going into receivership or liquidation. Follow Bernard Vogel's tips that we have just seen in case study 16 above for working in a true partnership with your investor: be completely transparent, disclose all news (in particular bad news), talk to your investor regularly and share your issues and views as often as possible.

## VC Tip #14

Keep your investors, bankers and advisers informed – they are there to help and do not like surprises!

If you do get into difficulties your investor may become particularly 'hands on' in order to protect his or her investment. It is essential that you have developed a good working relationship with your investor to see you through these hard times. And if the quality of the management team is questionable you may end up on the wrong side of Nigel Grierson's 'first immutable law of investing' that we saw in case study 14, ie 'the amount of time the investor has to involuntarily make available to the business is inversely proportional to the quality of the management team'. If the investor is experiencing declining confidence in the team, he or she corrects this by more frequent engagement. More frequent engagement often frustrates the founder or CEO, and hence the start of a deteriorating relationship is experienced.

### Watch for the danger signs!

Examples of danger signs in a business include the following:

- lack of response to changing environments;
- existence of fixed price contracts;
- increasing level of fixed costs;
- cash flow problems;

- breaches in bank covenants;
- failing to meet capital interest or dividend payments;
- increasing overseas competition;
- over-trading (ie taking on more work than the investment in working capital will allow);
- deteriorating credit control;
- uncontrolled capital expansion;
- inaccurate and/or untimely management information;
- autocratic management;
- financial impropriety;
- early success, but no staying power;
- over-expansion and loss of control;
- high turnover of key employees;
- extravagant executive lifestyle;
- dependence on too few customers and/or suppliers.

# DIRECTORS' RESPONSIBILITIES

As a company director you have onerous responsibilities to your share-holders and your creditors. The rules relating to directors' duties and responsibilities vary considerably from country to country in Europe. There are various forms of company in Europe and there are different rules for directors depending on the type of company used. Do seek professional advice for the rules relating to the country in which your business is incorporated or for advice on different jurisdictions. Be particularly careful of situations where you, and/or your fellow directors, including non-executive directors such as the VC investor, can be made personally liable in certain situations.

In the UK, many of the duties and obligations of a director are mandated by the Companies Act 1985 (shortly to be superceded by the Companies Act 2006). Others are governed by the Insolvency Act 1986 (you should be particularly aware of the 'wrongful trading' provisions contained therein) and the Company Directors' Disqualification Act 1986. Under the wrongful trading provisions a director may, by court order, be made personally liable for a company's debts if it is allowed to continue trading at a time when it was known, or should have been concluded, to be insolvent. Discuss any concerns with your private equity firm and other professional advisers before they become real problems and help to ensure success for you, your management team and your investors.

Also, in the UK you should review the Combined Code on Corporate Governance which is aimed at enhancing board effectiveness and improving investor confidence by raising standards of corporate governance.

## GUIDELINES FOR SUCCESS

The following guidelines apply to most successful business situations:

▌ Stick to what you know – avoid industries in which you are not experienced.

▌ Encourage a common philosophy of shared business goals and quality standards so that you meet and even exceed the expectations of your customers. Communicate these objectives and the results throughout your organization.

▌ Avoid information overload – concentrate your management information systems on what is critical to success.

▌ Build your team – as your business grows, recognize the need to direct the company and to not be personally involved in the day-to-day decision making which should be delegated to senior managers.

▌ Remember 'cash is king'; take care to manage your cash resources with the utmost care.

▌ Anticipate problems – know what is going to be critical as your company moves through its various growth stages.

▌ Keep your investors, bankers and advisers informed – they are there to help and do not like surprises.

▌ Watch your costs – ensure that the market price of your products gives a profit contribution in excess of the costs you incur. This may sound facile, but it is amazing how often this is not assessed regularly, resulting in unexpected losses.

▌ Do not anticipate sales – the costs can grow by themselves, but the sales will not.

▌ Use the network – a well-developed set of business contacts is one of the keys to business success. These could include customers, suppliers, trade associations, government agencies and professional advisers.

▌ Look for opportunities – the business plan is the agreed route forward for the business, but other opportunities will arise. Assess them, discuss them with your investors and pursue them if it makes sense for the business. Adapt your business plan as your company develops and new opportunities are considered.

# Exit routes

When you set up your business you probably had a time frame in mind in which you were looking to have grown your business to the point where it could be sold to another company or achieve a stock market flotation. Alternatively, you may have it in mind to hold on to the business and pass it on in due course to the next generation. Many business owners and management teams want to realize a capital gain and at some point they look to sell their investment or seek a stock market listing in order to realize a capital gain.

Whatever your aims for the company, if you have private equity firms involved, they will certainly require an exit route in order to realize a return on their investments. This will have been discussed at the time that you were negotiating the terms of the investment with them. You will also have indicated in your business plan how you believed that the venture capital firm would make a return on its investment.

The time frame from investment to exit can be as little as two years or as much as ten or more years. At the time of exit, the private equity firm may not sell all the shares it holds. In the case of a flotation, private equity firms are likely to continue to hold the newly quoted shares for a year or more. As we saw in Chapter 9, lock-up clauses included in the investment agreement will specify how soon after a flotation the management team and the VCs can sell their shares. This helps in making the shares attractive to public investors at the time of the IPO.

You need to be planning for the eventual exit as soon as you have a private equity or venture capital firm as your investor. As Frank Kenny and Joey Mason of Delta Partners stated in case study 6 on Neoss Limited, you need to remember that once you have an external investor on board, however small, you have started the process of eventually selling your business, be it through a trade sale or flotation. In fact, you need to be prepared to be tested on your exit plans at the business plan presentation stage, as Julian Davison of 3i states in case study 17 on e2v Technologies below.

## VC Tip #15

Start planning the exit for you and your investors as soon as you have the investors on board, if not before.

# EXIT OPTIONS

The five main exit options are listed below. If you are considering any of these, you will need the specialist advice of experienced professional advisers:

▌ *Trade sale*: the sale of your company's shares to another company, perhaps in the same industry sector. The majority of exits are achieved through a trade sale. This often brings a higher valuation to the company being sold than a full stock market quotation, because the acquirer actually needs the company to supplement its own business area, unlike a public shareholder.

▌ *Repurchase*: the repurchase of the private equity investors' shares by the company and/or its management. To repurchase shares you and your advisers will need to consult the regulations governing purchase of own shares in the country in which your company is incorporated, such as the Companies Act in the UK. Advance clearance from the tax authorities may also be required, as required by HM Revenue & Customs in the UK. Professional accounting and tax advice is absolutely essential before choosing this route.

▌ *Refinancing*: the purchase of the private equity investors' or others' shareholdings by another investment institution. This type of exit may be most suitable for a company that is not yet willing or ready for flotation or trade sale, but whose private equity investors may need an exit.

▌ *Flotation*: to obtain a quotation or IPO on a stock exchange, such as the Official List of the London Stock Exchange or AIM, the Deutsche Borse in Germany, Euronext and Alternext or NASDAQ in the USA. A stock market quotation has various advantages and disadvantages for the entrepreneur (see below).

■ *Involuntary exit*: where the company goes into receivership or liquidation.

## Data on exits

If we look at which types of exits are actually occurring the most in
Europe in practice, from the EVCA/Thomson/PwC private equity
survey, the total amount of divestments at cost made in 2005 was
€29.8 billion, an increase of 52% from 2004's total of €19.6 billion
(Figure 12.1).

Divestment by repayment of preference shares and/or loans was
actually the largest category by amount, representing 23% of the
total divestment amount in 2005, at €7.0 billion, up two-thirds from

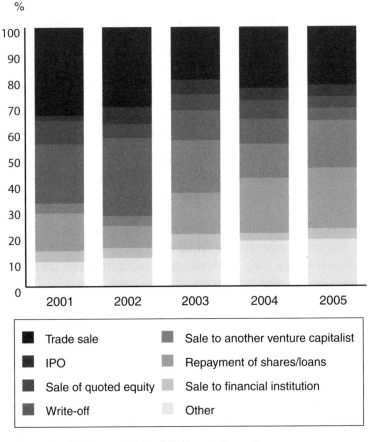

Source: EVCA/Thomson Financial/PricewaterhouseCoopers

**Figure 12.1** European private equity divestments

€4.2 billion in 2004. There were 1,633 divestments in this category in 2005 compared to 1,345 in 2004. These are largely financial engineering techniques, such as recapitalizations in order to release cash and return capital to investors.

Divestment by trade sale was the second largest category by amount, representing 23% of all divestments by amount in 2005 at €6.7 billion, a 46% increase from €4.6 billion in 2004. There were 1,317 divestments by trade sale in Europe in 2005 compared to 951 in 2004.

Secondary sales, which are sales by the private equity investor to another private equity firm, increased over two times to €5.5 billion in 2005 and represent 18% of total divestments by amount. There were 392 divestments in this category in 2005, compared to 292 in 2004.

Divestment by IPO (flotation or listing) remained relatively static at €1.3 billion in 2005, just a 4% increase in amount over 2004. There were 259 divestments by flotation in 2005, compared to 105 in 2004.

Overall, European divestments covered 4,824 companies in 2005 compared to 4,195 companies divested in 2004, representing an increase of average transaction size per company from €4.7 to €6.2 million.

Write-offs (where the private equity firm writes off its investment because it is non-performing and cannot be sold on to another investor, or it is in liquidation) decreased by 36% in 2005 to €1.4 billion, representing just 5% of the total divestment amount, compared to 10% in 2004.

So, with the exception of divestment by repayment of preference shares/loans, we can see that trade sales are easily the most popular form of exit, with divestment by IPO some way behind.

# TRADE SALE

The private equity firms tend to favour the trade sale exit route over an IPO because they can realize their investment in cash, or cash and shares where the shares can be sold for cash. With an IPO the private equity firms may not be able actually to sell their shares for some time (the so-called lock-up period). This also applies to the entrepreneur, founder or shareholder management team. The investment banks that underwrite IPOs generally insist upon lock-ups of at least 180 days from large shareholders (with 1% ownership or more) in order to allow an orderly market to develop in the shares. The shareholders that are subject to lock-up usually include the management and directors of the company, strategic partners and large investors such as the VCs.

For the entrepreneur/founder it is not all necessarily plain sailing with the trade sale exit route. Remember the story of Bob Jones and the sale of Equiinet to Dica in a share-for-share exchange in case study 13: the dot.com bubble burst at the end of 2000, the Neuer Markt crashed and Dica's attempts at an IPO failed. Dica went into administration and the original Equiinet investors, including Bob and Schroders, lost everything.

The entrepreneur/founder may want to continue with the business in some capacity following the sale and this will obviously be largely up to the needs of the new owner. In the case of Equiinet Dica took Bob Jones rather unexpectedly out of his executive role. If the entrepreneur has built up the business from start and/or been instrumental in growing the business he or she will likely have strong emotional ties to the company and will be concerned that there is the right cultural fit with the acquiring company and its management team. The entrepreneur will be concerned that his or her employees' interests are safeguarded. While the VC will achieve a complete exit with a trade sale and get their cash return, the entrepreneur may receive shares or even share options in the acquiring company.

Trade buyers can come from numerous sources. In recent years around one-fifth of merger and acquisition deals in the technology sector in Europe have been cross-border transactions, with the United States being the main player as its corporations seek out European target companies to acquire. The rationale for these deals ranges from establishing a European presence and buying best-of-breed solutions to complementing existing solution suites and acquiring sales and distribution networks.

## GOING PUBLIC

Going for an IPO or flotation has various attractions for the entrepreneur or shareholder management team, particularly when they want to carry on with their involvement in the business, but there are also several disadvantages to be aware of. There are various advantages and disadvantages of going public, as shown in Table 12.1.

The costs involved in the flotation process, underwriting, legal and accounting fees, can account for around 10–15% of the money raised from the flotation exercise (for a flotation on the LSE Main Market, for example). Then there are the ongoing compliance costs.

Also, do not underestimate the amount of time that it takes to go through the flotation process. While you are dealing with the investment

**Table 12.1** Advantages and disadvantages of going public

**Advantages of going public**

- Realization of some or all of the founder's/management team's capital
- Provides finance to expand the business (especially if VCs are not able to participate in a new round)
- Marketable shares available for acquisitions
- Enhanced status and public awareness
- Easier to recruit senior management and specialists from large companies
- Can re-energize management team as important milestone
- Increased employee motivation via share incentive schemes
- Potentially better job security for management and employees than with a trade sale
- A trade buyer may not recognize the full value in the company

**Disadvantages of going public**

- Possible loss of founder/management team control
- Requirement to reveal all price sensitive information which may also be of interest to your competitors
- VC investors locked in for 12 to 24 months, so not an exit for them
- Unwelcome (hostile) bids from suitors
- Continuing obligations – costs and management time incurred in complying with listed company regulations
- Increased scrutiny from shareholders and media
- Perceived emphasis on short-term profits and dividend performance

bankers, the VCs, various sets of lawyers and accountants, endless prospectus drafting meetings, warranties and indemnities etc, you also have to continue to run and grow your business. It is important not to take your eye off the ball during the arduous process. Expect to spend more of your time and that of your management team on the flotation than you did in raising private equity or venture capital. Following flotation you will also need to take the time to deal with investor relations, including spending time with the press.

## Increasing IPOs in Europe

The number of IPOs in Europe reached a peak in the year 2000 when well over 600 companies were floated on Europe's five most active markets at the time, corresponding with the boom in technology stocks. The number of IPOs subsequently dropped to 309 in 2001, 174 in 2002 and 149 in 2003, according to PwC's IPO Watch Europe Review. The number of IPOs jumped to 433 in 2004 and reached 603 in 2005. IPOs are on track to exceed 2005 levels as they reached 313 by the end of Q2 2006, despite several floats being cancelled due to severe market volatility. In 2005 Europe raised more new money from IPOs than the United States and attracted more international IPOs than the US stock exchanges.

# ALTERNATIVE INVESTMENT MARKET

AIM is the London Stock Exchange's international market for smaller growing companies. AIM was established in 1995 and is the leading secondary exchange in Europe. There are over 1,500 companies listed on AIM, with around 15% of companies coming from outside the UK. US companies are now looking to Europe for a listing on AIM or the other European markets in the aftermath of Sarbanes–Oxley with the high costs of compliance for companies listing on the New York Stock Exchange or NASDAQ.

AIM companies range from young, venture-capital-backed start-ups to well-established, mature organizations looking to expand. Many companies make the transition to the London Stock Exchange's Main Market following their experience on AIM.

To join AIM, companies do not need a particular financial track record or trading history. There is also no minimum requirement in terms of size or number of shareholders. Instead, all companies wishing to join AIM will need a nominated adviser ('Nomad') from AIM's approved register of Nomads who will ensure that the company is suitable for AIM and ready to be admitted to a public market.

The admission criteria for AIM and Main Market listings are summarized in Table 12.2.

The Main Market may provide better liquidity than AIM but many institutions are now prepared to invest in AIM companies. There is a lighter regulatory process on AIM: the ongoing compliance costs are less; an AIM company is not required to comply with the corporate governance requirements of the Main Market but still has to comply with public company requirements, such as preparing a prospectus for fundraising, preparing an annual report and keeping shareholders informed through scheduled six-month interim and full-year results announcements and making disclosures on an ongoing basis about other developments that might have an impact on the future performance of the company and/or its share price.

As discussed in Chapter 3, AIM has recently expanded into Europe. The London Stock Exchange is developing AIM to accommodate the demand among small- and medium-sized companies across Europe for equity growth capital. The LSE's goal is to develop AIM into a single pan-European trading platform for young, high-growth companies.

**Table 12.2** London Stock Exchange admission criteria: AIM versus Main Market

**AIM**

- No minimum shares to be in public hands
- No trading record requirement
- No prior shareholder approval for transactions (except reverse takeovers)
- Admission documents not pre-vetted by London Stock Exchange nor by the UK Listings Authority (UKLA) in most circumstances
- Nominated adviser required at all times (see above)
- No minimum market capitalization

**Main Market**

- Minimum 25% shares in public hands
- Normally 3-year trading record required
- Prior shareholder approval required for substantial acquisitions and disposals
- Pre-vetting of admission documents by UKLA
- Sponsors needed for certain transactions
- Minimum market capitalization (must be at least £700,000)

AIM is currently tightening up regulation of certain sectors, such as natural resources like oil, with AIM officials conducting compliance visits to the nominated advisers of companies and requiring more detailed disclosures of the value of assets, backed up with reports from independent experts.

# OTHER EUROPEAN ALTERNATIVE MARKETS

New junior markets have been created for the Deutsche Borse in Germany (its 'Entry Standard' segment of the Open Market) and Alternext was set up in 2005 by Euronext to meet the needs of small- and mid-sized companies seeking simplified access to the stock markets. Alternext streamlined listing requirements, and trading rules are suited to the size and business needs of small- and mid-cap firms seeking to finance growth and gain access to the financial markets of the euro zone. Euronext provides international services for regulated cash markets and derivative markets in Belgium, France, the UK (LIFFE derivatives market), the Netherlands and Portugal.

In June 2006 the New York Stock Exchange and Euronext agreed to complete a €15 billion merger creating the largest, and the world's first transatlantic, stock exchange.

EVCA continues to lobby hard for the creation of a pan-European stock market for young, high-growth companies in Europe. This could be achieved by close collaboration between the existing country exchanges or the broadening of one exchange to be pan-European. Some of the recent developments with AIM and Alternext are therefore encouraging in this regard.

The whole process of going public is quite onerous, fraught with potential pitfalls and requires careful planning. Take a look at the case study on Esmertec (case study 18) to see some of the issues faced by this company as it went public and post-flotation. You should seek specialist professional advice at the earliest opportunity if you are contemplating going the public route.

## Case study 17

### e2v Technologies – how the VC investor helped prepare for the management buyout and ultimate exit

3i originally invested €40m in e2v Technologies (e2v) when the company led a €82 million buyout of the then named Marconi Applied Technologies from Marconi in 2002. 3i recognized e2v as a company with strong potential that was, nevertheless, both poorly presented and poorly understood. e2v, in turn, wanted to work with 3i because it had a clearly defined plan to add value to the business.

3i's Julian Davison explained how 3i worked with the management team to effect the management buyout and later to achieve a successful exit through a listing on the London Stock Exchange.

### Background

The origins of e2v can be traced back to the 1940s, to the development of magnetrons for use in defence radar applications. e2v is now a specialist supplier of RF, microwave and sensing component and subsystems with strong, and in a number of cases leading, positions in global, niche markets.

e2v's range of high-power vacuum tubes is the enabling technology behind a diverse range of applications, from the transmission of TV signals to life-saving cancer radiotherapy machines. e2v also provides its customers with value-added product offerings, integrating power supplies and modulators around vacuum tube devices. Examples of this are e2v's high-power satellite uplink amplifiers and the compact modulator for driving magnetrons in a range of linear accelerator applications. e2v supplies image sensors for space mission instruments, such as the Hubble Space Telescope, and for use by dentists to capture digital images of teeth. The company's thermal imaging cameras are used by firefighters around the world and its Gunn diodes are the signal source for adaptive cruise control systems now found on the market in luxury cars. e2v has two manufacturing sites in the UK and exports over 65% of its output.

## Management buyout

Marconi was attempting to sell off its Applied Technologies division (now e2v) back in 2002 but was unable to find a trade buyer. The management team behind Marconi Applied Technologies put together a plan for a management buyout of the entity and an investment bank was engaged to market the opportunity to potential investors. Several private equity houses were approached, including 3i, who had already met the team through networking activities.

As noted above, e2v were attracted to 3i as an investor because of 3i's willingness to support the team and help to create value as e2v set up on its own away from Marconi. On its part, 3i saw the potential in the business and was impressed by the management team. Having decided to invest, 3i worked closely with the management team over the next few months in refining the business plan. 3i also introduced two turnaround specialists to the board as non-executive directors. 3i partner Julian Davison also joined the board.

The e2v buyout was a classic leveraged buyout structure with the management team holding an initial 20% of the equity and with a ratchet based on external returns – as target returns were exceeded the management team received proportionately more of the equity. 3i invested €40million in a mix of equity and shareholder loans, with the balance in bank debt.

With the management buyout successfully completed, and with a seat on the board, 3i continued to develop a strong relationship with the management team and board, and contributed significantly to strategic and operational decisions. This led to a number of successful operational improvements, from stock reduction to IT system implementations.

## Successful exit

3i also helped to improve the presentation of the business externally, making it much more attractive to potential investors and acquirers, and helped strengthen the board with the appointment of a further non-executive director with deep knowledge of e2v's end-markets. Trade buyers were approached and 3i also helped prepare the company for flotation, a six-month process.

In July 2004 e2v floated on the London Stock Exchange, achieving a capitalization of €162 million, and generated around €20million of free cash. In the period between the original buyout and its flotation, e2v's operating profits increased around 40% to €16 million.

## Julian Davison's tips for management teams looking to achieve a successful management buyout

Julian Davison has the following tips for management teams looking to achieve a successful buyout with the ultimate exit in mind:

▮ Have a clear plan about how to achieve sustainable earnings growth in the medium to longer term – don't just focus on short-term targets.
▮ Be clear about the business and its ability to support substantial acquisition debt and be careful to monitor and control the cash flow in the business.
▮ Be prepared to be tested on the business plan, particularly as regards exit plans: remember that the aim is to achieve maximum long-term value not only for the management team's own reward but with an ultimate purchaser in mind.
▮ Think about who might buy the business and why – groom the business to be attractive to a purchaser.
▮ Attempt to gain an understanding of the likely exit window, ie the right time for management to sell and the right time for a purchaser to buy.
▮ Develop links with potential purchasers well ahead of when you plan to exit.

www.3i.com

# Case study 18

## Esmertec (part two) – the issues that the company faced post-IPO

Subsequent to the €23 million financing in November 2003 to finance working capital and the development of applications on top of the core Java Virtual Machine (JVM) product (as discussed in case study 9), Esmertec completed a pre-IPO convertible note in October 2004, made several acquisitions, including operations in China and Japan, and started preparing for an IPO. Jean-Michel Deligny, managing director of Go4Venture, takes up the story.

In preparation for an IPO, Esmertec appointed a panel of prestigious board members, including Michel Bon, ex-chairman and CEO of France Telecom, Tony Reis, ex-CEO of Swisscom and Ulrich Schumacher, ex-CEO of Infineon. The IPO was planned for 30 June 2005 but postponed by one day due to an alleged patent infringement, a further three days due to one of its customers being placed in administration, and then postponed until after the summer period. The IPO finally took place in September 2005, priced at 18 Swiss francs, and was six times oversubscribed. The share price increased to 25 Swiss francs in November 2005.

In January 2006 Esmertec announced that it was having difficulty collecting royalties and that it was adapting its revenue recognition policy accordingly. The share price dropped back to around the IPO price of 18 Swiss francs.

The 2005 results announcement in March 2006 revealed US $39.2million in revenues (a 46% increase on 2004) with an operating loss of US $13.8million (versus US $5.4 million in 2004). The share price drifted down to around 15 Swiss francs.

In May 2006, the company announced the departure of the Chief Technology Officer (CTO) and two founders. A drastic drop in revenues occurred in the first half of 2006 and the CEO resigned. The chief operating officer, Jean-Claude Martinez, was appointed interim CEO. The share price dropped to around 4 Swiss francs.

In July 2006 Jean-Claude Martinez was confirmed as CEO. In November 2006 revenues of over US $24million were predicted and the share price increased to around 7 Swiss francs. Also in November 2006, the respected Swiss businessman, Ruedi Noser, was appointed chairman.

# Jean-Michel Deligny's comments on going public

Jean-Michel Deligny has the following comments and recommendations for management teams seeking a stock market listing based on the issues that affected Esmertec as it went through, and subsequent to, the IPO process.

## Business model (always easy to comment in hindsight!)

- Working capital requirements can be considerable in a business with substantial services revenues (25% of total revenues in the case of Esmertec) and large customers taking more than 90 days to pay.
- The best technology is not always sufficient in a market where price is key (mobile phones) and where customers may prefer a possibly inferior but cheaper technology.
- A handful of buyers may drive suppliers to engage in price wars (eg in the Japanese market).
- Revenue recognition policies are key!

## Bankers and board members

- Large banks (as appointed by Esmertec) may not be the most courageous in the face of adversity – they care about their reputational risk!
- Appointing prestigious board members is not necessarily a panacea. They are busy and cannot necessarily focus as much on the business. They will also worry about their reputation and may be inclined to push drastic measures to be seen as decisive during a crisis.

## European listing

- Read the small print of stock exchange rules: the Zurich Stock Exchange requires giving potential shareholders more time to absorb news in the case of a significant development during the book-building period.
- Public shareholders don't like surprises. Technology companies often spring surprises. The consequences can be devastating. The announcement of slower than expected revenue growth (even if it is still +40% pa) can still lead to a drop in share price by 30% in a day! This is explained mostly by the lack of liquidity, with a few sell orders having a disproportionate effect.

## PR

- Don't boast too much! Esmertec's entourage had been quite aggressive in touting their success. There was an element of *schadenfreude* when Esmertec blew up in such spectacular fashion.
- Pay attention to your communication. Esmertec acknowledged that their PR was less than stellar:
  - not explaining the stock exchange technicalities behind successive IPO postponements;
  - not being clear re bad debt risks, leaving observers to speculate;
  - announcing the departure of the CTO and two founders on the same day, with very little in terms of explanation.

## Finally

- Technology is a volatile business where execution is key (Esmertec was probably slow at diversifying away from its core JVM business) and companies are exposed to changing competition dynamics – caveat emptor (buyer beware).
- Going public has its own risks!

www.go4venture.com

# Concluding comments (and the 15 VC tips)

Despite some of the issues raised earlier in this book, the outlook for the European technology venture capital industry looks positive or at least 'cautiously optimistic'. There has been a more active mergers and acquisitions market over the past year and some successful IPOs of venture-backed companies in Europe. Several of the large, multinational technology companies have shown improved earnings. There is an improving entrepreneurial culture in Europe, one of the positive outcomes of the dot.com/internet era.

The time is now right for successful venture investing and raising finance for well-developed business propositions. But it is 'back to basics'. If you have a realistic, robust business model, innovative, commercially viable product(s), the ability to take a leading position in a growing market with evidence of your customer base and an experienced team, you have all the elements in place to raise venture capital finance for your business successfully. A tall order maybe, and you don't necessarily need to have all of these elements in place, but why should an external investor risk their fund's money in your venture if you haven't properly worked through these areas? I hope that this book has provided you with the practical guidance needed to raise venture capital finance in Europe.

As a reminder of some of the areas covered in this book I am including a listing here of the various 'VC tips' that featured in certain chapters. There is nothing 'earth shattering' here, just practical points for you to consider. And do also read through the personal tips of the venture capital firm investment executives, business angels and entrepreneurs included at the end of each of the 18 case studies which are a feature of this book. There is much excellent advice there from highly experienced individuals. You can refer to the cases again quickly via the listing of cases included after the contents list at the beginning of the book.

# THE 15 VC TIPS

## VC Tip #1

### *Assume nothing!*

Things may not be what they seem. Don't be afraid to ask questions and get feedback as you go through the venture capital raising process. (See Chapter 1)

## VC Tip #2

Get good people around you in your team, well balanced in terms of their skills and roles. (See Chapter 5)

## VC Tip #3

Plan for the unexpected/anticipate problems – know what is going to be critical as your company moves through its various growth stages. (See Chapter 6)

## VC Tip #4

Remember: 'Cash is king' – take care to manage and control your cash resources with the utmost care. (See Chapter 6)

## VC Tip # 5

Be selective in which VCs you contact – avoid the scattergun approach! (See Chapter 7)

## VC Tip #6

Get feedback on your business plan from one or two VCs before sending it to others on your list. (See Chapter 7)

## VC Tip #7

Practise your 'elevator pitch': a 60-second pitch about your business that *anyone* can understand. Must have a 'hook', USP and be delivered with passion and don't forget to follow up. (See Chapter 7)

## VC Tip #8

Network vigorously with VCs and other potential sources of finance, follow up your contacts and keep your contacts live. (See Chapter 7)

## VC Tip #9

Write the business plan yourself – investors want to learn what you and your team are planning to do, not see how well others can write for you! (See Chapter 8)

## VC Tip #10

Go overboard on the marketing section of the plan: it's often the most deficient part of the investment proposition. (See Chapter 8)

## VC Tip #11

Be patient: allow six to nine months for the investment process. (See Chapter 9)

## VC Tip #12

Properly prepare for your presentation to the VCs: have roles for all present, work as a team, keep the presentation simple, anticipate questions, don't bluff, and rehearse, rehearse, rehearse! (See Chapter 9)

## VC Tip #13

Be prepared to commit yourself financially when the VC invests – the time and money you have spent up to that point is not enough. (See Chapter 9)

## VC Tip #14

Keep your investors, bankers and advisers informed – they are there to help and do not like surprises! (See Chapter 11)

## VC Tip #15

Start planning the exit for you and your investors as soon as you have the investors on board, if not before. (See Chapter 12)

And a final point: Have fun and good luck! You really should be able to raise VC finance if you have the right ingredients in place, follow the guidance in this book and take professional advice as appropriate.

# References

Apax Partners and Economist Intelligence Unit (2006) *Unlocking Global Value: Future trends in private equity investment worldwide,* Apax Partners and Economist Intelligence Unit, London

Arundale, K (2004) Developing winning business plans, in *Taking Research to Market: How to build and invest in successful university spinouts,* ed K Tang, A Vohora and R Freeman, pp 103–113, Euromoney Books, London

British Venture Capital Association (BVCA) (2004) *A Guide to Private Equity,* BVCA, London

BVCA (2004) *A Guide to Venture Capital Term Sheets,* BVCA, London

BVCA (2005) *Creating Success from University Spin-outs,* BVCA, London

BVCA (2005) *The Economic Impact of Private Equity in the UK,* BVCA, London

BVCA (2006) *BVCA Private Equity and Venture Capital Performance Measurement Survey 2005,* BVCA, London

BVCA (2006) *Directory 2006/2007,* BVCA, London

BVCA (2006) *Report on Investment Activity 2005,* BVCA, London

Churchill, NC and Lewis, VL (1983) The five stages of small business growth, *Harvard Business Review,* May–June, pp 30–49

Cientifica (2006) *VCs to Nanotech: Don't call us!,* Cientifica, London

Coopey, R (1994) The first venture capitalist: Financing development in Britain after 1945, the case of ICFC/3i, *Business and Economic History,* **23** (1), pp 262–271

Deloitte (2006) *The Debt Markets: Will the good times keep rolling?* Deloitte, London

European Private Equity & Venture Capital Association (EVCA) (2002) *Survey of the Economic and Social Impact of Venture Capital in Europe,* EVCA, Brussels

EVCA (2001) *The Economic and Social Impact of Management Buyouts and Buyins in Europe,* EVCA, Brussels

EVCA (2003) *Private Equity and Venture Capital Incentives in Europe,* EVCA, Brussels

EVCA (2004) *Benchmarking European Tax and Legal Environments; Indicators of Tax and Legal Environments favouring the Development of Private Equity, Venture Capital and Entrepreneurship in Europe*, EVCA, Brussels

EVCA (2004) *Company Law across Europe*, EVCA, Brussels

EVCA (2004) *Taxation of Stock Options across Europe*, EVCA, Brussels

EVCA (2005) *Employment Law Issues for European Companies*, EVCA, Brussels

EVCA (2005) *Fulfilling the Promise of Venture-backed High Potential Companies – Why We Need to Fix the Small Cap Markets in Europe*, EVCA, Brussels

EVCA (2005) *Taxation of Corporate Profits, Dividends and Capital Gains in Europe*, EVCA, Brussels

EVCA (2006) *2006 EVCA Directory*, EVCA, Brussels

EVCA (2006) *Annual Survey of Pan-European Private Equity & Venture Capital Activity*, EVCA, Brussels

EVCA (2006) *Corporate Venturing 2005 – European Activity Update*, EVCA, Brussels

Kurtzman, J and Rifkin, G (2005) *Startups that Work*, Portfolio, Penguin Group (USA) Inc, New York

Mullins, JW (2003) *The New Business Road Test*, FT Prentice Hall, London

PricewaterhouseCoopers (PwC) (2005) *Money for Growth: The European Technology Investment Report*, PwC, London

PwC (2006) *IPO Watch Europe: Review of the year 2005*, PwC, London

PwC (2006) *Global Private Equity Report 2005*, PwC, London

Sahlman, WA (1997) How to write a great business plan, *Harvard Business Review*, July–August, pp 98–108

Tang, K, Vohora, A and Freeman, R (2004) *Taking Research to Market: How to build and invest in successful university spinouts*, Euromoney Books, London

# Index

# INDEX OF ADVERTISERS